I0114311

The Book of Earths

By

Edna Kenton

ISBN: 978-1-63923-502-5

Printed: November 2022

Cover Art By: Amit Paul

Published and Distributed By:
Lushena Books
607 Country Club Drive, Unit E
Bensenville, IL 60106
www.lushenabks.com

ISBN: 978-1-63923-502-5

The Book of Earths

Hollow Earth, Ancient Maps, Atlantis, and Other Theories

By

Edna Kenton

PUBLISHER'S PREFACE

About the Book

"This is a compendium of theories of the shape of the Earth, along with a great deal of 'Earth Mystery' lore. Richly illustrated, the Book of Earths includes many unusual theories, including Columbus' idea that the Earth is literally pear-shaped, modern theories that the Earth was originally tetrahedral, and so on. Kenton also covers many traditional theories including the ancient Babylonians and Egyptians, Hindu and Buddhist cosmology, and those of the Peruvians, Aztecs and Mongols. She also discusses modern alternative theories such as that of Reed and Koresh. Strangely enough, she misses or ignores the modern flat earth theory of Rowbotham. This is the only apparent omission in this definitive study.

Kenton has no apparent axe to grind: this is simply a very readable survey of the literature. If you have any interest in 'Earth mysteries'."

(Quote from sacred-texts.com)

CONTENTS

PUBLISHER'S PREFACE VII
ACKNOWLEDGMENTS 1
MAN'S QUEST IN SPACE 2
FIGURES OF EARTH 5
CREATION OF THE WORLD 18
UPHOLDERS OF THE WORLD 33
THE PRIMÆVAL EARTH 46
THE BABYLONIAN UNIVERSE 49
THE EGYPTIAN UNIVERSE 58
EARTH-MOON CATASTROPHE 62
THE DELUGE 70
THE LOST ATLANTIS 75
LOST LAND OF THE WEST 78
TREES OF THE WORLD 83
MOUNTAINS OF THE WORLD 112
THE WHEEL OF LIFE 124
EARTH THE MUNDANE EGG 136
SYSTEMS OF THE UNIVERSE 150
THE SQUARE EARTH OF COSMAS INDICOPLEUTES 166
THE PERUVIAN UNIVERSE 170
THE AZTEC UNIVERSE 174
TARTAR-MONGOL WORLDS 178
MAPS OF THE EARTH 182
THE EARTH OF COLUMBUS 190
DANTE'S UNIVERSE 192
EARTH THE HEART OF THE COSMOS 196
ST. HILDEGARD'S UNIVERSE 199
THE EARTHS IN THE UNIVERSE 208
WHEELS UPON WHEELS 210
THE WORLD OCTAVES 218
EARTH A HOLLOW SPHERE 223
THE TETRAHEDRAL EARTH 240
BIBLIOGRAPHY 246

ACKNOWLEDGMENTS

WITHOUT THE ROUSED INTEREST and cordial co-operation of many people this collection of representations of the Earth and its relation to the Universe would have been impossible. For permission to use copyright material I am indebted to D. Appleton and Company, the Clarendon Press, the Cambridge University Press, Cassell & Co., Ltd., Gall and Inglis, the Guiding Star Publishing House, the Kosmon Press, Luzac & Co., Marshall Jones Company, Macmillan & Co., Ltd., Popular Astronomy, Frederick A. Stokes Company, Edward Stanford, Ltd., and the New York World; and also to Col. James Churchward, Dr. E. A. Wallis Budge, Dr. William Fairfield Warren, Mr. Marshall B. Gardner, Miss Mary Elizabeth Litchfield, Mrs. Richard Folkard, and Mrs. Daniel G. Brinton. For assistance in tracing material I owe thanks to various members of the staffs of the Metropolitan Museum, the Museum of the American Indian, Heye Foundation, the Museum of the Hispanic Society of America, the Museum of the University of Pennsylvania, the American Geographical Society, the Swedenborg Library of the Church of the New Jerusalem, Brooklyn, the New York Society Library, and the New York Public Library. In various translations I was aided by Dr. Arthur Livingston of Columbia University, and by an unknown member of the staff of the Biblioteca Nacional de Habana. Mr. Andrew Dasberg gave valuable suggestions in the choice and arrangement of various figures and plates. Special thanks are due Mrs. Mabel Reber without whose researches through numberless volumes this book would have lacked many of the representations it contains. Special thanks are also due many members of the staff of the New York Public Library in which most of these figures of Earth and the Universe were collected.

EDNA KENTON

September, 1928
New York

MAN'S QUEST IN SPACE

THIS BOOK OF EARTHS began years ago, with a single little figure of Earth taken from what old book I do not know. For a long time it lay by itself; then another, come upon by chance, was laid beside it; and still others as I happened on them, always by chance. Old odd maps joined the casual collection--maps of the Earth, the Moon, the heavens. It was never a collection in the usual sense of the word, because it was so casual; but, such as it was, it is the origin of this book. For it occurred to me, not long ago, that it would be "fun" to put them all together, and many others with them, chosen to fill in the gaps of the original group.

Luckily for the fun of it, the search about to begin would not be limited to what we know about the Earth, else it would have ended before it began; for we live in a universe of which we know little, and on a planet of which we know perhaps less. It would include not only what we know, or think to-day we know, but also any-thing that has been believed or felt or no more than "guessed" to be the picture of the Earth and its place in the universe. It would include not only science, modern and ancient, but tradition, the older the better; diagrams or pictures based on little more than folk-lore; cosmogonies of religions great and small; cosmogonies of philosophers, of poets, and of savages. It would gather together pictured theories, guesses, hypotheses, or merely flights of pure imagination, whether "true" or "false" to-day; since history teaches us nothing if it does not teach us that one century's false doctrine is another century's truth, and that the mistakes of any age or race are quite as illuminating as any "truth" by which it lived.

This collection of pictures, therefore, would not be "scientific," not "selected" to prove one thing or to disprove another, not prejudged by any standard but that of a record told in pictures and diagrams of what man has guessed this Earth to be ever since he first began to wonder what the figure of the body was on which he lived. It would be free play through sources, once those sources were discovered; play unhampered by any necessity for judgment or criticism, since what was sought was the record only.

And so the search began, and the story of the search is personally as interesting as what it uncovered. It would be endless--that was clear from the beginning, and so it must be made deliberately brief. It could not include everything, even if "everything" came promptly to the surface. But there were high lights in the record, and these began to show dimly from the first. The rest was a matter of blazing an unpathed trail that would lead to the goal--the record; but that must allow for twists and turns, by-paths, now and then blind alleys in which often, as it proved, lurked the "tip" that had been lacking when one turned into them.

More and more, as the search went on, and one figure of Earth was added to another, it seemed worth while to bring a large number of them together. Inevitably, in such a collection of man's attempts to draw the planet on which we live and its relations to the heavenly bodies by which it is surrounded, there would be surprising similitudes, identifications, recognitions, even a queer unity. There would be, too, in such a collection, enormous differences, opportunity for endless comparison and endless wondering over the figures imaged by those supremely courageous men, the questioners of Space.

They are the men--anywhere, at any time--who have looked up at the unanswering heavens, and asked, "What and whence and why are those lights in the sky?" who have looked down at the unanswering Earth, and asked, "What is this land that forever gives everything--even to me my life, and forever takes everything--even from me my life? What are these waters around it that sustain its life and mine? this fire within it that pours through its mountain tops and heats its boiling springs, whose spark lies still within the rock and wood from which my father's fathers first struck out their own first fire? What is this air I breathe that is around the Earth and within it, in its secret caves? What is Earth? And what am I?"

They are the men who have questioned not idly but unceasingly; knowing all the while that to the tiny questioner below there is no great Answerer above; that any answer to the questions born of the speck in space that is man, must be born in its turn of just his questions; nothing more--but nothing less. There is no equipment for this lonely quest; there is only man the questioner and the universe--the Great Question; the answer lies within man himself. If ever we once realise this, we can never call them anything but supreme adventurers--those men curious enough to wonder enough to question enough to guess at last boldly enough to say, "Perhaps

it is like this," and set down the image, even though it is no more than a small triangular peak of land rising from a watery waste, with the arch of the heavens above it, and between it and heaven the Sun and Moon and stars.

For guesswork is the beginning and the end of knowledge--man's own answers to his own questions. They may be right or wrong, but they are his. To-day we give scientific "guesses" a statelier title; we call them hypotheses; they are nothing more than guesses shot into still un-answering Space. The "hypothesis," for instance, that the Earth is an island, plain, mountain, or whatever, was first advanced when the first man of the first race drew the first figure of Earth. The "guess"--only that--that the figure of Earth is an oblate spheroid is of our own era. Our hypotheses are continually changing; one supplants another, and is in its turn discarded for a new--or an old--one; and this has been the history of knowledge ever since that remote and notable day when the first brain, by sheer pressure of questioning, focused in a point that exploded into a "guess." It is the process of induced thinking that has carried man on; the heavens and the Earth have continued to revolve whether his answers are right or wrong.

Man could not equip himself for this quest in Space. But he had been equipped, after a fashion. He had a few resources, a few means.

First of all, long before science told him that he had within his body vestiges of all the life-strata of the world, he had a vague knowledge that he is an integral part of the universe. And, because he is a part of the universe, he had a vague knowledge of truth, or of segments of truth. He had numbers, he had signs, he had characters, he had symbols, all of these drawn in the heavens before he drew them on Earth. He had words. He had the capacity to be curious, the capacity to wonder, the capacity to draw analogies between seemingly unrelated things. From this scant handful of means, his faculty for guesswork developed. This is the whole story of all his perceptions of the universe and of his planet. For he has continuously dared the great adventure, and has returned sometimes with pure gold.

FIGURES OF EARTH

THE BELIEF THAT THE UNIVERSE is composed of five Great Elements is untraceably old. Even the savage knows very well four of these elements, Water, Air, Fire, and Earth, and has a vague sense of the fifth, Ether, or Space. From varying combinations of these five elemental substances, the ancients believed, all of the phenomena of Nature were formed. Earth itself was composed, in the last analysis, of these five. Man also, they believed, was a unique compound of these elements, and was, at death, resolved back into them. Each of these great "Creatures," as they were called, was symbolised by a certain shape, and the total figure of the five different forms, superimposed on one another in a regular order, is the stupa of China and India, the sotoba or go-rin of Japan, the "Five-circle" or "Five-zone" or "Five-blossom" funeral stone to be found everywhere in the Orient. The cube represents the Earth or stable foundation on which all builds; the sphere represents water; the pyramid or triangular tongue, fire or the elements in motion; the crescent or inverted vault of the sky, air or wind; the acuminated sphere or body-pyri-form, ether tapering into Space.

FIGURE I. The Stupa. (From Foe koue ki, by Fa-heen.)

Of course the old philosophers assigned particular places or grades to these five elements. Plato gave the first place to fire, the second to ether, then followed air, water, and lastly Earth. But Aristotle placed ether first, "as that which is impassable, it being a kind of fifth body," and after it he placed those elements "that are passable," in the order of fire, air, water, and Earth.

Sit down with pencil and paper, or, as the first mathematicians did, sit down on the sea shore and draw with a shell on the sands the simple or the complex geometrical figures, whatever you will. It will be a rather remarkable accident if you happen to put down a single figure that his not at some time represented either the figure of Earth directly, or a direct relation of the Earth to the universe.

FIGURE 2. The Tetrahedron.

Take the five regular solids, for instance: the tetrahedron, the octahedron, the icosahedron, the cube, and the dodecahedron. The Earth has been a tetrahedron, and it has been, many, many times, a cube. It has been conceived of as an eight-sided figure--one of the Siberian tribes believes today that the octahedron is the true figure of Earth. It was by way of the "five regular solids," "the five mathematical bodies," that Kepler, as we shall see later on, sought to solve the mystery of "distances" in the heavens. Seeking for some fixed relation of distances between the six planets and the Sun, he found, or believed he found, that the five regular solids fitted between the six spheres in a very curious order, and he elaborated on the nature of these solids and their relation to our solar system all of his life. The "nature" of the tetrahedron was of fire. The nature of the octahedron was of "flying birds." The nature of the icosahedron was of water. The nature of the cube was of Earth, even though it fitted into place between Saturn and Jupiter, and the nature of the dodecahedron was that of the celestial vault, or ether.

FIGURE 3. The Octahedron.

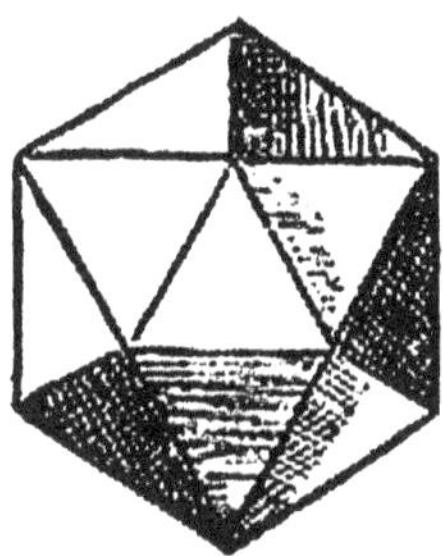

FIGURE 4. The Icosahedron.

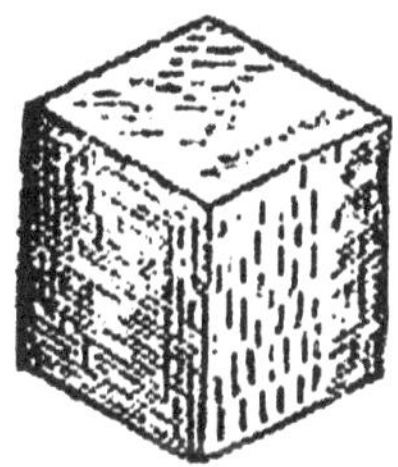

FIGURE 5. The Cube.

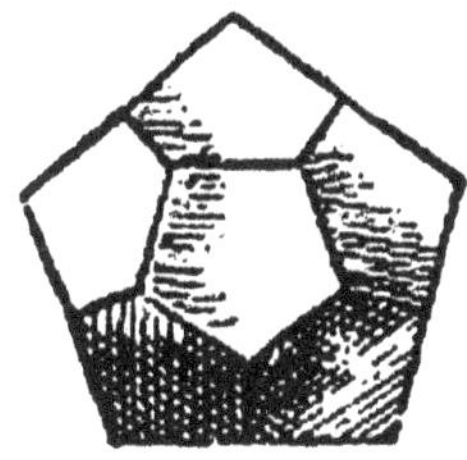

FIGURE 6. The Dodecahedron.

Earth has been given, also, at one time or another and in one way or another, all of the pyramidal forms. It has been figured as a three-sided and as a four-sided pyramid, and likewise as a cone. It has been a cylinder, filled with compressed air and balanced in the centre of the universe. It has been, at one time, a "rygge forme,"--"a three-cornered forme," says Recorde's The Castle of Knowledge (1556), "like the rygge of an house where one syde lyeth flatte, and the other two leane a slope. And thys forme they judged better for twoo causes. Firste they thought that it was more steddy than a cube forme, because it hath a broader foote, and a lesser toppe; and secondly for that they thought it a more apte forme to walke on and more agreeable to the nature of the earthe, where some-times there risyth highe hill, and sometimes again men may see greate vales descendyng. . . . Againe they thinke this Rygge forme meetest for the standing of the sea and for the running of rivers, for in the first forme [a cube] if the sea should rest on the outermost plaine, then wolde it over runne all that plaine, and so flow over all the earthe; where as in this seconde forme it mighter reste about the foote of the earthe, and yet the slope risyng wyll not permit it to over run all the earthe. And so for rivers if there is no slopenes (as in a cube there is none) then cannot the rivers runne well."

FIGURE 7. A "rygge forme" or three-sided tablet.

FIGURE 8. Five-sided tablet.

FIGURE 9. Cone.

FIGURE 10. Three-sided pyramid.

FIGURE 11. Four-sided pyramid.

FIGURE 12. Sphere.

FIGURE 13. Cylinder.

Already in these dozen geometrical figures we have collected two groups, one of which, the five regular solids, has been noted. The other one is that group from which all the known crystalline mineral forms--except radium and helium--can be constructed--"the eight basic elemental geometrical magnitudes," with eight definite bounding surfaces that compose a perfect series.

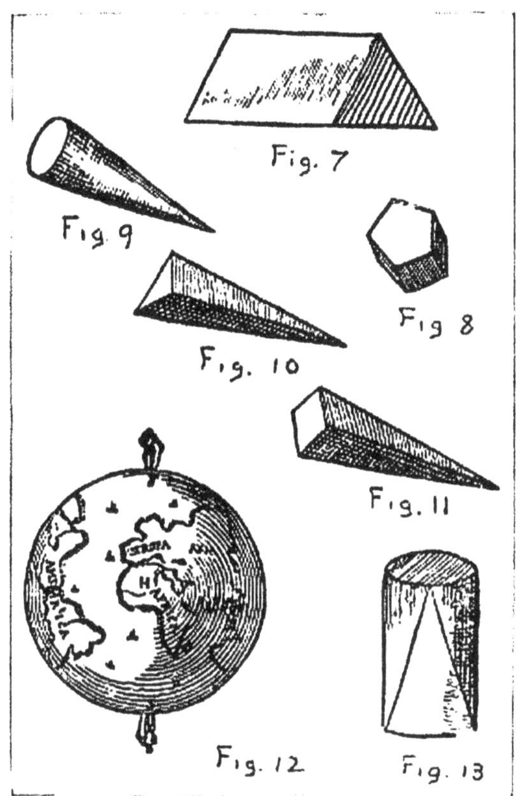

The first is the sphere with its one and only surface.

The second is the cone with its two surfaces.

The third is the cylinder with its three surfaces.

The fourth is the tetrahedron with its four surfaces.

The fifth is the three-sided tablet with its five surfaces.

The sixth is the cube with its six surfaces.

The seventh is the five-sided tablet with its seven surfaces.

The eighth is the octahedron with its eight surfaces.

And then again the Earth has been represented by a figure quite outside the angular figures. The sphere, for instance, as a figure of Earth, appears to be as old as any of the others, and, like all the others, has undergone the test of recurrence. But an even more curious form has been ascribed to this still mysterious planet of ours--a spiral. The beginning, or the end, that is, of a spiral form, like the vine, or like a watch-spring, which, stretched, or sprung, may reach from Earth to Heaven, along which all that lives in the universe may descend and ascend--a sort of Jacob's ladder without rungs. Before man had the watch-spring, his own creation, he had before him the vine--Nature's handiwork, and he used it to symbolise that for which he was always seeking, the connecting link, the path of communication between Earth and Heaven.

FIGURE 14. Spiral forms.

Of the spiral forms given in Fig. 14 the two small ones in the centre are modern drawings of radium and helium atoms, but their duplicates are to be found in the oldest, crudest pictographs of the cosmos--man's attempt to represent by a line either Earth's creative power and strength and energy, or the mysterious, potent force of Nature itself. The lower spiral is the ordinary right-handed (or dextral) curve found everywhere in Nature. The upper left-handed (or sinistral) spiral with its flying birds in opposition is a curious little drawing taken from Physiologia Kircheriana Experimentalis (1680), perhaps suggested by Leonardo da Vinci's Notebook on "The Flight of Birds," written nearly two centuries earlier, while he was making his marvellous studies of spiral formations.

For the great struggle of one element against another, suggested in this sinistral spiral, was itself to Leonardo the very secret of the mysterious force which shapes the structure of waves, of reeds, of animals, of man, of shells and horns and flowers and climbing vines. The force itself he could not define, but its movement he could trace; and its path was not a line or a closed circle but a spiral "twist," which might take the right-handed or the rarer left-handed way. There came to him what might be called a revelation of spirality; and he found the coil of a worm, the curve of the humblest shell, the wreathing smoke of a candle, the tiny whirl of street dust, the budding of a fern or a cyclamen, of an onion or a rose, just as significant as the spiral-like flight of birds or the spiral formations of water. But thousands of years before him, ancient temples and tombs and sacred rocks had been engraved with significant "studies" in spiral forms--many of those of the Eastern world based beyond all doubt on the struggle of the lotus with the elements and on the analogy of the lotus to the Earth--even to the cosmos itself. The ancient Stupa (Fig. 1) was not only a symbol of the five great elements, but it was also, for the Orient, an almost literal drawing of the lotus plant, rooted in Earth, climbing through water, by grace of its inner fire, to air, lifting there its acuminated spherical bud, and blossoming with a spiral twist into Space. To the ancient mind the secret path of Nature's immortal force was always most significantly symbolised by a spiral line, and it was suggested in a thousand ways.

A sphere or a hemisphere may be a solid body, or it may be merely a shell--and Earth has been again many times imagined as a half shell, swimming like an upturned basket or boat, on the surface of limitless waters, not sinking because its concavity was filled with air which, pressing on the water, balanced the hollow shell. Or, again, Earth has been, and is still to-day believed by some to be, "a playne Flatte." "They fantasied," wrote old Recorde, "that it wold reste most steddily, and so it was very easy to walke on. We are," he adds, "more beholdynge to those men, for devising our easy walkynge, than we are bound to them for their wise doctrine. The fourthe secte, fearyng least by this opinion they should loose the sea and all other waters, imagined the forme of the earthe more apte to hold water, and devised it hollow lyke a bolle."

FIGURE 15. "Halfe a Sphaere."

FIGURE 16. "Hollow lyke a bone."

FIGURE 17. "A playne Flatte."

It was always a problem for the early designers of the figure of Earth to account for the support of the heavens, and this idea of the habitable Earth "hollow lyke a bolle," was much more clearly and generally expressed by figurmg the Earth as a flat disc or plain surrounded by a continuous mountain wall on which the heavens rested. Only fourteen hundred years ago, with the theory of the spherical Earth the prevailing scientific one, but with all its vexing by-problems unsolved--not only that of an un-supported sky, but of men forced to walk like flies on the opposite ceiling of the Earth, one cosmogonist, Cosmas Indicopleustes, disposed of the whole matter by simply enclosing the entire visible universe in a hollow rectangular box and shutting down the lid. Man lived inside his box, like a squirrel in a cage.

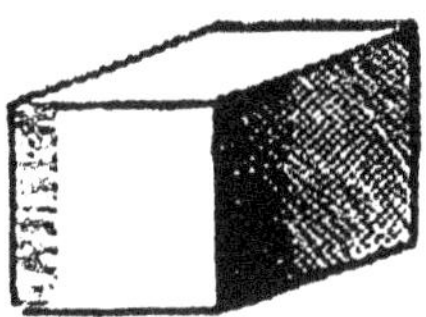

FIGURE 18. "Square like a box."

The Cosmasian idea was a simpler scheme of world-making than the model offered in Fig. 19, but it happens that this simple geometric figure is very similar to the Babylonian conception of the universe--Earth as a series of "stages" or steps, pyramidal in structure, enclosed within a series of concentric spheres. For the idea that Heaven is round and that Earth is square is very old, as old perhaps as the square and the circle--the foundation of measure. "Heaven is round like an opened umbrella," say the Chinese; "Earth is square like a chessboard." Or, "Earth is square like a box; heaven is round like the awning of a carriage."

Yet on what, if the Earth is square, may the dome of Heaven rest, not only that it may have firm support, but also that it may be tightly joined to the Earth? For the ancients greatly feared that Heaven, illy supported, might collapse and destroy its foundation; they feared also that, if Heaven and Earth were not hermetically cemented or glued together, untold horrors might creep into this universe from some fabulous "outside." For instance, the circular edge of the heavenly dome might find support firm enough by resting on the four quarters of the square Earth, in spite of the intervening arcs of water it must span. But there would be the open quarters; and unknown and unimaginable monsters might succeed in swimming through the depths of water under Heaven's unguarded edge, and so insinuate themselves into the Earth-waters, with the very probable result of the destruction of the world. Therefore, said some, Heaven's edge might very well begin as a square joined tightly to the Earth-square, and then melt insensibly into the rounded firmament. But, said others, Heaven is immeasurably high, Earth immeasurably deep; each covers the other, and both fit tightly together. Whether square or round, both must be one or the other.

A "six-faced tetrahedron," a solid giving the maximum of surface for the minimum of volume, represents, according to one theory, the figure of

Earth. This particular theory--a theory, by the way, of the latter nineteenth century--would seem to argue for the existence of an "economical" universe, with the Earth modelled on a plan designed to produce the greatest possible surface from the least possible substance.

FIGURE 19. Squares, or "stages," within circles.

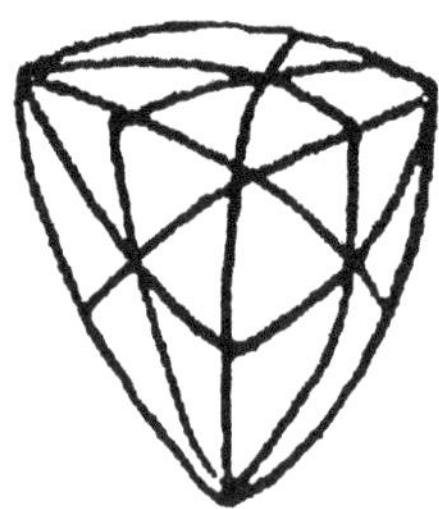

FIGURE 20. The six-faced tetrahedron.
(From Vestiges of the Molten Globe; William Lowthian Green, 1875, Plate I.)

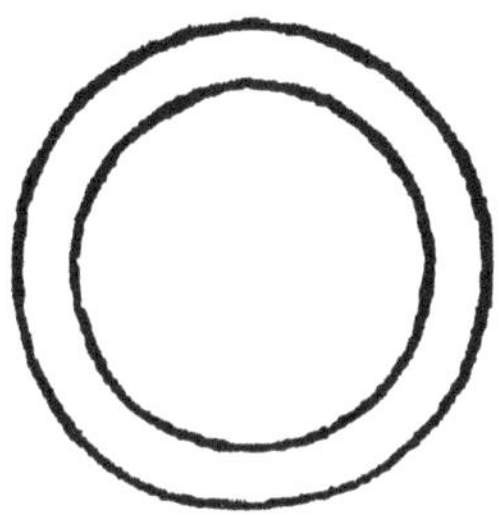

FIGURE 23. "*Parallel Circles.*"

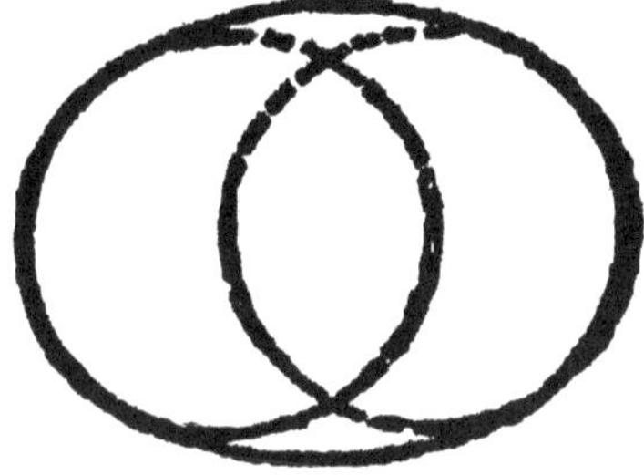

FIGURE 22. "*Circles within the Oval.*"

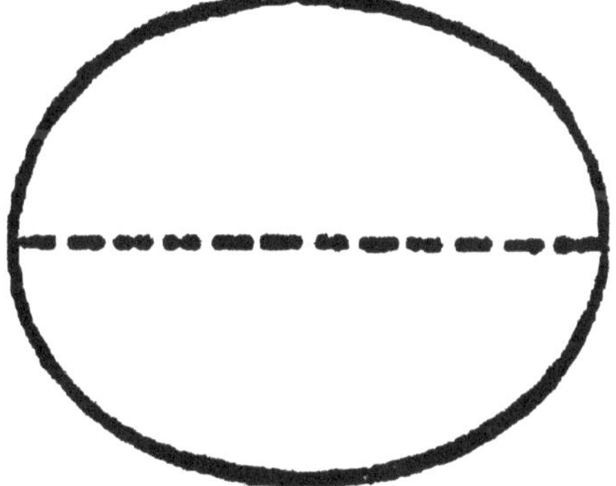

FIGURE 21. *The Oval, or "The Mundane Egg."*

FIGURE 23. "Parallel Circles."
FIGURE 22. "Circles within the Oval."
FIGURE 21. The Oval, or "The Mundane Egg."

And Earth is also the Mundane Egg, or an Oval form.

"There is another thing in Antiquity," wrote Thomas Burnet in his The Theory of the Earth (1697), "relating to the form and construction of the Earth, which is very remarkable, and hath obtained throughout all learned Nations and Ages. And that is the comparison or resemblence of the Earth to an Egg . . . this notion of the Mundane Egg, or that the World was Oviform, hath been the sence and Language of all Antiquity, Latins, Greeks, Persians, Egyptians, and others."

Burnet did not overstate his case, for this was his theory also. The concept of the Earth as the Mundane Egg or of the universe as the Cosmic Egg is one of the ancient of ancient figures of Earth. It appears everywhere, in the mythologies, cosmogonies, traditions, and folklore of all races and of all times. Heaven encloses the Earth from without as the shell encloses the yolk. Or the Earth's crust is the shell of the Mundane Egg; Burnet's whole theory of the Earth was built on this idea. There is no end to the analogy between the egg and the universe, or to the concept of the Earth as the Egg of the World.

FIGURE 24.

FIGURE 25. "Convex, concave."

These are some of the geometrical figures by which the Earth and the universe have been represented. But "shapes" also have been used to describe it. Shapes are irregular things compared with geometrical figures, but they may be accurate nevertheless. "Pear-shaped," for instance, is for descriptive purposes just as exact as "triangular" or "round." And so the Earth has been described and drawn, not only as "pear-shaped," but as "boat-shaped," as "heart-shaped," as "egg-shaped," as "tomato-shaped," as "turnip-shaped," "gourd-shaped," "onion-shaped," "lotus-shaped," "rose-shaped." It has been--many times--a tree; a great island-leaf with roots; a flower; a mountain; an octave in the cosmic series, or a note in the cosmic scale; or the living body of the "God of Heaven," the "Universal Man," spanning the space between the highest heaven and the lowest Earth.

FIGURE 26. "Right, Crooked, Mixt."

And for the last few hundred years it has been an "oblate spheroid."

But ask science to-day, What is the figure of Earth? and science will reply not with the geometrical figure of an oblate spheroid, nor with any definite "shape" drawn for the eye to see, but with a word: Earth is a geoid.

Ask, What is a geoid? and science will reply:

An Earth-shaped body.

Ask, What is an Earth-shaped body? and science will answer:

A geoid. A shape, that is, expressed by a word, but not yet by an image. The mysterious figure of the Earth, the shape peculiar to itself, has not yet been determined, with all of man's questionings and guesses.

CREATION OF THE WORLD

AND yet he has tried to determine it, with that handful of working means left him when the gods departed; his vague knowledge of truth--which has served him better for determining what is not truth than what is truth; his numbers, his signs, his characters, his symbols, his words, his capacity to be curious, to wonder, and to draw analogies between strange things. This was his equipment when he first began to question Space, and from this tiny handful of resources all the Creation stories of the world arose. Their outlines are remarkably the same. First of all a primordial substance and a Former to mould it--they sometimes called these two first forces the Maker and the Moulder, each contained within the other, but at rest. Then out of stillness came motion; out of motion light, out of light all created things; after Creation, evil; and, after evil, the deluge; out of the deluge the mountain top; and out of the ruins of the Old Earth, the New. Many of the Creation stories are familiar, but here are two which are almost unknown to the western world, though one of them is of that very world itself.

The first comes from Asia, land of the oldest recorded thought we have--at least nothing older is recognised as coming from any other source. The second is of America, youngest historically of all the continents, with all her prehistoric past practically stripped of records. The first is in words, one of man's most magnificent guesses at the original combining of the Great Elements which produced the Earth. The second is told in glyphs or pictographs. The first is taken from the Sanscrit Mahabharata; the second from the Walam Olum of the Lenape or Delaware Indians, a branch of the great Algonkin stock which roamed from east to west and west to east in North America, and styled itself the Sacred People," "the Mound Builders."

Bhrgu, in the Sanscrit epic, is answering the question, "By whom was this world with its oceans, its firmament, its mountains, its clouds, its lands, its fire, and its winds created? He replies that, first of all, the Primæval Being Manasa created a Divine Being Mahat.

Mahat created Consciousness.

That Divine Being created Space.

From Space was born Water, and from Water were born Fire and Wind.

Through the union of Fire and Wind was born the Earth.

Then follows a song to Mahat.

The Mountains are His bones.
The Earth is His fat and flesh.
The Oceans are His blood.
Space is His stomach.
The Wind is His breath.
Fire is His energy.
The Rivers are His arteries and veins.
Agni and Soma, otherwise the Sun and the Moon, are called His eyes.
The firmament above is His head.
The Earth is His two feet.
The Cardinal and subsidiary points of the horizon are His arms.
Without doubt He is incapable of being known and His Soul is inconceivable.

Of the extent of the firmament, of the surface of the Earth, and of the Wind:

Bhrgu said: The Sky thou seest above is infinite.

The Sun and the Moon cannot see, above or below, beyond the range of their own rays. There where the rays of the Sun and the Moon cannot reach are luminaries which are self-effulgent and which possess splendour like that of the Sun or of Fire.

This Space which the very gods cannot measure is full of many blazing and self-luminous worlds each above the other.

Beyond the limits of land are oceans of water. Beyond water is darkness. Beyond darkness is water again, and beyond the last is fire.

Downwards, beyond the nether regions, is water. Beyond water is the region belonging to the great snakes.

Beyond that is sky once more, and beyond the sky is water again.

Ever thus there is water and sky alternately without end. . . .

Formerly there was only Infinite Space, perfectly motionless and immovable. Without sun, moon, stars, and wind, it seemed to be asleep.

Then Water sprang into existence, like something darker within darkness.

Then from the pressure of Water arose Wind. As when an empty vessel without a hole appears at first to be without any sound, but when filled with Water, Air appears and makes a great noise, even so when Infinite Space was filled with Water, the Wind arose with a great noise, penetrating through the Water.

That Wind, thus generated by the pressure of the Ocean of Water, still moveth. Coming into unobstructed Space, its motion is never stopped.

Then, in consequence of the friction of Wind and Water, Fire possessed of great might and blazing energy sprang into existence with flames directed upwards.

That Fire dispelled the darkness that covered Space.

Assisted by the Wind, Fire drew Space and Water together.

Indeed, combining with the Wind, Fire became solidified.

While falling from the Sky, the liquid portion of Fire solidified again, and became what is known as the Earth.

The Earth or land, in which everything is born, is the origin of all kinds of taste, of all kinds of scent, of all kinds of liquids, and of all kinds of animals.

The Walam Olum (or "Red Score") of the Lenape. [1]

---

[1] This Creation and Deluge story of the Lenape or Delaware Indians is taken from Dr. Daniel G. Brinton's The Lenape and Their Legends (The Library of Aboriginal American Literature, Vol. V, 1885). Since "walam" means "painted," particularly

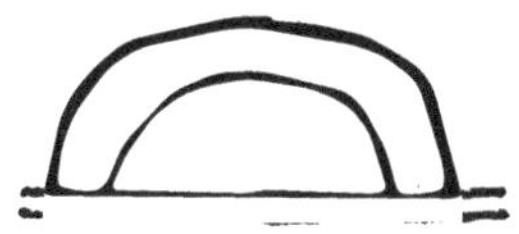

1. At first, in that place, at all times, above the earth,

2. On the earth, [was] an extended fog, and there the great Manito was.

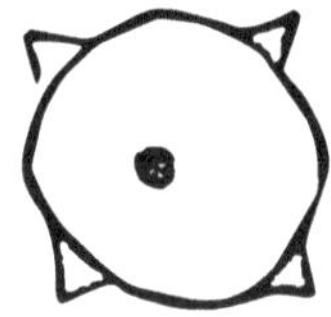

3. At first, forever, lost in space, everywhere, the great Manito was.

4. He made the extended land and the sky.

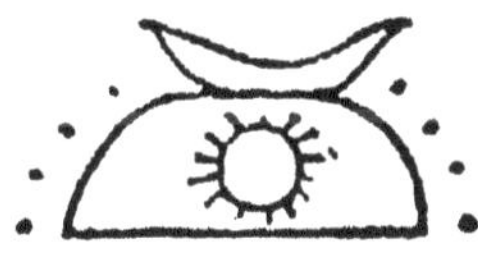

5. He made the sun, the moon, the stars.

"painted red," and "olum" signifies the scores or marks or notches or figures used on tally-sticks or record-boards, the sense of Walam Olum is variously rendered by "Red Score" (Dr. Brinton's choice), "Painted-engraved Tradition" (the translation left by Constantine Rafinesque, original copyist of these Algonkin pictographs), or "Painted Bark-Record." The pictographs or glyphs or signs were "notches" designed to keep the long chant in memory. The very beautiful translation is Dr. Brinton's.

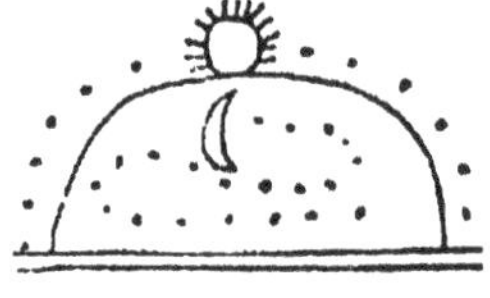

6. He made them all to move evenly.

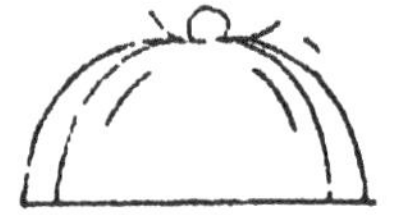

7. Then the wind blew violently, and it cleared, and the water flowed off far and strong.

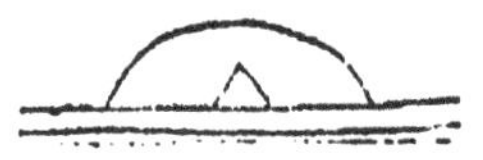

8. And groups of islands grew newly, and there remained.

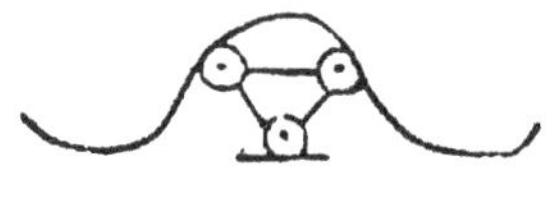

9. Anew spoke the great Manito, a manito to manitos,

10. To beings, mortals, souls and all,

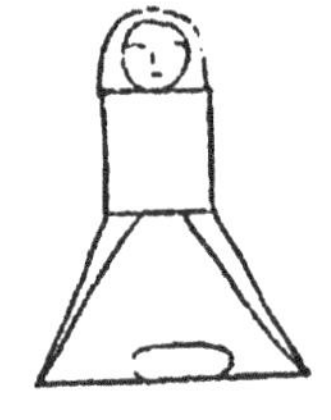

11. And ever after he was a manito to men, and their grandfather

12. He gave the first mother, the mother of beings.

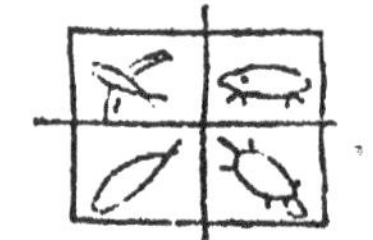

13. He gave the fish, he gave the turtles, he gave the beasts, he gave the birds.

14. But an evil Manito made evil beings only, monsters,

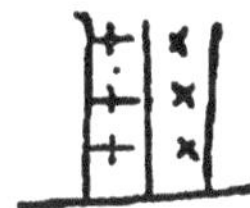

15. He made the flies, he made the gnats.

16. All beings were then friendly.

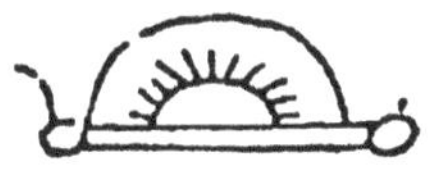

17. Truly the manitos were active and kindly

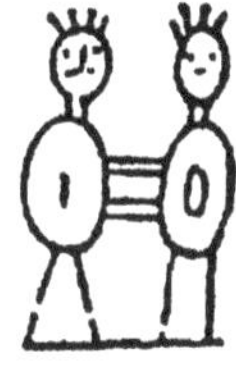

18. To those very first men, and to those first mothers, fetched them wives,

19. And fetched them food, when first they desired it.

20. All had cheerful knowledge, all had leisure, all thought in gladness.

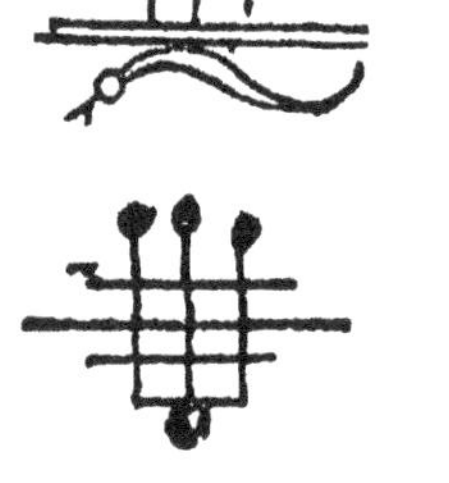

21. But very secretly an evil being, a mighty magician, came on earth,

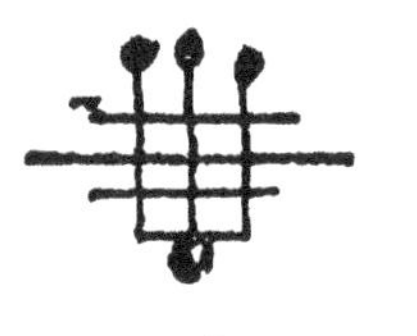

22. And with him brought badness, quarreling, unhappiness,

23. Brought bad weather, brought sickness, brought death.

24. All this took place of old on the earth, beyond the great tide-water, at the first.

II.

1. Long ago there was a mighty snake and beings evil to men.

2. This mighty snake hated those who were there (and) greatly disquieted those whom he hated.

3. They both did harm, they both injured each other, both were not in peace.

4. Driven from their homes they fought with this murderer.

5. The mighty snake firmly resolved to harm the men.

6. He brought three persons, he brought a monster, he brought a rushing water.

7. Between the hills the water rushed and rushed, dashing through and through, destroying much.

8. Nanabush, the Strong White One, grandfather of beings, grandfather of men, was on the Turtle Island.

9. There he was walking and creating, as he passed by and created the turtle.

10. Beings and men all go forth, they walk in the floods and shallow waters, down stream thither to the Turtle Island.

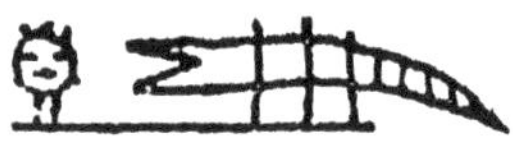

11. There were many monster fishes, which ate some of them.

12. The Manito daughter, coming, helped with her canoe, helped all, as they came and came.

13. [And also] Nanabush, Nanabush, the grandfather of all, the grandfather of beings, the grandfather of men, the grandfather of the turtle.

14. The men then were together on the turtle, like to turtles.

15. Frightened on the turtle, they prayed on the turtle that what was spoiled should be restored.

16. The water ran off, the earth dried, the lakes were at rest, all was silent, and the mighty snake departed.

Let us extract several of these primitive world-pictures from the Walam Olum and set them side by side for comparison. Quite apart from any meaning attached to them in the legend of the Lenape, these three signs illustrate very well indeed what were probably the first two world-concepts of man; either that the Earth was an island in a watery waste on whose waves the sky rested as best it might, or that it was a vast plain overarched by the solid vault of heaven and tightly enclosed within it. The first of the three needs only a writhing sea serpent inscribed beneath it to illustrate that heavy fear of primitive man, that portentous monsters, slipping through the deepest depth of the ocean, might creep under the edge of the firmament to work evil on Earth. So little has ever been done with these Lenape pictographs, as Dr. Brinton himself admits, that it is impossible to speak with certainty about the real meaning of any of them; and it is only a hazardous guess to suggest that Fig. 29, the last "sign" of the Deluge story--"The water ran off, the earth dried, the lakes were at rest, all was silent, and the mighty snake departed"--may represent the ocean surrounding the Earth as barred, perhaps forever, against the "mighty snake" which had wrought such desolation. The oblique lines would serve here, instead of an Earth-surrounding mountain wall, or a circular continental ring beyond the "River Ocean," to guard the Earth against invasion from without. In any case, here are primitive representations of "mountains of the world"--the "first Earth" before and the "first Earth" after the Deluge--and of that other "first" concept of the Earth as a vast plain, overarched by the solid vault of heaven.

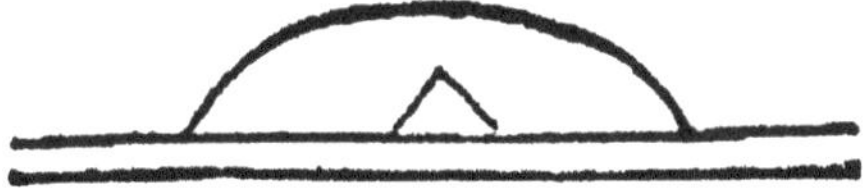

FIGURE 27.

FIGURE 28.

FIGURE 29.

There is another Creation story that we might glance at here, because it contains so many notions of the beginnings of things that are extraordinarily similar to other ideas we shall meet later on. It is the Creation story of the Maidus, an Indian tribe of northern California.

"When this world was filled with water," so Dixon translates the tradition, [1] Earth-Maker floated upon it, kept floating about. Nowhere in the world could he see even a tiny bit of earth. No persons of any kind flew about. He went about in this world, the world itself being invisible, transparent like the sky.

"He was troubled. 'I wonder how, I wonder where, I wonder in what place, in what country, we shall find a world!' he said. You are a very strong man, to be thinking of this world,' said Coyote. 'I am guessing in what direction the world is, then to that distant land let us float!' said Earth-Maker.

"In this world they kept floating along, kept floating along, hungry, having nothing to eat. You will die of hunger,' said Coyote. Then he thought. No, I cannot think of anything,' he said. 'Well,' said Earth-Maker, the world is large, a great world. If somewhere I find a tiny world, I can fix it up.'

"Then he sang, 'Where, little world, art thou?' It is said he sang, kept singing, sang all the time. 'Enough!' he said, and stopped singing. Well, I don't know many songs (?),' he said. Then Coyote sang again, kept singing, asking for the world, singing, 'Where, O world, art thou?' He sang, kept singing; then 'Enough!' he said. 'I am tired. You try again.'

"So Earth-Maker sang. 'Where are you, my great mountains, my world mountains?' he said. He sang, and all the time kept saying, 'Where are

---

[1] Maidu Texts: Roland B. Dixon. Leyden, 1912.

you?' He stopped singing. 'Enough!' he said. 'You try also.' Coyote tried, kept singing. 'My foggy mountains, where one goes about,' he said. 'Well, we shall see nothing at all. I guess there never was a world anywhere,' said he. 'I think, if we find a little world, I can fix it very well,' said Earth-Maker.

"As they floated along, they saw something like a bird's nest. 'Well, that is very small,' said Earth-Maker. 'It is small. If it were larger I could fix it. But it is too small,' he said. 'I wonder how I can stretch it a little.' He kept saying, 'What is the best way! How shall I make it larger!' So saying, he prepared it. He extended a rope to the east, to the south he extended a rope, to the west, to the northwest, and to the north he extended ropes.

II I

Plate I: STAGES OF CREATION
From right to left: I. Chaos: Division of Light from Darkness: Separation of Earth and Water. Vegetation. II. Sun, Moon, and Stars: Fishes and Birds: Animals and Man; Sabbath Rest.

"When all were stretched, he said, 'Well, sing, you who were the finder of this earth, this mud! "In the long, long ago, Robin-Man made the world, stuck earth together, making this world." Thus mortal man shall say of you, in myth-telling.' Then Robin sang, and his world-making song sounded sweet. After the ropes were all stretched, he kept singing; then, after a time, he ceased.

"Then Earth-Maker spoke to Coyote also. 'Do you sing, too,' he said. So he sang, singing, 'My world where one travels by the valley-edge; my world of many foggy mountains; my world where one goes zigzagging hither and thither; range after range,' he said, 'I sing of the country I shall travel in. In such a world I shall wander,' he said.

"Then Earth-Maker sang--sang of the world he had made, kept singing, until by and by he ceased. 'Now,' he said, it would be well if the world were a little larger. Let us stretch it.'--'Stop!' said Coyote. 'I speak wisely. This world ought to be painted with something so that it may look pretty. What do ye two think?'

"Then Robin-Man said, 'I am one who knows nothing. Ye two are clever men, making this world, talking it over; if ye find anything evil, ye will make it good.' 'Very well,' said Coyote, 'I will paint it with blood. There shall be blood in the world; and people shall be born there, having blood. There shall be birds born who shall have blood. Everything--deer, all kinds of game, all sorts of men without any exception--all things shall have blood that are to be created in this world. And in another place, making it red, there shall be red rocks. It will be as if blood were mixed up with the world, and thus the world will be beautiful,' he said. 'What do you think about it?' Your words are good,' he said, 'I know nothing.' So Robin-Man went off. As he went, he said, 'I shall be a person who travels only in this way,' and he flew away."

Only after all this was accomplished did Earth-Maker, commanding Coyote to lie down on his face, begin to stretch the world. With his foot he extended it to the east, to the south, to the west, to the northwest, and to the north. And yet again, saying to Coyote, "Do not look up. You must not," he stretched it again, as far as it would go in the five directions. Then Coyote, rising, began to walk to the eastward side, and Earth-Maker, after describing the entire circuit of the world, returned to the spot from whence he had set out, and began to prepare things. He made men, of different colours, two of each kind only, and as he made them in pairs, he counted them. "Then he counted all the countries, and, as he counted them, assigned them, gave them to the countries. 'You are a country having this name, you shall have this people,' he said. This sort of people, naming you, shall own the country. These people shall grow, shall keep on growing through many winters, through many dawns. They shall continue to grow until, their appointed winters being past, their dawns being over, this people having finished growing, shall be born,' he said."

So Earth-Maker created, to each country a name and a people with a name and speech, each different; until he arrived at the middle of the world, where he made two others and left them, saying, "'Ye here, growing steadily, when so many winters shall have passed, very many winters, many days, ye shall be fully grown,' he said. 'Then ye shall be mortal men, ye shall be born full grown. . . . Ye shall not be born soon,' he said."

Continuing on his way to the uttermost limit where mortal men were to live, he stopped, and created, first two, whom he laid down, and two more, and still another pair. "'Ye shall remain here,' he said, 'and your country shall have a name. Although living in a small country, in one that is not large, it shall be sufficient for you. This I leave; and growing continually . . . ye, being fully grown, shall be born,' he said. 'Then your food will grow--different sorts of food, all kinds of food; and ye, being born with sufficient intelligence, will survive,' said he. Then he pushed them down under a gopher-hill.

"He spoke again. 'Ye, too, shall possess a small country. "Come now, leave this country!" (this ye must not say to others wishing to take this land). Ye shall be people who will not drive others away, driving them off to another country. Ye shall be different, ye shall name your country.'"

To still another pair he spoke, saying, "'Ye shall have children, and when your children shall have grown larger, then, looking all over this country, ye must tell them about it, teach them about it, naming the country and places, showing them and naming them to your children. "That is such and such a place, and that is such and such a mountain." So when ye have caused them to learn this, teaching them, they shall understand even as ye do yourselves.' Then, placing them between his thumb and finger, he snapped them away.

"And when he had given countries thus to all that he had counted out, there was one pair left. 'Ye, also, ye shall be a people speaking differently. There will be a little too many of you for you to have the same sort of a

country also. So ye shall have that kind of a country, a great country,' he said.

"'Now, wherever I have passed along, there shall never be a lack of anything,' he said, and made motions in all directions. 'The country where I have been shall be one where nothing is ever lacking. I have finished talking to you, and I say to you that ye shall remain where ye are to be born. Ye are the last people; and while ye are to remain where ye are created, I shall return and stay there. When this world becomes bad, I will make it over again; and after I make it, ye shall be born,' he said. Long ago Coyote suspected this, they say.

"'This world will shake,' he said. 'This world is spread out flat, the world is not stable. After this world is all made, by and by, after a long time, I will pull this rope a little, then the world shall be firm. I, pulling on my rope, shall make it shake. And now,' he said, 'there shall be songs, they shall not be lacking, ye shall have them.' And he sang, and kept on singing until he ceased singing. 'Ye mortal men shall have this song,' he said, and then he sang another; and singing many different songs, he walked along, kept walking until he reached the middle of the world; and there, sitting down over across from it, he remained.

"But in making the world, Robin-Man sang that which was pleasant to hear. He, they say, was the first created person--a man whose song passed across the valleys, a man who found the world, a man who in the olden time sang very beautifully--sounding songs. And Earth-Maker, going along, and having passed by the middle of the world, made a house for himself, and remained there. That is as far as he went. That is all, they say."

UPHOLDERS OF THE WORLD

FLAMMARION'S OLD DRAWING of The Earth Floating is a peculiarly desolate rendering of the ancient idea that the Earth was nothing more than an island in a sea. This idea would of course have its probable origin among races living near great seas or oceans whose other side they had tried in vain to reach. The mind of men likes symmetry; if water stretching endlessly away bounded one side of their "island," even though that island were a continent whose other edge they did not know, water must lie also on its other sides. If the Sun rose from their eastern waters, say, at dawn, it must sink in some unknown western waves at night, if for no other re ason than, by swimming through them, to arrive again by the next dawn, in the eastern sky. We may smile at this childish notion if we will, but it may very well be that no great "system" of the harmonious orbits of Sun and Moon and

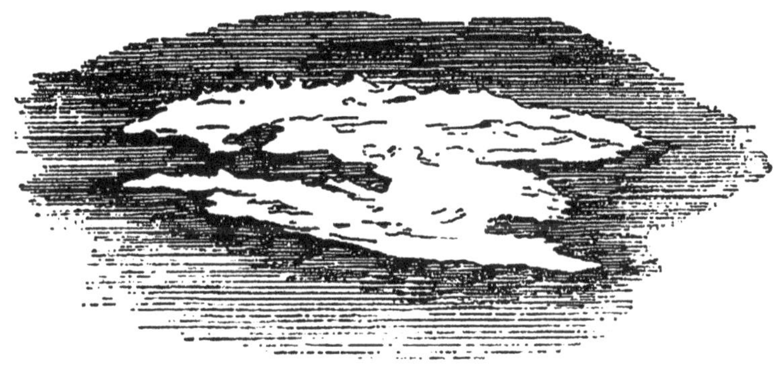

FIGURE 30. The Earth Floating.
(From Flammarion's Astronomical Myths, 1877.)

A. Quetzalcoatl upholding the Heavens. From an original Mexican painting preserved in the Imperial Library at Vienna.

(From Kingsborough's Mexican Antiquities. 1831, Vol. II)

A

B

C

PLATE II: SUSTAINERS OF THE EARTH

B. Atlas upholding the Earth.

(From Engravings after Stoddard: a collection in The New York Public Library)

C. A Hindu Earth.

(From Flammarion's Astronomical Myths, 1877)

Earth explain the mystery of the "rising and the setting of the Sun" any more or any better than the primitive idea that darkness came when the Sun was submerged in the sea, and that light came when the Sun sprang out of the sea. Perhaps all that we know to-day--really know--is that in the hour of dawn the Sun appears, and in the hour of twilight the Sun has vanished.

The precise nature of the element in which the Earth-island floated came to be a matter of concern and much speculation. At first it was assumed to be simply water; later it was defined as "water or some other liquid," and finally it was believed to be a liquid not unlike the composition of the waters directly under the firmament or lower heaven, which were supposed to be a crystalline, congealed water, specially combined to resist the flame of the Sun, Moon, and galaxy of stars, to be itself full of fire, and yet not to burn. It was water, yet not water, air yet not air, fire, yet not fire. Probably this was an attempt to describe the medium in which the Island Moon floated, all sustaining, yet clear.

Doubtless too the roundness of the Sun and Moon, their discs so broad, yet thin enough to float in space, or aethereal waters, had as much to do with giving men the idea that the Earth's shape might also be flat and round, as the circular defining line of the horizon. Again, if the Moon was like a leaf, floating in the heavenly water, the Earth, like a leaf, floated on the world water, and like a leaf in water would develop roots. Ages ago, as we have already noted (p. 14), the ancient world, India, China, Egypt, made the lotus the water-flower that symbolises Earth and Heaven and all that lies between. For as a tree, rooted in the Earth, is a part of it, so Earth, rooted in the universal waters, must be a part of the universe from which it derives life and nourishment. And again, though the roots of an Earth-island might not be as firm as the roots of a great Earth-tree might, that is, be as supple and flexible as those of water plants, nevertheless it was an anchorage of the Earth to something outside itself.

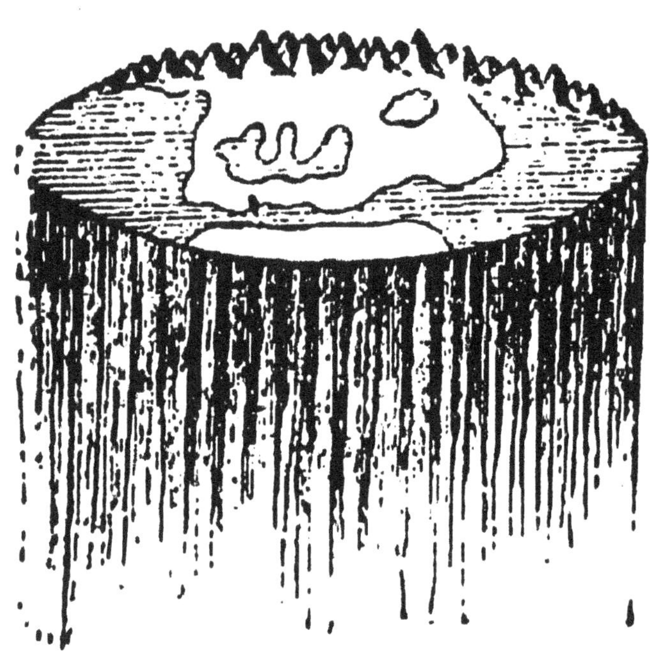

FIGURE 31. The Earth with Roots.
(From Flammarion's Astronomical Myths, 1877.)

Naturally evolving from this would rise an Earth set on solid pillars, an established, firmly founded disc. Fig. 32 is an old picture of just such an Earth--"the Earth of the Vedic priests." Its upper side is its only habitable side; its under side rests on twelve columns, these columns resting in turn on the Twelve Great Sacrifices of the Virtuous,--the aimful deeds, that is, of men aware of duty. Without this subterranean foundation, said the ancient priests, the pillars of the Earth would dry up, and the Earth would fall down. These pillars, says Flammarion, accounted more reasonably for the rising and the setting of the Sun, than the rather lazy guess that it swam through water from west to east every night; though there was another speculation that it might reach the eastern heavens by traversing a complicated system of tunnels, like great connecting caves, which pierced the Earth-disc from occident to orient.

FIGURE 32. The Earth of the Vedic Priests.
(From Flammarion's Astronomical Myths, 1877.)

But the twelve pillars, quite as little as the roots of the Earth-island leaf, failed to satisfy man's wonderings over the problem of what supported the Earth, or on what the Earth rested. One of the old familiar figures of Earth is that hemispherical Earth of the Hindus (Plate II, C) supported on the backs of four elephants, which stand on the hemispherical shell of a gigantic tortoise floating on the surface of the world-waters. Sometimes, in addition to these three supports, there is a fourth, the coiled ring of the great world-serpent on which the tortoise rests--four foundations for Earth, and five for Heaven which must rest on the Earth.

But the elephant, the tortoise and the serpent are only three of the great animals which folk-lore and tradition say may support this planet. The Altaic people of Northern Siberia affirm that their mighty Ulgen created the Earth on the waters, and placed under its disc, to support it, three great fish, one in the centre and one on either side. The head of the middle fish being placed towards the north, floods occur there when it presses its head down; and, should it ever sink too low, the whole Earth will be deluged

again. They believe that these fish are attached to heaven by a rope through their gills, whereby their heads can be lowered or raised, and that at the three posts of heaven to which these ropes are tied, the Bodhisatta Mandishire, or guardian of Earth, always watches. According to another tradition, only one great fish supports the Earth; when he changes his position earthquakes occur. In Hebrew myths, this mighty animal is the "fish-shaped Leviathan." Where the turtle or the tortoise is unknown, as in far northern lands, the "world-supporting Frog" will take its place; if its finger ever moves, the Earth shivers. Among Tartars and many of the tribes of Asia-Europe, the Earth is believed to be supported by a great bull; sometimes the Earth rests on its back, sometimes it is held aloft on the horns. Or, another variation, in the world-ocean there is a great fish, and, upon the fish, a bull which bears the Earth. Or again, in the world-ocean there is a giant-crab which gives support to the Earth-bearing bull. Some say that the terrible weight of the Earth has already broken one of the great horns, and that when the other breaks the world will come to an end. Another of the Tartar tribes says that after the Great Mammoth was created, it was found that the Earth was not strong enough to bear its weight, and so, to avoid a waste of creation in the universe, the Great Ruler solved the difficulty by commanding the Great Mammoth to bear the Earth.

On what did the Earth rest? Not only on literal water, and great beasts. On a whirlwind, said Empedocles; on roots rooted in the Infinite, said Xenophanes; on a Soul of the World, said Plato and his school; on Twelve Pillars, said the Vedic priests, which must have for their foundation the "sacrifices of the virtuous." Earth, that is, depended ultimately on man for its support. And sooner or later, in all cosmologies and mythologies, we come upon some lurking or developed concept that the burden of supporting both Earth and Heaven rests on the shoulders of man. In countries as widely separated by race and by oceans as Greece and Mexico, we find an "Atlas of the World," a sustainer of the universe (Plate II, A and B). In Greece it is Atlas the "Endurer," brother of Prometheus the rebel bringer-of-fire, who supports the globe. Son of Poseidon, he knew the depths of the whole Ocean-world; it was his task to guard the pillars which held Heaven and Earth apart. According to one story, it was because he had attempted to storm the heavens that he was condemned to carry its vault on his head and hands. According to another version, it was only after the loss of his great Island realm Atlantis, that he was forced to become the sustainer of the sky.

PLATE III. ATLAS SUPPORTING THE UNIVERSE
(From Margarita Philosophica, 1517)

Mexico appears to have had four--at least--heaven-bearing gods, and each of these appears to have exercised a number of functions other than the sufficiently onerous one of supporting the universe. Quetzalcoatl, although a Sun god and an earthquake god, was also, like Atlas, a water god. If Atlas, interpreted, means the Endurer, Quetzalcoatl, interpreted, means Heart of the Sea. God of the Sun, of the earthquake, and the water, he also up-held the heavens of the Mexicans. In the eastern world and in the western,

thousands of years ago, these different races believed alike that some great force never to be understood and never to be overcome had wrenched the heavens from the Earth, but that, at the same time it separated them, it united them by another force, which each race represented by a human figure, a great man-god. Explain it as we will, call it naïve or arrogant, it expressed one of man's few entirely admirable qualities, his lonely necessity to share, or to believe that he shared in the work of carrying on the universe. And it found expression in countless ways.

A curious old drawing of the Middle Ages (Plate III) shows how the Atlas-myth persisted even into modern time. The Earth still occupies the centre of the universe, with all the other heavenly bodies revolving about it. From pole to pole of the firmament--his head marking the "Polus Arctic" and his two feet the "Polus Antarctic," stretches Atlas, or the Macrocosm, or the Great Man, or Adam Kadmon, whichever you will. To mediæval Europe Atlas represented the Macrocosm, or the long great world, in contrast to the Microcosm or man--little, but the epitome of all that had combined to produce him. Very often, in such circular designs, the two lower corners will be filled each with a toiling figure, the burden-bearer man, with his shoulders bent to the wheel. Only by his microcosmic, microscopic effort, they seem to say over and over again, may the Wheel of Life be kept revolving. Not only does the Earth--the pillared Earth of the Vedic priests--rest on the sacrifices of man, but, since Heaven itself leans on the Earth, without man's aid the whole universe must collapse.

It is easy to see how this ancient image of the Great Man rose before the eyes of the "little men" of the Earth. This was a being infinitely stronger, infinitely better, almost yet not quite a god because he was Man, who somehow stood or moved between the two worlds and kept them in touch with one another. He came to be called by many names, to be pictured under many disguises. He was the Being praised in the Creation chant of the Mahabharata; he was the "manitou to men and their grandfather" of the Lenape Creation story. He was the cosmic P'an Ku of the Chinese, who came into being "in the midst of the cosmic egg," whose very name P'an means "the shell of an egg," and who was hatched out of the cosmos. He created in the middle, out of the pure elements, Heaven; out of the mixed elements, Earth. Every day Heaven grew ten feet higher, Earth ten feet deeper and he ten feet taller, for 18,000 years. When he died, his breath became wind, his voice thunder, his four limbs the four directions, his five extremities the five sacred mountains, his left eye the sun, his right eye the moon, his blood the rivers, his beard the stars, his hair the trees and plants, his flesh the soil, his teeth metals, his bones rocks, his marrow precious stones, his perspiration rain, and his parasites men. The old Chaldeans drew a Great Man across the sky in such a way that the signs of their zodiac corresponded to the parts of his body. And, proof once again that the ancient peoples separated by the Earth's diameter from each other were inexplicably one in many of their fancies, the Tewa Indians regarded Opa--the world, the universe--as a living being, and worshipped it as the "Universal Man," whose backbone, they said, is the Milky Way. And the old Norse sagas have in their giant Ymir almost the facsimile--or it may be the original, who may say?--of the Chinese P'an Ku; for from Ymir's body was made the world, from his flesh the Earth, from his blood the rivers and oceans, from his bones the mountains, from his eyebrows the "encompassing" of Mitgard the Earth. From his skull was shaped Heaven, and his brains were changed into floating clouds and fogs.

What is interesting about all this is the fact that primitive man arrived without the aid of science at the tremendous idea that definite figure is an attribute of the heavens. It was the idea that so fascinated Herschel, discoverer of Uranus, and curious inquirer into the mysteries of the Milky Way. He was possessed by the "guess" that not only is our galaxy a stratum or confined bed of stars, but that this stratum is measurable, and that by comparison of his gauging or sounding lines, he might actually draw a chart of it. He "guessed" again that in the main--and this guess was wrong--the stars are scattered equably throughout our immediate Space, which would mean that, seeing as far in one direction as another, the figure of the heavens would tend towards a circular form. In an old book of 1848, Thoughts on Some Important Points Relating to the System of the World, by John Nichol, there is a very odd "Figure of the Universe," based on Herschel's gauging system, which illustrates as well as any other the method employed (Fig. 33)

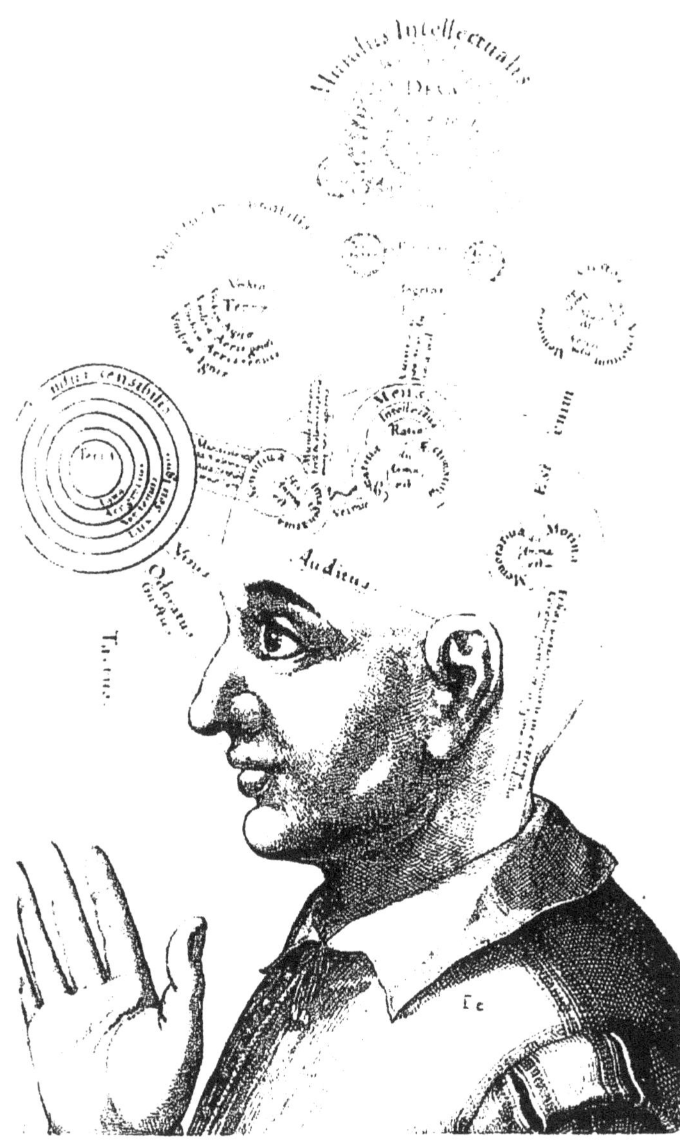

PLATE IV. A very clear demonstration of the three kinds of vision in the Microcosm (or soul of Man) of the location of their objects, and of the manner of discerning them. (From Microcosmi Historia; Robert Fludd, 1619)

If, says Nichol, we were in the centre of a circular group, it would mean that whether we looked through the line C A or the line C B, the number of stars that could be counted would be the same. But if the group were an irregular one, the number of stars in the direction of C A would be much less than that along the line C B, and the proportions of their numbers would give the pro-portions of the two lines C A and C B. Supposing S (lower figure) the place of our Sun, "or," says Nichol, "what is the same thing, of the Earth, on which the observations are recorded," let a number of lines be drawn answering in direction to the position of Herschel's telescope, and in length to the number of stars revealed in that direction. Then, if the extremities of these lines were joined, the result would be "a figure which, however strange, must approximate to a section of our vast and dazzling vault." He goes on to imagine one with the power to depart from Earth, proceeding through Space towards the Milky Way, leaving behind the constellations which we know, coming upon new configurations, passing even through the Milky Way, until, looking back, he sees this universe so dwindled away as to present the appearance of nothing but a speck in Space, shining with a faint, irregularly diffused illumination corresponding in its rays to the outlined figure.

NATURALLY MOST OF THE EARLY STORIES of the "Great Man" of the heavens are odd mixtures of perception and fancy, of clumsy literalness and real imagination. All too often this Opa Being was more earthly than heavenly, much more man than god, but, whatever his guise or disguise, he was always much more than man, and in some of his incarnations he was very close to divine. As Adam Kadmon he has meant not only the First Man created in the true image of God, but something more, "the divine man-forming power" capable of transforming a questioning little man cut off from wisdom into a divining Great Man who could know. Precisely such a conception of Adam Kadmon has been lying in Robert Fludd's Microcosmi Historia since 1619 (), "A very clear demonstration of the three kinds of vision in the Microcosm (or soul of man); of the location of their objects, and of the manner of discerning them." Surely no figure of "Earth" was ever drawn before or since so lightly poised, so aethereally supported.

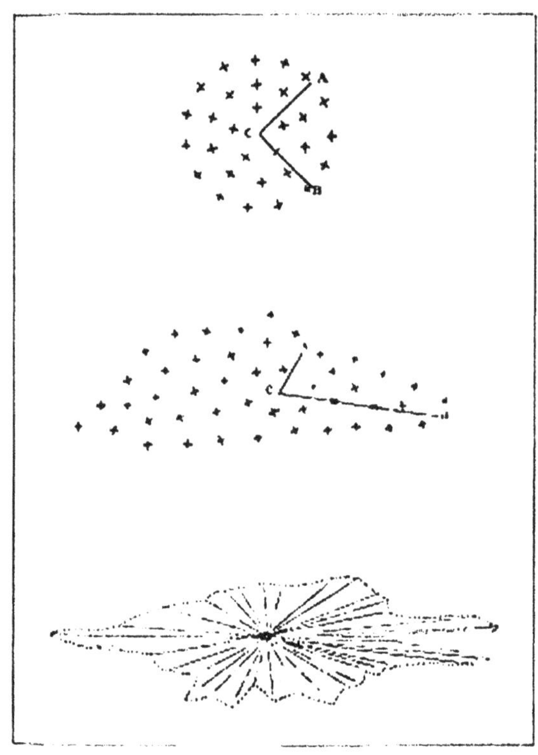

FIGURE 33. A Figure of the Universe.
(From The System of the World; John Nichol, 1848.)

Unless it is the tiny figure of Earth as the end and the beginning of the Spiral World (Plate V) which immediately follows in the Microcosmi Historia: "Another demonstration showing how the soul rises in a spiral ascent from the sensible things of the world to unity, through twenty-two stages, beginning with the Earth, and ascending upwards to God; that is, from multiplicity to unity." This is drawn in twenty-two whorls or "grades," beginning, by numbers, with "Terra" and ending with "Deus." Or, by the order of the Hebrew alphabet, beginning with "Deus" and ending in "Terra." These spiral grades or stages have each four signs to mark them; first, the letters of the Hebrew alphabet, beginning with the outer whorl and winding continuously inward to the centre. (The Hebrew alphabet, according to the Kabbala, is based on the primitive alphabet in which Gods were Letters, Letters were Ideas, Ideas were Numbers, and Numbers were perfect Signs.) Second, the names of the procession of grades, from the first manifestation of the Godhead, Mens or Mind, to its final expression in Terra or Earth. Third, numbers, from 1 to 22. Fourth, the tiny winged heads common to each completed whorl. The spiral, reaching from Heaven to Earth, is shown here as lying in a flat coil, like a spring. But it may be re-imaged as the winding line described about a sphere that tapers irresistibly out to a point. It is just that line, says this figure, described by a point moving in space, beginning in Heaven and ending in Earth, which at once separates and unites them. Beyond Earth there is nothing. But in Earth there is everything--even the power to make the descending spiral an ascending one. It can be re-imaged as an ascending vine, climbing back by way of the great World-tree. For life, said the ancients, flows never in one way. Rooted in Heaven, it descends to Earth, and rooted in Earth it may ascend to Heaven.

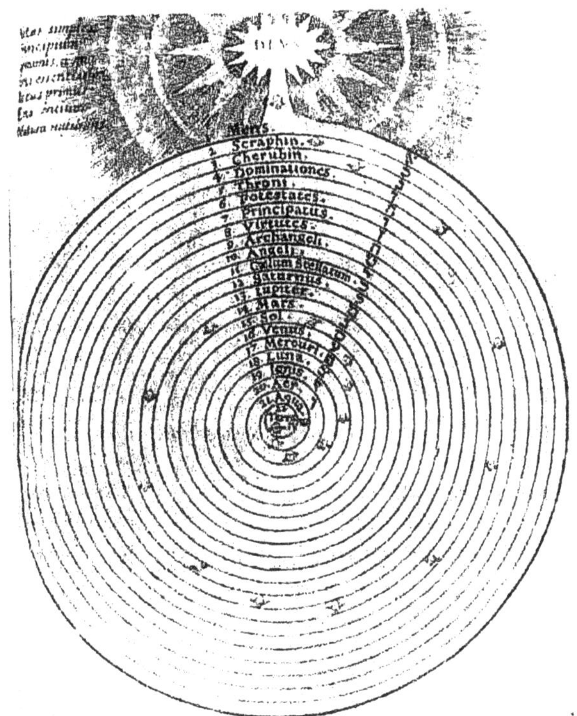

PLATE V. Another demonstration showing how the soul rises in a spiral ascent from the sensible things of the world to Unity.
(From Microcosmi Historia: Robert Fludd, 1619)

THE PRIMÆVAL EARTH

"BECAUSE IT PLEASETH more and makes a greater impression upon us," wrote the old English Platonist Thomas Burnet, "to see things represented to the Eye, than to read their description in words, we have ventured to give a model of the Primæval Earth, with its Zones or greater Climates, and the general order and tracts of its Rivers. Not that we believe things to have been in the very same form as here exhibited, but this may serve as a general Idea of that Earth, which may be wrought into more exactness, according as we are able to enlarge or correct our thoughts hereafter . . . . The Rivers of that Earth, you see, were in most respects different, and in some respects contrary to ours, and if you could turn our Rivers backwards, to run from the Sea towards their Fountain-heads, they would more resemble the course of these Antediluvian Rivers; for they were greatest at their first setting out; and the Current thereafter, when it was more weak, and the Chanel more shallow, was divided into many branches, and little Rivers, like the Arteries in our Body, that carry the Blood, they are greatest at first, and the further they go from the Heart, their Source, the less they grow and divide into a multitude of little branches, which lose themselves insensibly in the habit of the flesh as these little Floods did in the Sands of the begins to divide and subdivide into dozens of lesser streams, all of which finally dwindle away into the Earth instead of rising from it.

What was the state of the primæval Earth before man appeared, and with him, trouble? All the Creation stories give a common answer--harmony; harmony of all the spheres. It is in the song to Mahat, with its ordered account of the separation of the five great Elements from Chaos, and their recombinings into the bodies of the universe. "He made them all to move evenly," says the Creation legend of the Lenape, after the Great Manito had formed land and sky and moon and stars; and in the pictograph the even movement is a spiral line. In Sebastien Muenster's Cosmographia Universalis (1559), at the beginning of the chapter on "The creation and disposing of the primordial Earth and Sea," is an old drawing evidently intended to show the paradisaical state of terrestrial affairs at the end of the Fifth Day of Creation, with the great stage built and the great scene set and lighted for the entrance of man and the beginning of his drama (Plate VI). It is a picture in successive planes of the Genesis story, with a charming addition--the boat with sails, floating in the foreground; and, on it, a little three-storied house--the Ark, perhaps, whose part in the coming drama had been already foreseen by the Creator, and which was to become, of all the vanished treasures of a drowned and broken Earth, man's single precious possession.

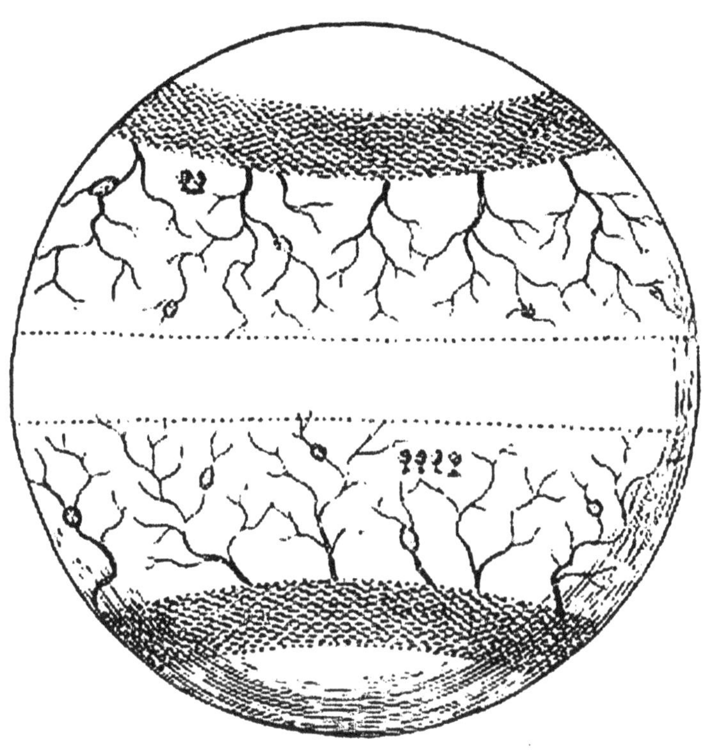

FIGURE 34. The Primæval Earth, with its Zones or greater Climates, and the general order and tracts of its Rivers.
(From The Theory of the Earth; Thomas Burnet, 1697.)

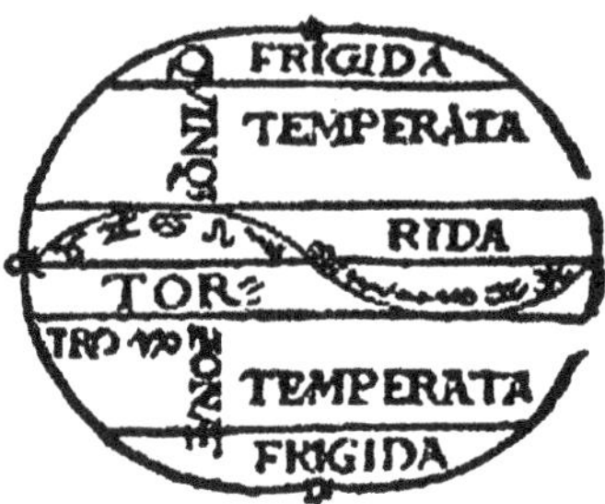

FIGURE 34A. Zones or Climates of the Earth, with the Zodiac. (From Sphæra emendata; Joannes Sacro Bosco, Cologne, 1601.)

THE BABYLONIAN UNIVERSE

WHAT PEOPLE AT WHAT TIME first imagined the Earth as a hollow hemispherical shell floating on the world-waters we cannot know. But it is another of the "oldest figures of Earth." This idea of the Earth as "boat-shaped" had its origin probably in the almost universal myth of the Deluge; the transition from an Ark floating right side up, to the Earth, itself a boat, floating upside down, is an easy one. But "boat-shaped" is a word which, thanks to our modern patterns, has lost its early significance. The ancient world had, however, among a certain people, a boat built on exactly such an hemi- spherical model. To-day, on the Euphrates River, these same kufas float--the round boats of the ancient Chaldeans, made of skins, stretched and sewed into a hollow hemisphere. And to-day, likewise, on the same river, fishermen ride at ease on the same inflated cushions or air-boats of skin that were in use thousands of years ago. Nothing skimmed the waters more swiftly than these circular boats, and nothing floated more safely than these hollow hemispheres of stretched skin upturned on the waters.

There is a curious relation between the ancient boats and the Assyrian story of the Creation. If these boats were hemispheres of stretched skin, so were the Heavens and the Earth. Merodach, the world-maker of this legend, lay for a long time helpless like the other gods under the blind rule of Chaos-Tiemat, from whom sprang everything and who created unceasingly, but who had yet created neither Heaven nor Earth. From her issued spontaneously monstrous animals and figures, men with two wings and others with four, with two faces or four, with goats' legs and horns, or with the hindparts of a horse and the foreparts of a man; animals with human heads or fishes' tails; other forms in which every sort of animal shape was united in confusion, and this confusion of creation run mad never ceased.

PLATE VI. THE PRIMORDIAL EARTH AND SEA
(From Cosmographia Universalis, Sebastian Muenster, 1599).

But finally Merodach arose, alone of all the gods, to meet her, and then it was that Space witnessed its most terrific combat. He finally slew her, but matters were hardly bettered, for Tiemat's great dead body stretched throughout all Space. "He placed his foot upon her," reads the Assyrian story, "and with his unerring knife he cut into the upper part of her; then he cut the blood vessels, and caused the blood to be carried by the north wind to the hidden places. . . . He contemplated the great corpse, raised it and wrought marvels. He split it in two as one does a fish for drying; then he hung up one of the halves on high, which became the heavens." The other half he spread out under his feet to form the Earth, and immediately all the creatures that were in her disappeared. Merodach again surveyed the empty world; then he cut off his own head, and, having kneaded the blood flowing from it with the Earth, formed men, who were thus endowed with a surviving particle of understanding and with a surviving particle of divine thought.

This odd conception of the heavens as made of "skin" is found over and over among primitive races. The Yakuts say that the sky is made of several skins, tightly stretched and overlapping. The Buriats call the Milky Way a "stitched seam" in the sky, and they speak with awe of a "certain being" who murmurs from time to time, "Long, long ago, when I was young, I sewed the sky together."

The picture of the kufa (Plate VII, A) is given to make clearer what most of the writers on the old Akkadian cosmogony mean when they say, "The Akkadians or Chaldeans considered the Earth to be hollow and boat-shaped." For "boat-shaped" meant to them no elongated oval figure, but distinctly a hollow hemisphere, a round shell, even a "stretched skin." Plate VII, B shows Myer's construction of their world on just this model, and his interpretation is followed below. [1]

Briefly, E is the convex side of the hollow Earth shell. From C to E stretches the Lower Firmament, or zone of the atmosphere--winds, storms and clouds; this zone rests firmly upon the convex Earth shell. From C to A is the Upper Firmament, divided into two layers; from A to B is the zone of the spirit of the heavens; and from B to C is the zone of the planets--"sheep," or "wanderers," or "watchers." This is the zone also of lightning and of thunder. A, in this diagram, represents the Zodiac, which is "in Space and the Great Celestial Ocean," called also the "Deep" and the "Abyss." T'hom, the Great Dragon of this Great Sea, was also called Tiemat, and it was really looked upon as the Primordial Abyss out of which everything in the Universe, including Heaven and Earth, came. The arrangement of the seven planets, between B and C, are, according to Myer, a. Saturn, b. Jupiter, c. Mars, d. Sun, e. Venus, f. Mercury, g. Moon, and Earth the centre.

F F is the concave side of the Earth shell, with seven zones described, "answering," says Myer, "as shadows, to the orbits of the seven planets." This was the realm of the king of the ghost-world, the king of the dead. Curiously enough, it was believed to have been ruled over at one time by Ea, deity of Wisdom. G was the Nadir, and I was the mountain of the East, or the mountain of the world, which supported the Upper Firmament and the Great Celestial Ocean. II is the Great Chaotic Crystalline Sea, extending to an unknown distance beyond the Zodiacal zone. III is the pivot of the Star zone, on the top of the World mountain, upon which the firmament

---

[1] Qabbalah; Isaac Myer, 1888, pp. 448-450.

revolves. IV are the guarded gates to the Underworld, abode of the dead, or home of the dark spirits, or a place for punishment. Yet in it are concealed the waters of life, and through this region of the Underworld the nightly journey of the Sun takes place, from west to east.

Disregarding any number of merely technical differences between them, this diagram of Myer's will serve as a fair picture of any cosmogony based on the idea that the Earth is a hollow hemisphere with an underworld. But there is sharp disagreement over whether after all the ancient Assyrian people--certainly the Chaldeans and Babylonians--believed that the Earth was a hemispherical shell, or whether they believed that it was something quite other than that.

Babylon was mighty, and it perished utterly. Of all its wisdom, only battered fragments of texts remain; which present-day scholars have worked for years to interpret. Within a period of just twenty years, from 1888 to 1908, eight different diagrams of the supposed figure of this Babylonian Universe were offered by eight different men, of which Myer's diagram was the first. The last of these is Dr. William Fairfield Warren's, first published in The Journal of the Royal Asiatic Society, 1908. As he points out, no two of the other seven agree; certainly no one of the other seven bears any likeness to this beautiful construction of eight crystalline spheres surrounding a cubical, pyramidal, antipodal Earth-figure (Plate VIII).

"For the reconstruction of the Babylonian universe," he says, "we have no less than twelve most valuable data derived from the study of ancient Babylonian texts." Following is an abstract of the twelve data on which he modelled this translucent universe. [1]

1. In the Babylonian conception of the universe the earth occupied the central place. It was the accepted centre of their planetary system.

2. The northern half of the earth was called the upper, associated with life and light. The southern half was called the under, associated with darkness and death. The South and the Underworld are identical.

3. The upper or northern half of the earth was regarded as consisting of seven stages (tupukati), ranged one above the other in the form of a staged

---

[1] Journal Royal Asiatic Society of Great Britain and Ireland, 1908, pp. 977-983.

pyramid. The staged Temple of Nippur, according to Sayce, was a model of the Earth according to the belief of those who built it.

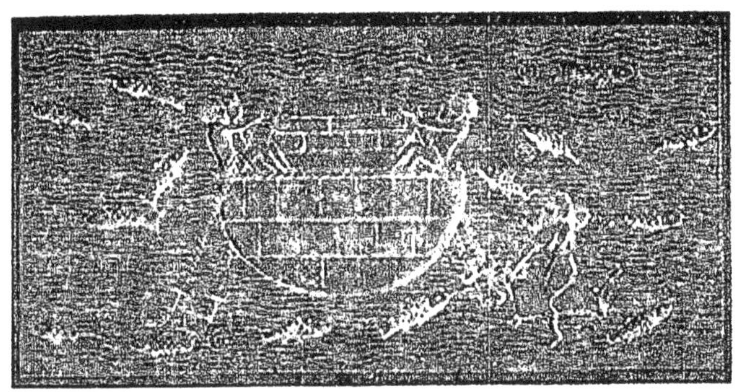

PLATE VII. A. A kufa laden with stoner and manned by a crew of four men. Drawn by Faucher-Gudin from a bas-relief at Koyunjik.
(From The Dawn of Civilization; Gaston Maspero, 1894)

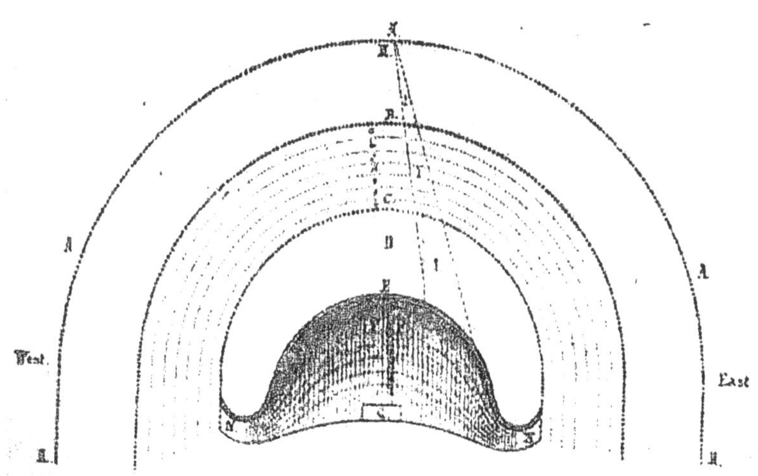

PLATE VII. B. Construction of the Akkadian, Chaldean and Babylonian Universe.
(From Qaballah; Isaac Myer, 1888)

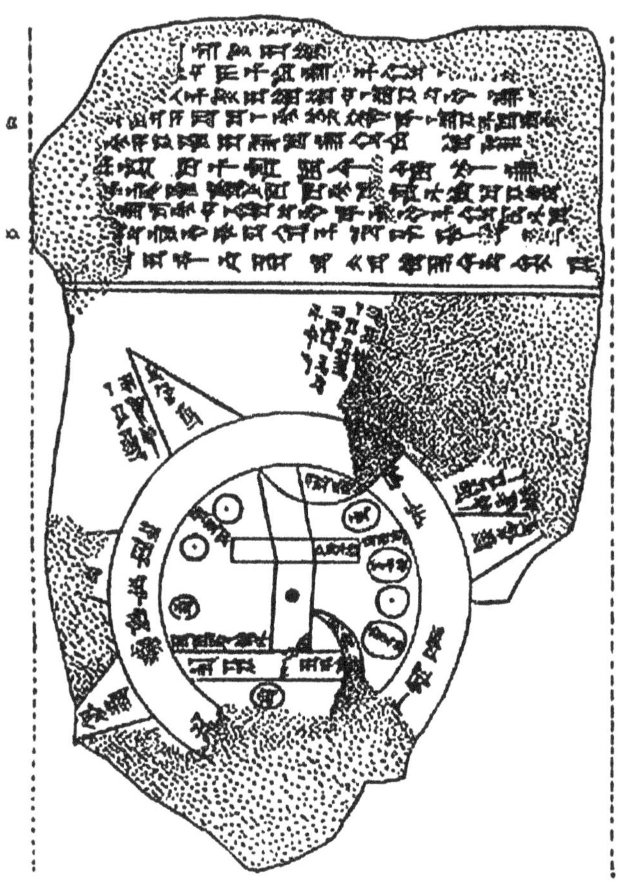

FIGURE 35. Babylonian "Mappa Mundi" inscribed on a Babylonian geographical tablet in the British Museum, No. 92,687. Showing the ocean surrounding the world, and marking the position of Babylon on the Euphrates as its centre. It shows also the mountains at the source of the river, the land of Assyria, Bit-lakinu, and the swamps at the mouth of the Euphrates.
(From Cuneiform Texts from Babylonian Tablets, etc., in the British Museum, 1906: Part XXII, Plate 48. The reading is taken from The Babylonian Legends of the Creation. Brit. Mus. Pubs., 1921, p. 3.)

4. Correspondingly, the antarctic or under half of the Earth was supposed to consist of seven similar stages. The seven tupukati of the underworld are a facsimile of the seven tupukati of the over world.

5. Like the quadrilateral temple modelled after it, the Earth of the Babylonians was four-cornered. In this particular it agreed with the conception ascribed to the ancient Egyptians, Hebrews, Chinese, and to the Indo-Aryans of the Rig-Veda period.

6. In Babylonian thought there were seven heavens and seven hells. This belief is one of untraceable antiquity.

7. Above the seventh heaven was another, the "highest heaven," that of the fixed stars, called by the Babylonians the "heaven of Anu," after the name of one of their oldest and highest gods.

8. This eighth heaven was divided by the Zodiac into two corresponding portions, an upper, or Arctic, and an under, or Antarctic. At the upper pole Anu had his palace and throne.

9. In Babylonian thought, the north pole of the heavens was the true zenith of the cosmic system, and the axis of the system upright; consequently the diurnal movements of the sun and moon were regarded as occurring in a horizontal plane.

10. Proceeding outward from the central Earth, the order of the seven known planets was as follows: Moon, Sun, Mercury, Venus, Mars, Jupiter, Saturn. That their respective distances from the Earth were not uniform was already known.

11. In order to pass from the upper half of the Earth to its under half, that is, from the abode of living men to the abode of the dead, it was necessary to cross a body of water which on every side separated the two abodes.

12. According to Diodorus Siculus, the Babylonians considered that the twelve designated stars south of the Zodiac stood in the same relation to the dead as do the twelve corresponding stars north of the Zodiac to men in the land of the living. This representation clearly makes the living and the dead the residents respectively of antipodal surfaces of one and the same heaven-enclosed Earth. According to the Babylonian Creation Tablets (V,

line 8) Anu and Ea are antipodally located gods, Anu being enthroned at the north pole of the heavens, and Ea at the south pole.

These twelve propositions, says Dr. Warren, are the fundamental features of the ancient Babylonian world-concept, and each of the twelve requirements is met by this figure. The upright central line represents the polar axis of the heavens and Earth in perpendicular position. The two central seven-staged pyramids represent the upper and lower halves of E-KUR, the Earth; the upper is the abode of living men, the lower the abode of the dead. The separating waters are the four seas. The seven dotted half circles above the Earth represent the "seven heavens," and the corresponding seven hemispheres below the earth, the "seven hells." The seven inner concentric spheres are respectively the domains and abodes of Sin, Shamash, Nabu, Ishtar, Nergal, Marduk, and Ninib, each being a "world-ruler" in his own planetary sphere. (The order of these spheres has been given above as Moon, Sun, Mercury, Venus, Mars, Jupiter, and Saturn.) The outer-most sphere (with its upper half cut away, as are the upper seven heavens, to show better the interior of the system) is the sphere of the antipodal gods, Anu and Ea, and the heaven of the fixed stars. It is to be noted further, Dr. Warren explains, that the spaces between the spheres widen rapidly at each remove from the Earth, so rapidly that in a world-view the size of this, they cannot be represented other than as in this plate.

Dr. 'Warren calls this "The Babylonian Universe" principally because Babylonia is almost the limit of our back-ward reach to the wisdom of the past, and our retracing of the persistent recurrences of so many of these principles--the "four-cornered Earth," or the cubical Earth, the "seven heavens," "Earth and counter-Earth," the "crystalline spheres," the "mountains of the world," and so on--must end there. But its origin, he says, was among a people antedating the Babylonians. "A truer name therefore for the system would be the Pre-Babylonian. The East-Semites received it from their predecessors in the possession of the Euphratean valley, the Akkado-Sumarians. At least such is the opinion and the teaching of our highest experts. Did the system originate among those non-Semitic predecessors in the valley? This has been assumed, but no man can pretend to know."

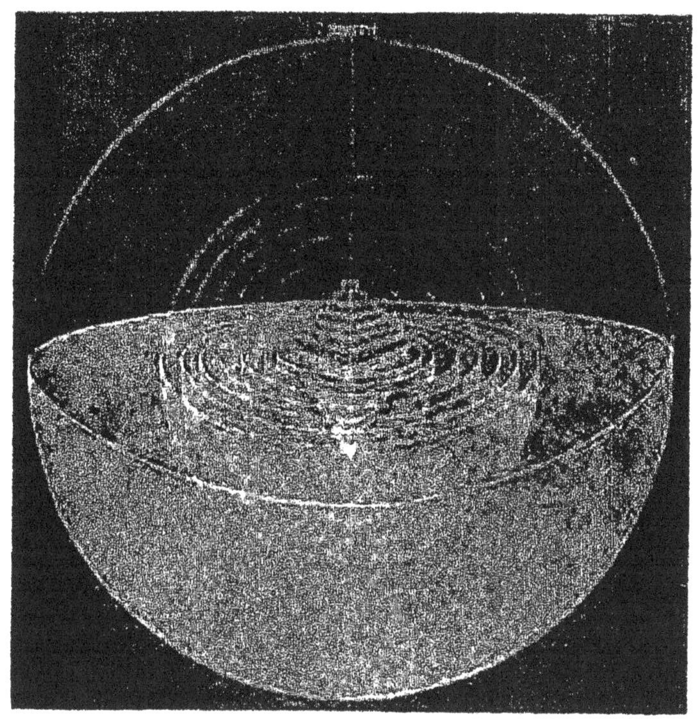

PLATE VIII. THE BABYLONIAN UNIVERSE
(From The Universe as pictured in Milton's Paradise Lost;
William Fairfield Warren, 1915)

THE EGYPTIAN UNIVERSE

IN THE METROPOLITAN MUSEUM of the City of New York, rests the grey diorite sarcophagus of Uresh-Nofer, one time priest of the "watery" goddess Mut, in Egypt. On the upper half of the sarcophagus lid is engraved the figure of the Sky goddess Nut "bending over the Earth," a marvellous picture of the Egyptian Universe.

"The Sky Goddess Nut bending over the Earth," and the succeeding Plate, "The Goddess Nut represented Double," bring up so clearly the first of the major traditional catastrophes of the Earth, that it would be timely just now to consider them briefly. There have been five, one so dimly related that it shall be left till the last. But there are four great timeless traditions of great disasters. The first is the violent separation of Earth from Heaven. The second is the appalling Earth-Moon catastrophe. The third is the Deluge, and the fourth is the sinking of Atlantis. Or, it may be, the third in point of "time" is the sinking of Atlantis, and the fourth is the Deluge. Or, again, it may be that these two catastrophes, though individual, were coincident with each other. Tradition however is, happily, not logic, and so, even in a disorderly order, we may take up the outstanding afflictions of the planet we call Earth.

First, then, the violent separation of Earth from Heaven, which these Egyptian world-pictures illustrate so beautifully.

Nut was goddess of the starry sky. Sometimes she is represented as powdered with stars; sometimes, as here, with but a line of them along her spine; once at least, on the sarcophagus lid of Uresh-Nofer, with the three discs or spheres of universal significance--body, spirit, soul--connected by eight stars and by six. Sometimes the band of stars was accompanied by a band of water flowing over her spine--the celestial Nile, as the Egyptians called the mysterious heavenly waters that covered the world. Sometimes the path of the celestial Nile is called the path of the Milky Way; and often the path of the Milky Way is called the path of souls." Through her husband, Seb, she gave birth to the Sun, which was ever after re-born each morning: daily it made its journey from east to west beneath her body until, sinking below the western horizon, it passed into the mouth of Nut, traversed her body during the night, to be born again at dawn. Nut also gave birth to the Moon, which came forth from her breasts as milk. And to countless other heavenly bodies as well whose genealogy would take us too far.

This is the story of Nut or Heaven and of Seb or Earth.

PLATE IX THE SKY GODDESS NUT BENDING OVER THE EARTH
From the Sarcophagus of Uresh-Nofer, Priest of the Goddess Mut (XXXth dynasty, 378-341 B.C.)
(In the Metropolitan Museum of the City of New York)

In the beginning--that stirless rest in which all myths of the original Creation begin--Heaven and Earth were together, wedded gods, from whom was to spring all that has been, is, and shall ever be. Time was not yet, sings one of the old world-hymns, nor Universal Mind, nor Thought, nor Word. Bliss was not. Misery was not. Darkness alone filled the boundless All, for Father-Mother-Son were once more one, and the Son had not yet awakened for the new Wheel and his new Pilgrimage. The Universe was still concealed in the Divine Thought and the Divine Bosom.

But the day of Creation came, and a new god, Shu, god of Air or of Sunlight, sprang out of the primordial waters. He slipped between the two, and tearing Nut with force from the body of Seb her husband, raised her to the sky. Her star-spangled body marked the extent of the firmament; and her hands and feet hanging down were the four pillars of the firmament and the four quarters of the Earth. There ever since she has remained, bending over the Earth, eternally watching the Earth and the children of Earth.

Of Seb the Earth it is related that he did not endure the violent separation from Nut without a struggle. He sought to rise, that he might fight and overcome the newly created god. But as he struggled, just roused from deep dreamless sleep, he was arrested and held in the curious position he has ever since maintained (Plate X, B), without power to change it. He has been veiled each spring with plants and herbs and grasses; and winter has wrapped him in ice an now; while along his back has passed the endless panorama of the generations of animals and men. Through him is given to them all they have; he gives and they ungratefully take, never asking if he has a need they might supply, a sorrow they might soothe. Often he sleeps, and, sleeping, dreams of Nut, forgetting for a time his grief and pain; forgetting for a time that between him and his mate, forever separating them, stands Shu, god of Air or of Sunlight. But he may never again sink into dreamless sleep; sooner or later the circle of his dreams rounds on itself, and he is roused by pain to his state of suffering again. This is why Earth eternally questions Heaven until, wearied with waiting for answers that never come, he sinks again into slumber. Some say that Heaven answers Earth when he dreams, but because the path of his dreaming is a circle, he has forgotten most of Heaven's answers when he awakes.

And some have quite another story of Seb the Earth; namely, that Seb is concealed under the form of a colossal gander, whose mate laid the Sun Egg, and perhaps still lays it every day. Or again there is another story of

Shu, which is that as the divine Son, he had later in his turn begotten Seb and Nut, the two deities he had separated.

Such then is the first catastrophe--every religion has recognised it; that the Earth is cut off, disinherited, a troubled, troublesome, perturbed, perturbating, turbulent, storm-swept, dream-sodden, staggering, breathless, complaining planet; and that all of its children have inherited its qualities.

EARTH-MOON CATASTROPHE

THE second catastrophe to afflict the Earth in the beginning of things was the Earth-Moon catastrophe; and this, by the way, is not only one of the most ancient of traditions, but it is also a modern theory of causes with which science has been flirting for half a century. So difficult is it to find anything new, even a new theory, which cannot be traced back along some old tangled thread of folk-lore. It is difficult, however, to find anything older in man's consciousness than the riddle of the Moon. What is it, that changeless, ever-changing, flat-faced disc in the sky, forever turning about the Earth, yet never turning its other face to the Earth? What mysterious other-world, under-world, over-world, dead or alive, lies on its secret side? What is the relation of the Moon to the Earth and to man? what the relation of the hidden life of the Earth and of man to the Moon? Tradition had doubled these two bodies as a pair acted upon by the Sun, long before astronomers had given us the image of Earth-Moon as a beautiful double planet moving among the stars; long before mathematicians had constructed from the interrelated "pull" of Sun and Moon and Earth the baffling "problem of three bodies," before which many a wise man has fallen.

PLATE X. A. The Heavenly Goose.
(From Ancient Mythology: Jacob Bryant, 1774, Vol. II)

PLATE X. B. The Sky Goddess Nut represented double.
(From The Dawn of Astronomy; J. Norman Lockyer, 1894)

FIGURE 36. Lunar and Solar Eclipses.
(From Sphæra Mundi; Joannes Sacro Bosco, Venice, 1482.)

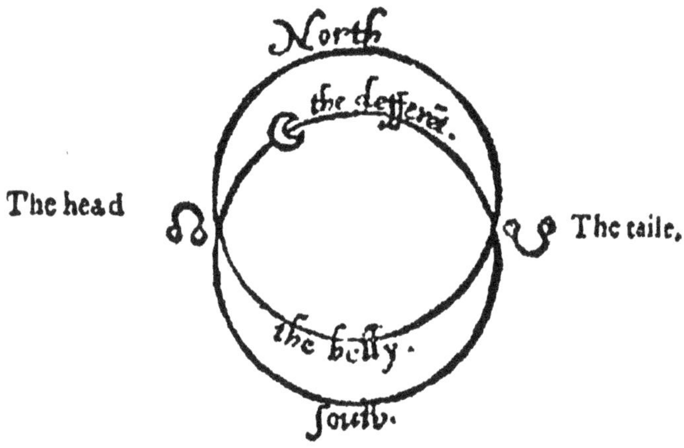

FIGURE 37. The Figure of the Dragon: the Lunar Nodes.
(From Blundeville His Exercises; London, 1606.)

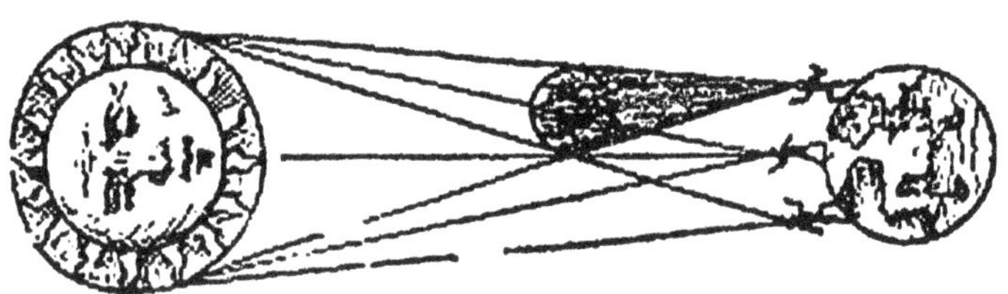

FIGURE 38. "When the Moone is betwixt the Sunne and the Earth."
(From Blundeville His Exercises; London, 1606.)

Here is the ancient story of the genesis of the Moon.

Long after the separation of Heaven and Earth, and while Earth was still in process of being made ready for human life, but before man had been yet created, it chanced that the line of its course in the heavens was crossed by that of a great Comet, and that by some heavenly accident, the two enormous bodies collided. The terrific impact resulted in the cracking of the Earth's hard shell, and a huge fragment--some traditions say two--was torn away as violently as Nut was torn, in the Egyptian myth, from the body of Seb. This fragment of Earth promptly went into space, and became known as the Moon; and ever since that time Earth and Moon, Mother and Daughter, have been following each other through the heavens. As to which is the pursued, which the pursuer, old accounts vary. But there is always the stable myth of Ceres and Proserpina to fall back on.

Very soon after Galileo made the first drawing of the Moon, in 1610, John Wilkins, Lord Bishop of Chester, devised a highly curious little book, entitled The Discovery of a New World in the Moone, or, A Discourse tending to Prove that 'tis probable there may be another habitable World in that Planet. Wilkins bulwarks his "guess" with similar ones of the ancients: "Pythagoreans in general did affirm," he says, "that the Moone also was Terrestrial, and that she was inhabited as this lower World.

To this opinion of Pythagoras did Plato also assent . . . we may read often in him and his followers of an æthera terra and a lunares populi--an Æthereal Earth and Inhabitants in the Moone." As their world is our Moon, so our world is their Moon, he declares, and quotes others of antiquity, whose Heavens and Elysian Fields were there, where the air is most quiet and pure. In the frontispiece to his book, he attempts to show just this relation between them. He goes back to the old Greek myth of the Earth, and calls the two Ceres and Proserpina. "By the fable of Ceres," he says, "continually wandering in search of her daughter Proserpina, it meant nothing else but the longing desire of Men, who live upon Ceres, Earth, to attain a Place in Proserpina, the Moon or Heaven," and he held that "'tis possible for some of our Posterity to find out a Conveyance to this other World; and, if there be inhabitants there, to have Commerce with them."

Buffon seems to have been the first of modern scientists to voice the modern theory of the genesis of the Moon from this then moonless planet. He followed the push of tradition and made a Comet responsible for the split. This was in the eighteenth century. But in 1879, George H. Darwin lifted tradition to the dignity of an hypothetical guess, and suggested, as a part of his theory of Tidal Evolutions, that the Moon was formerly a part of the Earth; that it was originally much nearer the Earth than it is at present, and is now slowly receding from it; that at the time of the separation of the Earth into Earth and Moon, the planet was hardly larger than it is to-day; that it was hot, solid, ellipsoidical, with an interior more or less liquid, revolving on its axis once every four or five hours, its density increasing and its volume diminishing as it cooled; that, as its volume lessened, its speed of rotation increased, until by centrifugal force, the Moon was born, carrying with it, in its flight into Space, three-quarters of the Earth's crust.

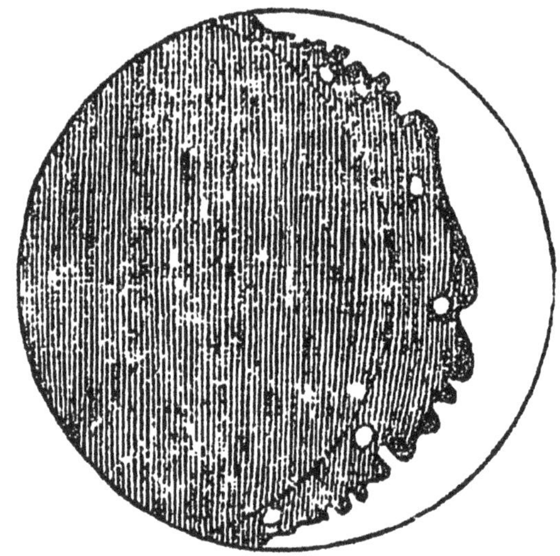

FIGURE 39. The first drawing of the Moon, by Galileo, 1610.
(From The Discovery of a World in the Moone; John Wilkins, 1638.)

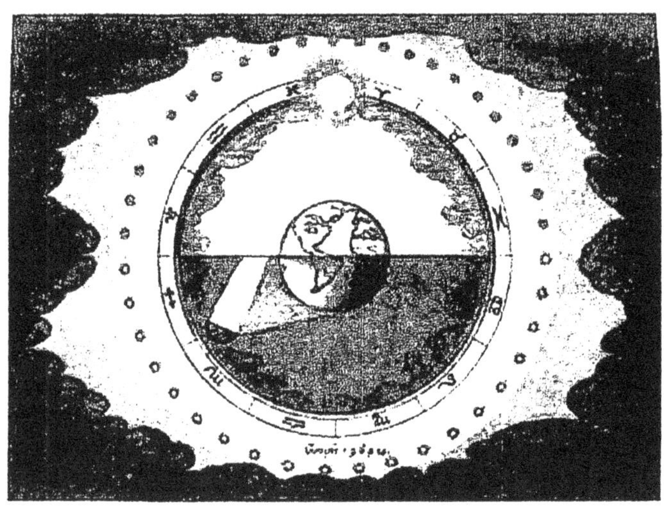

OMNIA PER IPSUM FACTA SUNT
Matter in motion, figure, rest: adde Grade. This is the very somme of All God made: Att first of nought by's power in six dayes space. Now nature acts it's part; here after Grace. (From Bybel Printen; Matthaeus Merian, 1650)

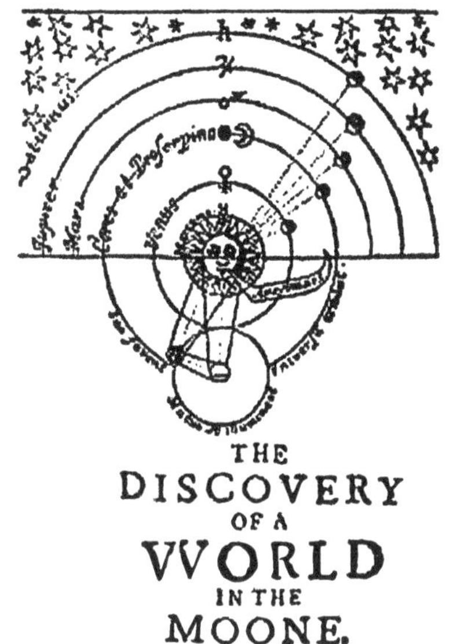

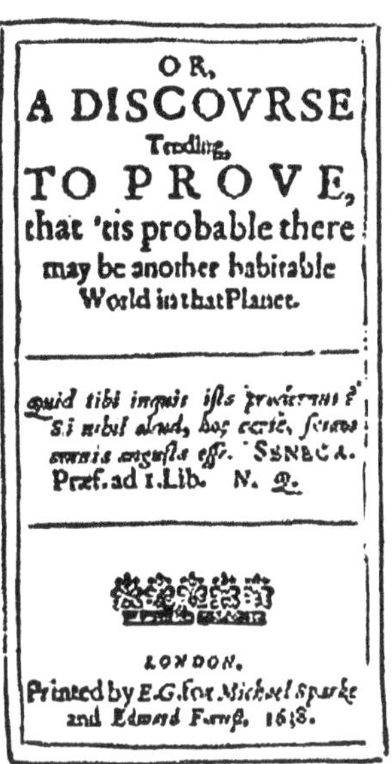

OR,
A DISCOVRSE
Tending,
TO PROVE,
that 'tis probable there
may be another habitable
World in that Planet.

SENECA.
Præf. ad 1.Lib. N. Q.

LONDON,
Printed by E.G. for Michael Sparke
and Edward Forrest, 1638.

FIGURE 40. Frontispiece and Title-page of "The Discovery of a World in the Moone"; John Wilkins, 1638.

A good deal of interesting discussion followed this new type of Darwinian theory, and a number of scientists began to speculate on the precise place of the origin of the Moon, granted that Darwin was right. Of course--and here again tradition guided them--or had at least preceded them--they chose the Pacific Ocean basin that holds apart the scarred coast lines of western North and South America, and eastern Asia, the East Indies, New Zealand, and the Antarctics. One of these speculators amused himself to good purpose: Plate XII, shows George D. Swazey's extraordinarily imaginative "quarter Earth" which remained after the Moon had flown, cracked by great lines of cleavage that were to slowly split the plastic floating crust into two major continental masses.

PLATE XII. THE EARTH AFTER THE EARTH-MOON CATASTROPHE
(Drawn by George D. Swazey for Popular Astronomy, Aug.-Sept., 1907.)

Among the old drawings of the Moon, it is difficult to choose--they are all so beautiful. One drawing, however, must always stand for an example of the miracles man has wrought in this quest of his--the first drawing of the Moon (Fig. 39), made in 1610 by Galileo through his "Glasse." That tiny lens, compared to the gigantic telescopes of to-day, amounted to considerably less than a child's toy. But it magnified a surface three times, and with it Galileo essayed to prove or disprove Aristotle's theory that "the form and images of the Ocean appear in the Moon as in a Mirror." "Leaving aside these terrestrial things," he said, "I have directed my researches towards the. heavens, beginning with the Moon." He decided very quickly that the Moon had no mirror-like surface, for he discovered mountains, circular hollows, and many bright spots which he compared to the eyes in a peacock's tail. Before he died, he had succeeded in making a glass which magnified surfaces thirty-two times, and it was not long before the surface of the Moon was mapped out and named. It was a world so similar in many of its formations to those of the Earth, that its first map-maker, Hevelius, simply transferred to the Moon the names of the cities and seas and mountains of the Earth. But Riccioli, in 1651, renamed its mountains and craters and supposed lakes and seas, not after places of the Earth, but after the learned men of the Earth, choosing rather to place their names in the sky. Instead of lunar Alps or Apennines, there arose on the Moon great mountain ranges, or plains, or craters bearing the names of Plato, Ptolemy, Copernicus, Kepler, Tycho; instead of lunar seas called Caspian, Mediterranean, and the like, there were instead the Seas of Storms, of Clouds, of Rains: the Seas of Tranquillity, of Serenity, and the Lake of Dreams--enchanting names which linger to this day.

THE DELUGE

THE third and fourth catastrophes of the Earth are the Deluge, and the sinking of Atlantis--Atlantis the fabulous continent, not the little Island remnant. Their time sequence in the old traditions is a little mixed, not that it matters. Suppose we take first the Deluge.

The Comet, that blazing terror of the skies, that erratic wanderer of the heavens, has always been given more than its probable share of blame for terrestrial bad luck. It has been called the cause of the birth of the Moon; it has also been held responsible for the universal Deluge. This is another of those untraceably old traditions, but we begin with the Comet of 1680, and the remarkable egg laid at Rome on December 4 of the Comet-year; because this Comet and this egg are responsible for two "Theories of Earth" written within the next twenty years, both by Englishmen. William Whiston worked out a complete theory of a deluged, because Comet-riven, Earth, and Thomas Burnet developed his theory of Earth as the Mundane Egg whose broken shell unlocked the "waters of the deep."

The evidence in the case is at hand in the shape of the elaborate frontispiece to Lettre d'un gentil-homme de province à une dame de qualité sur le sujet de la Comete, a brief little labour of informative love published anonymously in 1681, but known now to have been written by Claude François Manestrier. "An extraordinary freak of nature," it reads, "occurred in Rome, at the time of the appearance of the Comet, in the Palace of the Maximi, which was seen by His Holiness, by the Queen of Sweden, and by all persons of the first rank in Rome. The design of it was sent to Paris, as an entirely new thing, by a per-son greatly interested and worthy of confidence. On the 4th of December, 1680, in the Palace of the Maximi, a hen laid an egg, on which could be discerned the figure of the Comet, accompanied by other markings such as are here represented. All the most skilled naturalists of Rome saw and examined it, and found it to be a freak of nature unique and unparalleled. It is left to the curious gentlemen of Paris to make profitable use of it and to seek the cause."

PLATE XIII. One of the oldest drawings of the Moon. by Pere Capucin Marie de Rheita (1645). At the top Tycho is seen in full view, with its diverging rays. (From Iter Exstaticum Coeleste; Athanasius Kircher, 1660)

Now it has always been extremely difficult for the extremely exact among the theorists to account for the sources of waters great enough to bring about a universal Deluge. No rains of forty days and nights explain it, even when these rains from heaven are united with all the external waters of the Earth. There were, to be sure, the "fountains of the great deep," but how were they to be broken up! And it is said that the Comet-Egg of this Comet-year gave good Will Whiston the idea he needed for solving the mystery of the Deluge. He published, in 1690, A New Theory of Earth, in which he set forth "the other main Cause of the Deluge, the breaking up of the fountains of the great deep," by the deadly weight of the waters in the tail of a Comet active in the heavens while Noah was building the Ark. "For when the near approach of the Comet to the Earth had rendered the Shape of that internal dense Fluid, on which its upper Crust rested, so very oblong and oval, and its Surface so much larger than before, as to occasion the opening of its perpendicular Fissures, which are visible at this day, . . . the vast weight of the additional Waters from the Comet would attempt to press this upper Earth deeper into the dense Fluid below . . . and so join the subterraneous to the cometical waters, for the supply of a Quantity sufficient for so vast a Purpose as that of a universal Deluge."

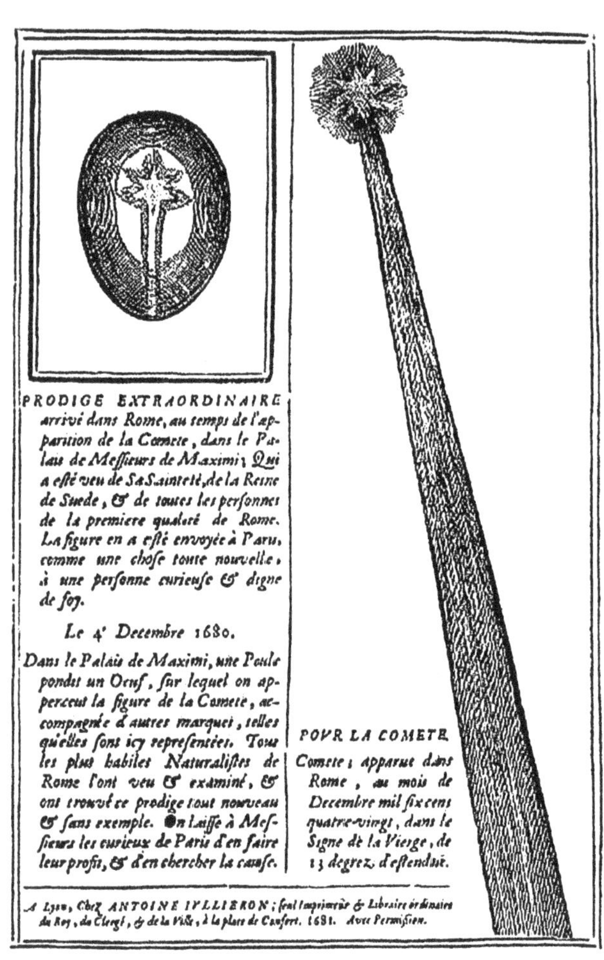

FIGURE 41. The Comet of 1680 and the marvellous Egg.
(Frontispiece of Lettre d'un gentil-homme de province à une dame de qualité sur le sujet de la Comete; Claude François Manestrier, 1681.)

Whiston went even farther in his "cometical" theory; he supposed the Earth to have been originally a Comet; to have had a lop-sided form without beauty or proportion; subject to all the misfortunes of Comets, "sometimes a thousand times hotter than melted iron; at other times a thousand times colder than ice." These alternations of hot and cold were "Chaos," a dense though fluid atmosphere which surrounded the solid contents of the Earth, and which was in a state of continuous agitation and shock from its unharmoniously mingled substances. It was the Comet's atmosphere or tail, filled with water, which "struck" the Earth and broke its surface; and Whiston describes minutely just how the antediluvian Comet involved the antediluvian Earth in its tail, until all of Earth, even the mountain of the world, was submerged.

Burnet's theory of the Earth as the Mundane Egg will come farther on, but no better place could be found in this collection of world-pictures than just here, for one of his beautiful drawings of the Deluge, the second Chaos, when, "upon this Chaos rid the distrest Ark that bore the small remains of Mankind," a ship whose cargo was no less than a whole world (Plate XIV). It is at once a picture of the Deluge after the dove was sent forth from the Ark, and a "Roughe Globe"; a delicate tracery of the broken Earth seen through water, as one looks down into a clear lake. There are vague glinting hints of lost or sunken continents that never emerged when the Earth dried and the waters ran off; a misty figuration of the new Earth, its pattern defined long before the Ark of Noah came to rest on Ararat; with some lost Lemuria, some sunk Atlantis, some shattered Pan or Mu still lingering along the declining edges of the continents about to be. Many of the modern "maps" of the Atlantean and Lemurian lands resemble very much this drawing of Burnet's, where continent seems to overlay continent until the oceans seem little more than spring floods in mountain valleys. Burnet speaks of Plato, who "supposeth his Atlantis to have been greater than Asia and Africa together, and yet to have sunk all into the Sea," and he concludes that great alterations in the face of the land and the sea would take place for a long time after the Deluge; that many of the fragments of land would change their posture, and that there would be a succession of sinkings and eruptions and lesser floods until all became poised and settled once again.

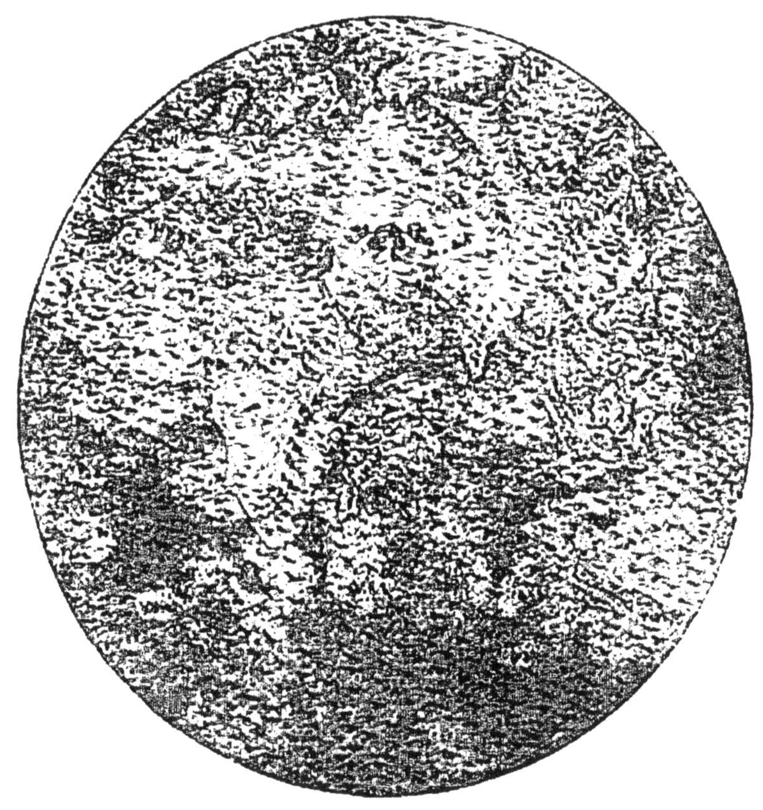

PLATE XIV "AND AGAIN HE SENT FORTH THE DOVE OUT OF THE ARK"
(From The Theory of the Earth; Thomas Burnet, 1697)

THE LOST ATLANTIS

THE fourth--or the third--catastrophe of the world-tradition is the sinking of Atlantis, the great prehistoric continent. A generation ago scientists would have smiled at the idea of taking this particular tradition seriously. But they do not smile to-day; they give the theory the Scotch verdict--"not proven." Even that conservative storehouse of factual knowledge, the Encyclopædia Britannica, says of this tradition, "It is impossible to decide how far this legend is due to Plato's invention, and how far it is based on facts of which no record remains." Fortunately for us, however, world-pictures are not based on proven facts, or they would never have been drawn, and Plato's story of the lost Atlantis, even if eventually proved "true," will always remain one of the most charming of fantasies. If you have not read it, in the Timaeus and the Critias, read it--his story of a golden world, when men were sons of gods and had not lost their heritage; of a civilisation that soared to heights of knowledge ours has never known--and sank. A few escaped this continental Deluge--Atlas escaped, says the old story, to support Heaven and Earth, in order that the Universe might not sink also.

Every one has seen somewhere Kircher's drawing of the Island of Atlantis--this was the last remnant of the continent, which tradition says sank 12,000 years ago--but it is doubtful that any one has ever seen it reproduced as it appeared in his Mundus Subterraneus of 1678 (Plate XV).

It is always reversed, relettered, and made to conform to the right geography. The ship in the upper right-hand corner is turned bottom side up, and made to lie at anchor in the lower left-hand corner. Let the old mistake stand, if mistake it was--and mistake it was surely. Turning it upside down will put everything into right relation with modern geography. Only the ship will be wrong, like a mirage in the waters. Plate XVI is Kircher's accompanying illustration of "Ocean mountains," whose highest peaks may be island remnants of sunken continents, a little ground plan of the ocean floor.

Kircher, whose bold "guesses" on things he could not prove brought him less fame than blame, guessed again on the combined problems of the Deluge and lost continents, and in his Arca Noë, 1665, presented, in a world-map, a "conjectural geography of the Earth's translation after the Flood, from the opinions of various geographers, to which the author subscribes" (Plate XVII). This is a very odd map, by the way, and one evidently little known to modern geographers. Imagine a little German scholar, sitting in Rome under the shadow of St. Peter's during the Thirty Years' War, and guessing simply, not only at the form and extent of the then discovered but by no means explored Americas, and not only at the form and extent of the still unknown Arctic and Antarctic "continents," but also at the conformation and extent of the "ocean-mountains," and of the sunken antediluvian continents. To say he guessed wrong is to say a little less than nothing. This map represents more clearly than his little drawing of Atlantis, his then novel theory that the Lost Island had been situated west of Gibraltar, and that the Canaries and the Azores are to-day its only remnants. But what it really does, of course, is to send the conjectural Atlantean continent straight west into the Americas, and almost across them. Who knows? We are still guessing, and the Mayan excavations are furnishing golden material for further guesses. It may very well be that half a century from now this old "guess-map" of Kircher's will be even more interesting than it is to-day.

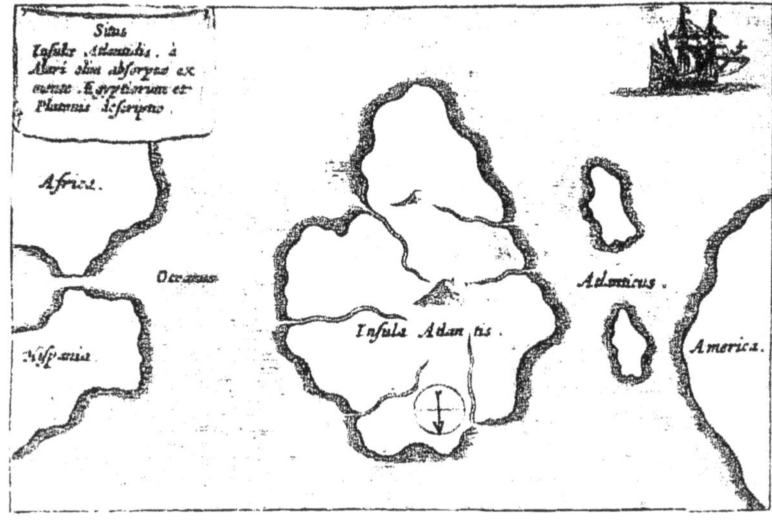

PLATE XV Situation of the Island of Atlantis, according to the ideas of the ancient Egyptians and the description of Plato.
(From Mundus Subterraneus; Athanasius Kircher, 1678)

According to the beautiful maps of W. Scott-Elliot 1--Kircher's map may serve as a guide for Scott-Elliot's slightly different theory--the Atlantean continent extended from a point a few degrees east of Iceland to, approximately, the site of Rio de Janeiro in South America, and across the ocean to the African Gold Coast. It took in Texas, and the Gulf of Mexico, the southern and eastern States of America up to and including Labrador, and stretched across the Atlantic to the British Isles, embracing Scotland, Ireland, and part of northern England. Atlantis is, by this assumption, the parent land of America--a great continent surrounded by water at a time so far away as that in which the Sahara Desert was an ocean floor.

LOST LAND OF THE WEST

BUT there is another obscure tradition of a fifth catastrophe which seems to have antedated the sinking of Atlantis. This concerns another lost continent in the Pacific Ocean, a great catastrophe in the western waters. Old records are riddled with allusions to vanished "Lands--and peoples--of the West." Old Aztec and Mayan records, that is; the Asiatic records speak of the vanished lands and peoples "of the East." This old tradition appeared first in modern times through the assumption of Sclater, an Englishman seeking for some "lost links," that long, long ago a great southern continent lay stretched about the South Pole very much as the continental land to-day surrounds the arctic zone. He named this continent Lemuria, to fix more firmly thereby his supposition that on such a continent animals of the Lemuroid type must have been developed. It is a curious instance in scientific history that when Ernst Haeckel, most material of materialistic scientists, came upon this Lemurian hypothesis, he promptly incorporated it into his own working scheme, and in his The History of Creation and The Evolution of Man he speaks of Lemurian creatures and Lemurian traces as if the existence of such a land had been already scientifically proved. His explanation, which failed to satisfy all scientists, was that the Lemurian time-cycle was the only supposable thing that explained certain otherwise inexplicable gaps in the evolutionary theory.

This prehistoric, pre-Atlantean continent, existing--if it existed--hundreds of thousands of years ago, has also been called the Continent of Pan. In Oahspe, A New Bible in the Words of Jehovih, published by John Ballou Newbrough in 1882, there is a world-map showing the location of this lost Pan in the Pacific Ocean. Oahspe makes its sinking coincident with the Deluge. The sacred people of Pan, the I'hins--otherwise the Algonkins--had been warned of the coming flood, and were building ships in which to escape--138 Arks of the Deluge set out from this Continent of Pan. ". . . in the same day the gates of heaven and Earth were opened. And the Earth rocked to and fro, as a ship at sea, and the rains fell in torrents, and loud thunderings came up from beneath the floor of the world. . . . And the vortex of the Earth closed in from the extreme, and lo, the Earth was broken! A mighty continent was cut loose from its fastenings, and the fires of the Earth came forth in flames and clouds with loud roarings. And the land rocked to and fro like a ship at sea. And again the vortex of the Earth closed in about on all sides, and by the pressure the land sank down beneath the water, to rise no more." The Algonkins, oddly enough, have a fascinating word with a fascinating meaning for just such shadowy fables as these. "It is only Nitatahakau," they say; which is to say, "I relate a fable. I am telling an old story invented for amusement."

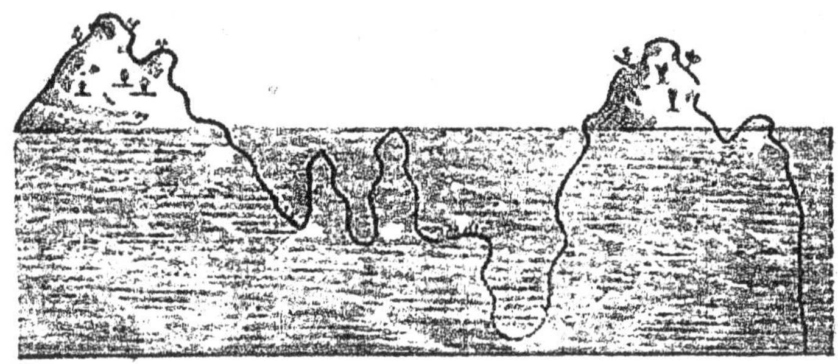

THE SUBTERRANEAN BRIDGE
(From Mundus Subterraneus; Athanasius Kircher, 1678).

FIGURE 42. Outline map showing the locality of Pan, the submerged continent.
(From Oahspe, A New Bible in the Words of Jehovih; John Ballou Newbrough, 1891, Plate 62.)

This dim continent has also been called the Continent of Mu. And by "this dim continent" I do not mean to say that Lemuria and Pan and Mu, or even that conjectural "western crust" of the Earth from which the Moon hypothetically sprang, are identical except in this way; that they all hang together on the same thread of tradition, that something at some far distant time happened in the centre of the space that is now called the Pacific basin. We have already seen that a serious modern scientific theory assigns the origin of the Moon to this planet, and that a supplementary theory suggests the Pacific basin as the place of the split. We have seen too that a southern continent, antipodal to Atlantis, has been assumed by evolutionists because something like it had to be assumed. Col. James Churchward's recent book on The Lost Continent of Mu is a unique and serious study of this traditional catastrophe in the western waters, carried on over a period of fifty years, during which time he collected all the collectable evidence on this theme, that once upon a time in the western ocean a great continent went down to rise no more.

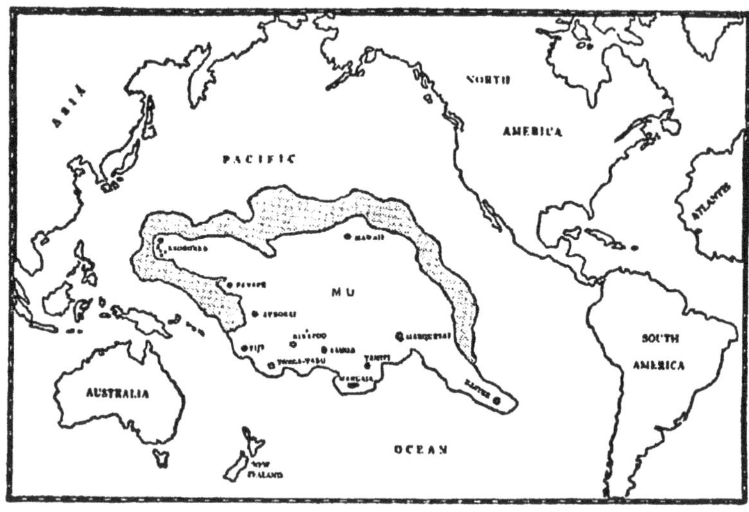

FIGURE 43. The geographical position of Mu.
(From The Lost Continent of Mu; James Churchward, 1926.)

His material is very interesting. Long-forgotten sacred tablets of India describe, he says, among other things, the creation of man in the land of Mu, the mother country of humanity--which land was not the land of Asia.

Records of later date describe the destruction of the land, "when the earth's crust was broken up by earthquakes, and then sank into a fiery abyss. Then the waters of the Pacific rolled in over her, leaving only water where a mighty civilisation had existed." He finds the land of Mu mentioned by Plato; he finds "the Land of Mu," or "Lands of the West" in the Troano Manuscript, an ancient Mayan book, and in the Codex Cortesianus, another Mayan book; he finds it in the Lhasa record, and in hundreds of other writings in all parts of the world, including India, Egypt, Greece, Central America, and Mexico.

He says that this continent was a vast one, extending from the north of Hawaii down towards the south. A line between Easter Island--with its massive sculptured stones for which no man has ever accounted--and the Fijis formed its southern boundary. It measured over 5,000 miles from east to west, and over 3,000 miles from north to south. The continent consisted of three areas of land, separated from each other by narrow seas or channels, and on it dwelt 64,000,000 people divided into "ten tribes" or "peoples." It was called the "Empire of the Sun," and it was the centre of the whole Earth's civilisation, of its learning, its art, and its commerce. Its great cities were seven, and its people, being skilled navigators, had sent out colonists to all parts of the Earth.

But the final one of a series of earthquakes came to Mu, and Col. Churchward quotes from old records: "'The whole continent heaved and rolled like the ocean's waves. The land trembled and shook like the leaves of a tree in a storm. Temples and palaces came crashing to the ground and monuments and statues were overturned. The cities became heaps of ruins.' As the land rose and fell, quivered and shook, the fires of the underneath burst forth, piercing the clouds in roaring flames three miles in diameter. There they were met by lightning shafts which filled the heavens. A thick black pall of smoke overshadowed the land. 'Huge cataclysmic waves rolled in over the shores and extended themselves over the plains.' Cities and all things living went down to destruction before them. 'Agonizing cries of the multitude filled the air. The people sought refuge in their temples and citadels only to be driven out by fire and smoke, and the women and the men in their shining garments and precious stones cried: "Mu, save us!"' . . . 'During the night' the land was torn asunder and rent to pieces. With thunderous roarings the doomed land sank. Down, down, down she went, into the mouth of hell, 'a tank of fire.' As the broken land fell into that great abyss of fire, 'flames shot up around and enveloped her.'

The fires claimed their victim. 'Mu and her 64,000,000 people were sacrificed.'"[1]

PLATE XVII. A Conjectural Geography of the Translation of the Earth after the Deluge.
(From Arca Noë, Athanasius Kircher, 1665).

These are the five great traditional catastrophes of the Earth. After each one of them, according to tradition, the generation of man began again. Again he began to rebuild his world; again began the quest for the knowledge--even for the crafts--that he had lost. Almost like the first men of Earth, he questioned the silent heavens, with no knowledge or wisdom of his own to aid him in his questions or their answers--nothing but vague old tales of something that had happened in a recordless past which had robbed his fathers of a heritage, and had put him where he was, ignorant and alone. What? and how? and why?

[1] The Lost Continent of Mu: James Churchward, 1926, pp. 29-30.

TREES OF THE WORLD

THERE ARE TWO UNIVERSAL WORLD-FIGURES, found everywhere, among all races--the World Tree, and the World Mountain. For man could draw analogies--his traditions prove it almost better than his written records. He knew that he had been born, that he was living, that he must die; yet of birth he remembered nothing, and death he would not know until too late. But in the animal world--above all in the vegetable world, he could watch the recurrent miracles of life and death, rebirth and growth, sleeping and waking states more easily than he could note the same miracles in his own sphere. And so he came very early and easily to see a correspondence between humanity, greatest of the animal world, and the Tree, mightiest of its kingdom. It is true that in every great cosmological system and in great and lesser cosmogonies, there stands the figure of the World Tree, with its seed, its roots, its trunk, its resting perches, its knitting knots, its pith, its main branch, its leaves, its flowers and their sweet smell, its refreshing shade, its immortal sap, and the spot where it grows, all brought into close and exquisite analogy with man and his universe.

"Without doubt," sings one of the greatest of the Vedic poets, "though possessed of density, trees have space within them. The putting forth of flowers and fruits is always taking place in them. They have heat within them in consequence of which leaf, bark, fruit and flower are seen to droop. They sicken and dry up. That shows they have perception of touch. Through sound of wind and fire and thunder, their fruits and flowers drop down. Sound is perceived through the ear. Trees have, therefore, ears, and do hear. A creeper winds round a tree and goes all about its sides. A blind thing cannot find its way. For this reason it is evident that trees have vision. Then again trees recover vigour and put forth flowers in consequence of odours good and bad, of the sacred perfume of various kinds of dhupas. It is plain that trees have scent. They drink water by their roots. They catch diseases of divers kinds. Those diseases again are cured by different operations. From this it is evident that trees have perception of taste. As one can suck up water through a bent lotus stalk, trees also, with the aid of the wind, drink through their roots. They are susceptible of pleasure or pain, and grow when cut or lopped off. From these circumstances I see that trees have life. They are not inanimate. Fire and wind cause the water thus sucked up to be digested. Accordingly again, to the quantity of water taken up, the tree advances in growth and becomes humid. In the bodies of all subtile things the five elements occur. In each the proportions are different."

According again to the races of men, the type of the World Tree varied. The Date-palm was the sacred Asherah of the Assyrians. To the Greeks, and to the Norsemen, the cosmic Ash was the World Tree. But also to the Greeks, and to the Germans, the Oak was the life-giver and the life-sustainer. And the Greeks made the vine the "sacred tree" of Dionysos. Persian legends centre about the haoma tree, and the Egyptians had a mythical golden gem-bearing tree of the heavens, where the Sky goddess Nut had her abode. The Japanese believed that a great metal-pine grew far to the north at the centre of the world, and the Russians have a legend of an Iron Tree whose root "is the power of God," and whose head sustains the three worlds--the heavenly ocean of air, the Earth, and Hell with its burning fire. To the branches of the Jambu or Rose Apple tree, the Hindu dead clung and climbed to immortality. India has also her incredible banyan tree, declared to be more like man than man himself. Unlike plants, man can move at will over the surface of the Earth, but this sacred Indian Fig Tree bears the name of the Tree of Many Feet, because its seed, rarely rooting in the ground, ordinarily sends down its hanging garden of roots from its nest in the crown of palms, where it has been deposited by birds. These aerial roots, touching the Earth, sink into it, glide through it and from it spring upward again to send down other drooping branches that root themselves, and so, over and over, until the prodigious grove--myriad parts of a single tree sprung from one air-nested seed--eventually destroys the Palm that cradled it.

Countless books have been written about the origin of the myth of the Cosmic Tree, but the gist of them all can be stated very briefly. First of all, Heaven and Earth are separated. They must be, therefore, at one and the same time held apart--lest the heavens fall down and crush the Earth--and they must be also united by some subtle path of communication, some bridge over the monstrous interval. If a mushroom, delicate as a butterfly, can work a miracle in a night and raise a rock, a tree rooted in the Earth may support the sky. But no tree of Earth could reach to heaven unless it were itself divine, born somehow of the gods; and so we find a host of literal "parent trees," said to be produced from the body moisture of deities, and capable therefore, in their turn, of producing man. In its more developed form, this parent tree became the Tree of Life, the Tree of Knowledge, offering men immortality and the wisdom of the gods. There is a Tibetan tree called Tarayana or the Way of Safety which grows by the side of the great river separating the worlds, and only by grace of its overhanging branches may men pass from the mortal to the immortal bank.

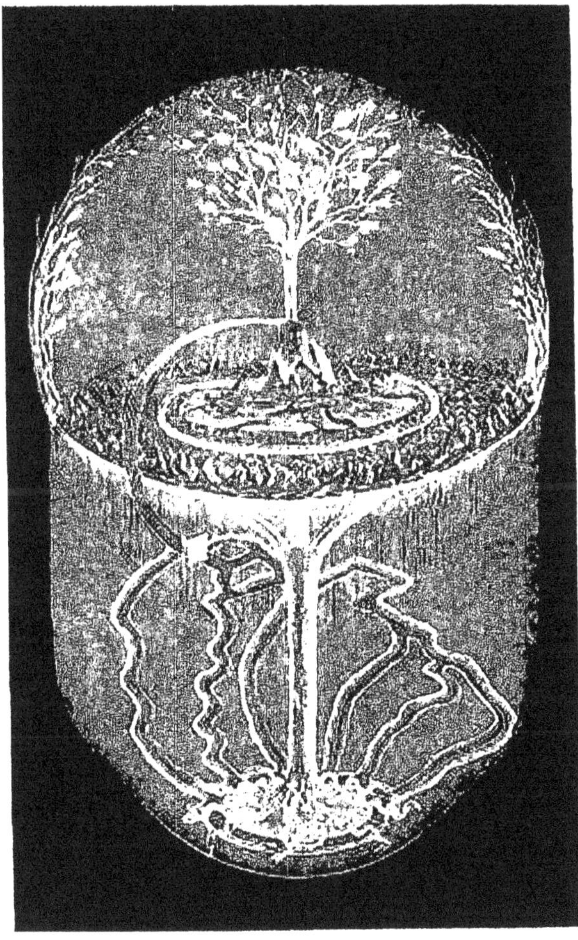

PLATE XVIII. Yggdrasil, the World Tree of the Norsemen.
After Finn Magnusen's

The oldest World Tree? who shall say? When in search of the "oldest" we always think of the ancient East; but no one can assert--and prove--that Yggdrasil, the Cosmic Ash, the World Tree of the Norsemen, had its origin in the Orient, however remarkably its ideas coincide with the sacred trees of Asia. Let us begin for a change with the Occident and Yggdrasil.

"The chief and most holy seat of the gods," say the Eddas, "is by the Ash Yggdrasil. There the gods meet in council every day. It is the greatest and best of all trees. Its branches spread over the world and reach above heaven. Three roots sustain the tree and stand wide apart; one is with Asa; the second is with the Frost giants; the third reaches into Niflheim, and under it is Hvergelmar, where Nidhug gnaws the roots from below. But under the second root, which extends to the Frost giants, is the well of Mimir, wherein knowledge and wisdom are concealed. The third root of the Ash is in Heaven, and beneath it is the most sacred fountain of Urd. Here the gods have their doomstead. The Asa ride thither every day over the Bi-frost, which is also called Asa-bridge. There stands a beautiful hall near the fountain beneath the Ash. Out of it come three maids. These maids shape the lives of men, and we call them the Norns. On the boughs of the Ash sits an eagle, who knows many things. Between his eyes, sits the hawk, called Vedfolner. A squirrel, by name Ratatösk, springs up and down the tree and bears words of hate between the eagle and Nidhug. Four stags leap about in the branches of the Ash and bite the buds. The Norns that dwell by the fountain of Urd every day take water from the fountain, and clay that lies around the fountain, and sprinkle therewith the Ash, in order that its branches may not wither or decay." [1]

There are a number of interesting things to note here, because of their constant recurrence in other world-concepts widely separated in time and race. One is the close association of the World Tree with the World Mountain; one springs from the other, take them in what order we will. Another is the division of the Universe into nine worlds. Another, for the sake of comparison with a Mayan World Tree farther on, is the squirrel Ratatösk. Another is the Bi-frost or Asa-bridge.

PLATE XVIII. Yggdrasil, the World Tree of the Norsemen. After Finn Magnusen's

[1] The Prose of Younger Edda, translated by G. W. Dasent, p. 16.

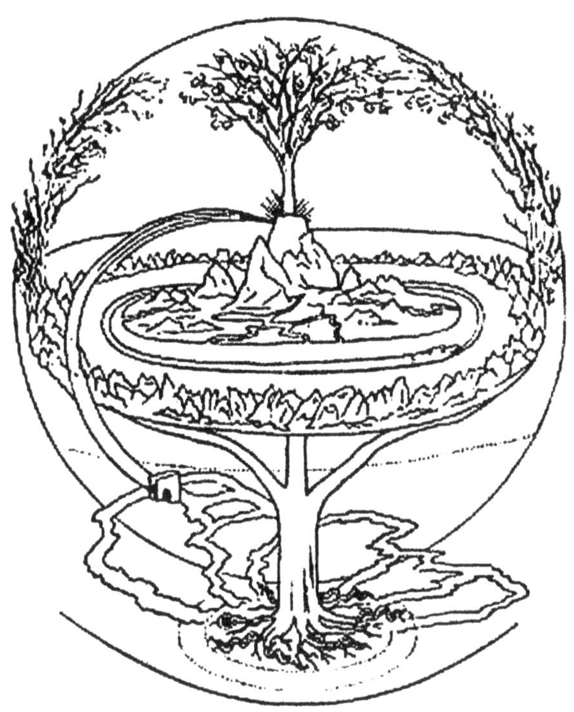

FIGURE 44. Yggdrasil, the Cosmic Ash (From Finn Magnusen's "Eddalæren.") (From The Sacred Tree, or The Tree in Religion and Myth; Mrs. J. H. Philpot, 1897.)

In the beginning of all things, says the Norse story of the Creation, there were two worlds, Niflheim, the world of ice in the north, and Muspelheim, the world of fire in the south, with all the space between an empty abyss, called Ginungagap. The fierce flames in Muspelheim blew constantly over into the abyss many sparks which confronted only nothingness, until, from the ice-bound Niflheim, a great spring opened and sent down twelve rivers, some of which flowed into the abyss and formed great layers of frozen vapour. At last the sparks of fire met the frozen air, and Ymir the giant was created, and then, in turn,

From Ymir's flesh
the earth was formed,

and from his bones the hills,
the heaven from the skull
of that ice-cold giant
and from his blood the sea.

Of the nine worlds Asgard was the highest and was the world of the gods. Below it was Mitgard or Earth, the world of men, a flat disc surrounded by the River Ocean.

Beyond the River Ocean, but surrounding Mitgard, was Jötunheim, the upper giant world, and, beneath the Earth plane, was the great underworld divided into four worlds. In the North was the lower giant world of Niflheim; at the South Urd and her two sisters ruled over the kingdom of the dead, and between North and South was Mimir's land, where dwelt the wisest of the gods, and, with him, Day, Night, Dawn and the Sun and Moon. Below Niflheim again was the world of torture, and below Urd's realm of the dead, the land of subterranean fire.

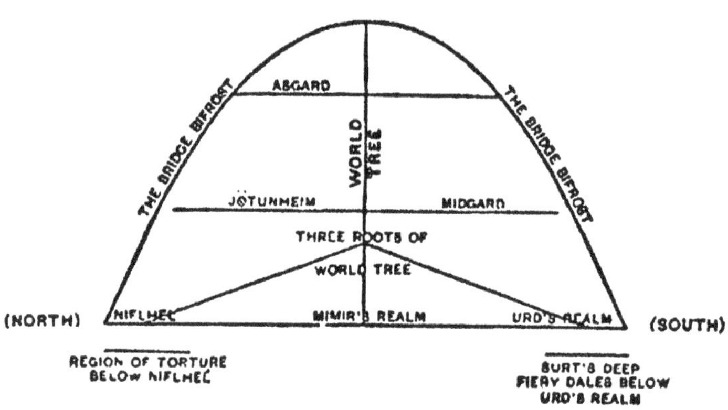

FIGURE 45. Diagram of the Nine Worlds, supported by the World Tree Yggdrasil.
(From The Nine Worlds; Mary Elizabeth Litchfield, 1890.)

Just two things bound these worlds together, the tree Yggdrasil, and the Asa-bridge, or Bi-frost. And a third--the spirit of heaven, the great Energiser, passing ever to and fro, guiding, controlling all the universe, from the first world to the ninth; at home everywhere, abiding no-where, stirless when moving and moving when still; that without which there would be nothing--here shown as merely a tiny timid nimble squirrel.

But what was the binding and the separating bridge, the Bi-frost?

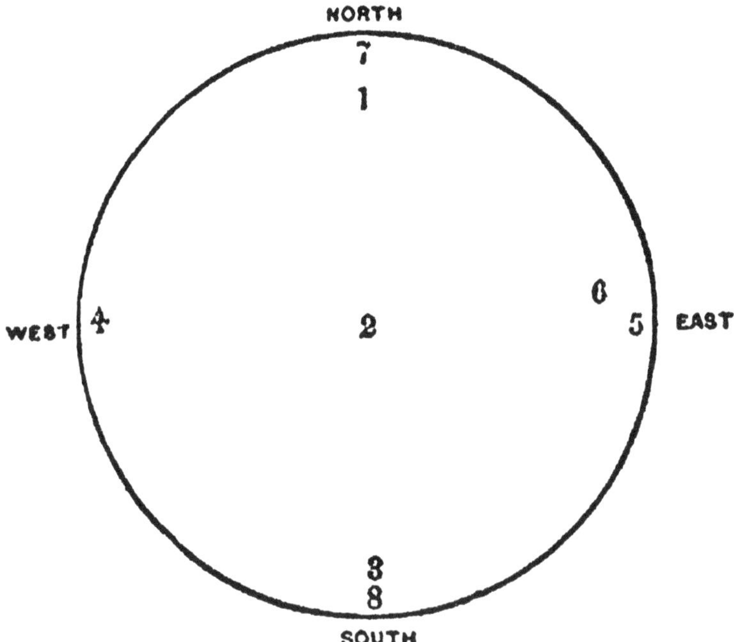

FIGURE 46. Diagram of the Scandinavian Cosmos.

1 Spring Hvergelmir, in Niflhel or Niflheim, under Yggdrasil's northern root.
2 Well of Wisdom in Mimir's Realm, under Yggdrasil's middle root.
3 Urd's Well in her Realm, under Yggdrasil's southern root.
4 Home of the Vanir.
5 Home of the Elves in Mimir's Realm.
6 Castle where Baldur dwelt with the Asmégir.
7 Northern End of Bifröst, guarded by Heimdall.
8 Southern End of Bifröst, near Urd's Well.

(From The Nine Worlds; Mary Elizabeth Litchfield, 1890.)

Again, who knows? Its arch was over Asgard, world of the gods; its northern tip resting upon the mountains of the ice-girt Niflheim; its southern end in the realm of the dead, where Urd and her sisters ruled. Some say the Milky Way is the original of Bi-frost or the Trembling Bridge, as some say the Milky Way is the very trunk of the Celestial Tree. Others believe that the Rainbow is the prototype for Bi-frost and all the "bridges of the world." For the World bridges are as universal as the "trees" and "mountains" of the world. Earth was cut off from Heaven--yet somewhere, if man could only find it, there was a path that might lead back home. The Bi-frost at its northern end was inviolately guarded by the great Heimdall, "World-Judge" or "World-Divider," "whose ears were so good that he could hear the grass pushing up through the ground, and the wool growing on the backs of sheep, and he needed less sleep than a bird." The gods crossed it every day on their way to the judgment hall in the realm of Urd, but the way was barred against all others, lest some thief in the night should find his way into Heaven. Yet it was the bridge also on which the souls of all the dead began their passage to the land of Urd.

The Persians had their Chinvat bridge, which is to say also, the Bridge of the Judge, over which all souls, good and evil, passed--"that bridge," says one of their sacred books, "like a beam of many sides, of whose edges there are some which are broad, and there are some which are thin and sharp; its broad sides are so large that its width is of twenty-seven reeds, and its sharp sides are so contracted that in thinness it is just like the edge of a razor." Mohammed too placed a way over the middle of hell, "which is sharper than a sword and finer than a hair, over which all must pass."

Certainly the North American Indians considered the Milky Way to be the "bridge" to the Land of Souls--a great village situated "where the Sun sets." "They call the milky way Tchipai meskenau, the path of souls, because they think that the souls raise themselves through this way in going to that great village," wrote Paul Le Jeune in 1634 of the Montagnais. One hundred years later Pierre Aulneau wrote of the Crees of upper Lake Superior, that they believed in a paradise of feasts and great hunts for the immortal souls of the dead. "But, before reaching it, there is a spot of extreme peril--the souls have to cross a wide ditch. One side of the way it is full of muddy water, offensive to the smell and covered with scum; while on the other the pit is filled with fire, which rises in fierce tongues of flame. The only means of crossing it is on a fir tree, the ends of which rest. on either bank. Its bark is ever freshly moistened and besmeared with a substance which makes it as slippery as ice. If the souls who wish to cross to the enchanting plains have the misfortune to fall at this dangerous passage, there is no help left; they are doomed forever to drink of the foul stagnant water or to burn in the flames, according to the side on which they fall." Sometimes the "bridge-building fiend" made the bridging spar a snake or a swinging log.

A "Sketch of the World," by a Thompson River Indian, illustrates this exactly. They believe that the Earth is square, level in the centre and rising towards the north from whence comes the cold, that it rises also in great mountain ranges about its borders, and that these mountains or lands are topped by mountains of air--the clouds and mists rising from the encircling lake of the world. All the rivers of the world rise in the north and flow south.

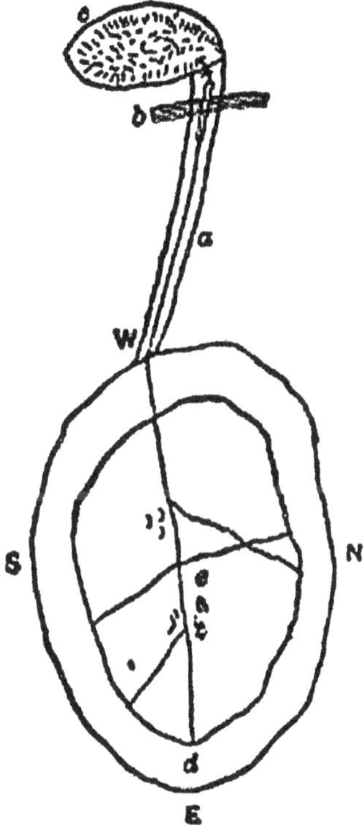

FIGURE 47. Sketch of the World, by a Thompson River Indian.

a. Trail leading from the earth to the land of the ghosts, with tracks of the souls; b. River and log on which the souls cross; c. Land of the ghosts and dancing souls; d. Lake surrounding the earth; e. Earth, with rivers and villages; N. S. E. W. points of the compass.

(From Memoirs of the American Museum of Natural History, Vol. II, 1900, p. 343.)

This trail to the soul-world has been minutely described by James Teit in his The Thompson River Indians of British Columbia. [1] According to him, the country of souls is underneath us, towards the sunset, and its path is one of perils, storms, narrow bridges, and gaping chasms. The trail leads through a dim twilight; along it are always visible the tracks of the people who last went over it, and also the tracks of their dogs, if they had any with them. It winds along until it meets another road, which the shamans, or medicine-men (their nearest approach to priests) use as a short cut when trying to intercept a soul. From here on, the trail is much smoother and straighter, and is painted red with ochre. Farther on it winds to the westward, descends a long gentle slope, and ends at a wide shallow stream of very clear mirror-like water. This stream is spanned by a long slender log, on which the tracks of souls may be seen again. After crossing the "bridge," if the traveller is fortunate enough to hold his footing on the slippery edge between the worlds, he finds himself again on the trail, which is now an ascending one. At a certain height is heaped a great pile of clothes; this marks the spot on the journey where the souls must leave behind them all that they have brought from the other world. And from here on the trail not only seems level, but little by little the dimness and twilight confusion disappear.

Three guardians are stationed along the trail of the souls--one on each side of the river that must be crossed, and the third at the very end of the trail of the ghosts.

The first of these, on the hither side of the stream, has built for himself a sweat house where he spends most of his time. It is the duty of all three to send back to the land of the living any soul not yet ready to enter the land of the dead, even though he may have by some miracle of accident crossed the bridge. For sometimes it happens that a soul succeeds in passing the first two guardians, only to be turned back by the third, who is the chief of the three, and who now and then, being a great orator, sends back messages to the world of the living through the medium of souls who,

---

[1] Memoirs of the American Museum of Natural History, Vol. II, 1900, pp. 342-43.

having survived all other tests of courage and merit, fail in the final test of being judged worthy by the guardian of the gate of life to pass through.

But, having been permitted by him to pass, the soul at last reaches a large lodge at the end of the trail. It is made of a hard white material, like limestone or white clay. It extends a long distance from east to west, and is much shorter from north to south. Its top is "like a round mound or ant-hill." The doors to this white lodge are at the east and west, and the trail leads up to the eastern door, which is very small, barely large enough to let a soul pass through. But the western door, through which the soul passes to the land of ghosts, is much higher and wider. Through the entire length of the lodge there is a double row of fires, for when the deceased friends of a person expect his soul to arrive, they go in a body to this lodge to talk about his death and prepare to welcome him. As the newly arrived soul reaches the entrance to the lodge of the dead, he finds some one standing at the door to greet him and call him by name, while others sing, dance, and beat upon drums. The air is always pleasant and still, and it is always light and warm. There are sweet smells of flowers, an abundance of grass, and berry-bushes laden with ripe fruit. The rest is hunting, feasting, and dancing through eternity, for the dancing, or immortal, souls.

The Wak wak Tree is a fabulous tree growing on a fabulous island somewhere in the Southern Ocean--or somewhere near Japan, or near the western (or the eastern) coast of Africa--it all depends on the traveller who tells the legend. It appears to have had nothing to do with America or the American Indians; yet here is a curious bit of Sioux lore, which, in connection with one of the legends of the lost continent of the Pacific, has an odd interest here.

The Sioux Indians have a special reverence for what they call the waka da cedar. Waka da, according to W. J. McGee, [1] who has made a special study of the word in his The Siouan Indians, is a very curious word indeed. It has, he says, as many connotations as the Sanscrit word Karma, and, like Karma, is not to be translated by any single English word. The Sun, for instance, is not "the" or "a" waka da, but simply waka da. So is thunder, so is lightning, the stars, the winds, and especially waka da cedar, by which they mean precisely the state of being which makes a cedar human and more than human. Even a man might be waka da. The term, he says, may be trans-

---

[1] U.S. Bur. Ethnol. Rep., 1893-94, p. 182."

lated by "mystery" more satisfactorily than by any other single English word; nevertheless, with its vague implications of "power," "sacred," "ancient," "grandeur," "animate," "immortal," "not even an English sentence of ordinary length could quite convey the sum total of the aboriginal idea expressed by the term waka da." Perhaps all its meaning is conveyed when, applied to the cedar, they say it is that state of being which makes a cedar human and more than human.

Now of the Wak wak tree which bore human fruit, Turkey, Arabia, Persia, and India all had a tradition; that in the Southern Ocean--or some other unexplored waste of waters--was an island called Wak wak--or a great mountain called Wak wak--because on it grew a tree which produced fruit with a human head, or fruit in the form of a human body, or even in the form of animals, and these beings, at dawn and at sunset, cried aloud, so that all might know the passage of the Sun, "Wak! wak!" The island and the mountain are mentioned in The Thousand and One Nights--Hasan al-Basri went there to find his wife and children. The tree is described without being named by Friar Odorico of Pordenone who in the fourteenth century left Italy to make the grand tour of the East. Arrived at Malabar, he wrote thus: "And here I heard tell that there be trees which bear men and women like fruit upon them. They are about a cubit in measurement, and are fixed in the tree up to the navel, and there they be; and when the wind blows they be fresh, but when it does not blow they are all dried up. This I saw not in sooth, but I heard it told by people who had seen it." Plate XIX gives a drawing of the Wak wak tree, taken from an old Turkish History of Western India and Its Wonders, published at Constantinople in 1729. It represents the fruit of this fabulous tree not by human heads but by seven pendent bodies. The two great birds at the foot of the tree are as fabulous as the rest of it.

Sometimes these souls were imagined as suspended with their heads downwards, alive, but clinging and climbing on a reversed path back to heaven. In an old Hindu legend it is related that Garuda, lord of all birds, coursing one day towards a gigantic banyan tree, with the fleetness of the mind, to sit thereon and "eat the elephant and the tortoise," in alighting broke one of the branches. As it broke he caught it and saw to his wonder that a tribe of Rishis called Valikhilyas were hanging from it head downwards, engaged in "ascetic penances." And gathering together all of his strength, the lord of birds soared high into the heavens with his burden of hanging men, and saved them. Sometimes, when the air is quiet, trees will move and their leaves rustle--this very common phenomenon had for the ancients a mystic meaning; at such times the invisible souls were talking to each other of their trials and triumphs on the journey back to heaven.

PLATE XIX. THE WAK WAK TREE
(From Ta'rikh al-Hind al-Gharbi. Constantinople, 1729)

FIGURE 48. The Tree of Judas.
(From Maundevile's Voiage and Travailes, 1839 reprint.)

In their "Sketch of the World," the Thompson River Indians incorporated one form of the World Tree, in the bridge between the worlds, literally, "the path of life." The Osage Indians, in their chart of the universe, have another. Few world-pictures can be found more simply and beautifully drawn than this by Red Corn, with its Earth plane, its "stages" or heavens, and its Tree of Life. Like the Lenape pictograph, it is the "score" of a tradition chanted by members of a secret society of his tribe. It is explained by J. Owen Dorsey as follows: [1]

The tree at the top represents the tree of life. By this flows a river. The tree and the river are described later in the degrees. When a woman is initiated, she is required by the head of her gens to take four sips of water (symbolising the river), then he rubs cedar on the palms of his hands, with which he rubs her from head to foot. If she belongs to a gens on the left side of a tribal circle, her chief begins on the left side of her head, making three passes, and pronouncing the sacred name three times. Then he repeats the

[1] Picture Writing of the American Indians: Garrick Mallery, 1894, pp. 251-252.

process from her forehead down; then on the right side of her head; then at the back of her head; four times three times, or twelve passes in all.

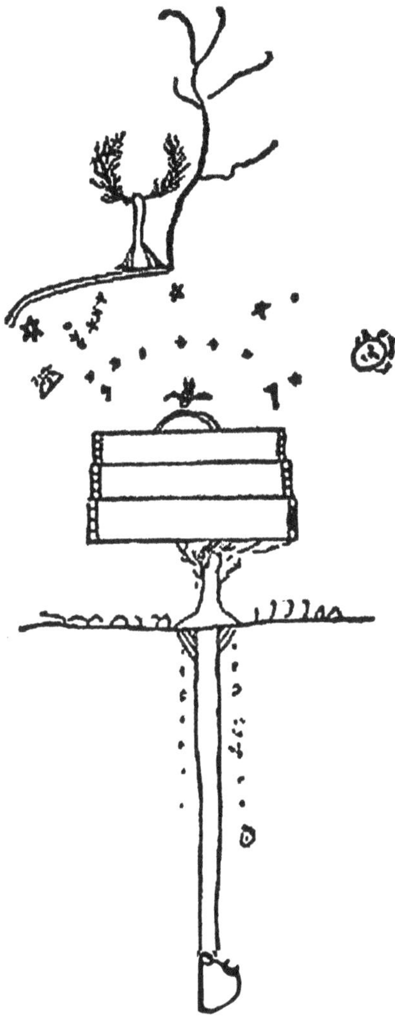

FIGURE 49. Osage Chart of the Universe, drawn by Red Corn.
(From Picture-Writing of the American Indians; Garrick Mallery, 1894, p. 251.)

Beneath the river are the following objects: The Watse tuka, male slaying animal (?), or morning star, which is a red star. 2. Six stars called the "Elm rod" by the white people in the Indian Territory. 3. The evening star. 4. The little star. Beneath this are the moon, seven stars, and sun. Under the seven stars are the peace pipe and war hatchet; the latter is close to the sun, and the former and the moon are on the same side of the chart. Four parallel lines extending across the chart represent four heavens or upper worlds through which the ancestors of the Tsicu people passed before they came to this earth. The lowest heaven rests on an oak tree; the ends of the others appear to be supported by pillars or ladders. The tradition begins below the lowest heaven, on the left side of the chart, under the peace pipe. Each space on the pillar corresponds with a line of the chant; and each stanza (at the opening of the tradition) contains four lines. The first stanza precedes the arrival of the first heaven, pointing to a time when the children of the "former end" of the race were without human bodies as well as human souls. The bird hovering over the arch denotes an advance in the condition of the people; then they had human souls in the bodies of birds. Then followed the progress from the fourth to the first heaven, followed by the descent to earth. The ascent to our heaven, and the descent to three, makes up the number seven.

When they alighted, it was on a beautiful day, when the earth was covered with luxuriant vegetation. From that time the paths of the Osages separated; some marched to the right, being the war gentes, while those on the left were peace gentes, including the Tsicu whose chart this is.

Then the Tsicu met the black bear, called in the tradition Káxe-wáhü-sa^{n}' (Crow-bone-white), in the distance. He offered to become their messenger, so they sent him to the different stars for aid. According to the chart, he went to them in the following order: Morning star, sun, moon, seven stars, evening star, little star.

Then the black bear went to the Waciñka-cutse, a female red bird sitting on her nest. This grandmother granted his request. She gave them human bodies, making them out of her own body.

The earth-lodge at the end of the chart denotes the village of Hañka utaka^{n} tsi, who were a very war-like people. Buffalo skulls were on the tops of the lodges, and the bones of the animals on which they subsisted whitened on the ground. The very air was rendered offensive by the decaying bodies and offal.

The whole of the chart was used mnemonically. Parts of it, such as the four heavens, and the four ladders, were tattooed on the throat and chest of the men belonging to the order.

Another Siouan tribe, the Sia Indians of New Mexico, believe that in each of the six regions of the world--they name these as the four quarters, zenith and nadir--there was a giant mountain bearing a giant tree, at whose foot was a spring, in which dwelt one of the "cloud-rulers," each attended by one of the six primal priestesses of the Sia, who interceded constantly with the six cloud rulers to send rain to the Sia. The six varieties of their World Trees were the spruce, the pine, the aspen, the cedar, and two varieties of the oak.

It would be a brave, not to say a reckless scientist, who would say to-day how young or how old the Mayan civilisation is. Thirty years ago, answers would have come easily enough; but that was before the excavations of the great buried cities in Central America began, which may very well result in the uncovering of records which ante-date the oldest we have. Already we know that America, youngest of the continents historically, is older prehistorically than we yet dare to say. And, although we never knew more than a little about the Mayas and their beliefs, we know to-day how fragmentary and isolated those bits of knowledge are, and how untrustworthy the conclusions we have drawn from them.

Nevertheless, under the date of 1640, there has come down to us a picture of the Mayan Universe, copied by Father Cogolludo from the central design of the Chilam Balam, or Sacred Book, of Mani, and inserted in his Historia de Yucathan, written at the end of twenty-one years spent among the Mayas (Plate XX).

At the bottom of the "universe" lies a cube, which has long been recognised as representing in the Mayan cosmogony the Earth. Above the Earth cube, resting on four legs which rest in turn on the four quarters of the Earth, is the heavenly vase, Cum, which holds the celestial waters--the treasures of the snow and of the hail, of the rains and the showers, on which all life, vegetable, animal and human, depends. Above this vase hang the rain clouds, and within it grows the Yax che, the Green Tree or the Tree of Life, its upper branches bearing on their tips the flowers or fruits of life on Earth, ol or yol; that is to say, the soul or immortal principle of man. Under the Green Tree Yax che, the souls who have passed through Mitna or the underworld, dwell in happiness, while the others sink into a region where they suffer eternal cold and hunger. In Brinton's Primer of Mayan Hieroglyphics, the inner figure of the cube, the vase, the clouds and the tree, is reproduced, lettered according to readings from other of the Sacred Books. The Earth cube in that picture is not lettered IUM, Earth, but tem, the Altar. "The Earth signifies the great Altar of the gods, and the offering upon it is Life."

The thirteen heads surrounding the World Tree signify, according to Brinton, the thirteen ahau katuna, or greater cycles of years. They also may signify the thirteen possible directions of Space. That is, the complete terrestrial globe is symbolised by the four cardinal points, zenith, and nadir, with man in the centre making the seventh, and the complete celestial sphere is symbolised by adding the six directions, with man, the focal point, remaining the same. "The border therefore," says Brinton, "expresses the totality of Time and Space, and the design itself symbolises Life within Time and Space."

Another Mayan world-picture is shown in Fig. 50, which is the central design of the Tableau of the Bacabs. Instead of the thirteen ahau katuna or greater cycles of years, this design is surrounded by "the signs of the twenty days," which extend in the original design, beyond the figure here given, to the four cardinal points and to the gods and time-cycles connected with them. "Again," says Brinton, "it is Life within Time and Space."

Here, sitting beneath the shade of the Green Tree, at its root, are the divine First Pair, Cuculcan, the feathered or winged serpent god, and Xmucane his spouse,--"the Creator and the Former," says the Popol Vuh, "Grandfather and Grandmother of the race . . . two-fold grand-mother, two-fold grandfather . . . the Maker, the Former, the Ruler, the Serpent clothed in feathers, they who beget, they who impart life, they rest upon the waters like a glowing light, they are clothed in colour green and blue, therefore their name is Gucumatz, 'Feathered Serpent.'"

PLATE XX. THE WORLD TREE OF THE MAYAS
(From Historia de Yucathan; Diez Lopez Cogolludo, 1640)

FIGURE 50. Our First Parents. From the Codex Cortesianus.
(From A Primer of Mayan Hieroglyphics; Daniel G. Brinton, 1894.)

The resemblances between the divisions of this Mayan tree and the Norse tree Yggdrasil are obvious, but here is a correspondence in ideas that is very curious. Between the nine Norse worlds, it will be recalled, from the roots of the tree to its topmost branch, ran Ratatösk, scamperer between men and gods, matter and spirit, Space and Time--the great Energiser under the guise of a tiny squirrel. It is rather interesting to discover that under the green cosmic tree Yax che of Yucatan sits a figure whose name, Cuculcan, is derived from a Mayan verb, cucul, meaning to "revolve," "to move round and round," as they moved their great calendar wheels to accomplish the rotation of time; and that this rotation itself is called cuceb, "the squirrel," derived directly from the same verb cucul, "to revolve, to move round and round."

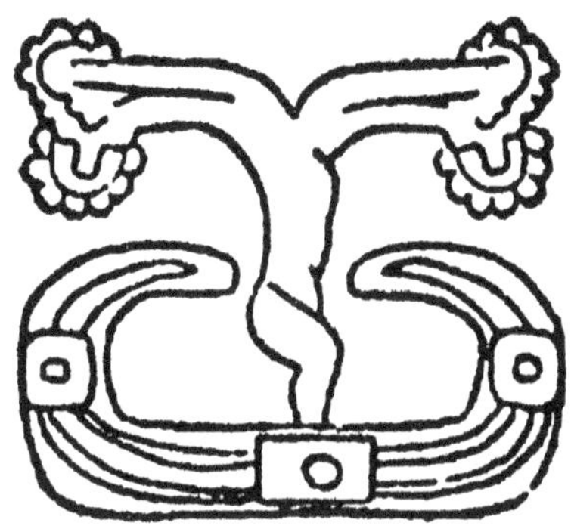

FIGURE 51. The

One more Mayan Tree of Life, too beautiful not to be included in any group of "Cosmic Trees," particularly as it shows the mystery of metamorphosis almost in the act of transmutation from one form to another is given in Fig. 51. In the original drawing the god of the north star rests upon it, as it rises from the heavenly vase that holds the heavenly waters. And, to show that Egypt and Yucatan were not separated in fancy at least by oceans Atlantic or Pacific, here is a little drawing of the Sacred Tree of the Egyptians, with Heaven, or the Sky goddess Nut, bestowing knowledge on man and his soul.

FIGURE 52. Sacred Tree of the Egyptians.
(From Egyptian Mythology and Egyptian Christianity; Samuel Sharpe, 1863.)

"THE WHOLE WORLD," says an old Hebrew writing, "is like a gigantic tree full of branches and leaves, the root of which is the spiritual world of the Sph'roth; or it is like a firmly united chain the last link of which is attached to the upper world; or like an immense sea, which is constantly filled by a spring, everlastingly gushing forth its streams."

When we take up the Kabbala, to interpret anything in it, we touch a book on which literally thousands of interpretative books have been written. The Arber Sephirotheca is perhaps its keystone figure, and the interpretations of the relation and meaning of the ten Sephiroth which compose the "tree" differ so that any summary of them is not only hopeless but useless here. It is possible, however, to sketch largely and with no detail, a general explanation of this Hebrew World Tree.

First of all, what are the ten Sephiroth? First of all then, they are indicated by the first ten letters of the primitive alphabet in which, as we have noted before, Gods were Letters, Letters were Ideas, Ideas were Numbers, and Numbers were perfect Signs. They may mean either "to count" (that is, they may mean "numbers"), or "brilliance" or "spheres." Or they may mean "qualities," standing for the several grades or stages of wisdom. Or they may mean "emanations."

The Arber Sephirotheca (Plate XXI) shows the Hebrew scheme of Creation--the esoteric side of the Genesis story, beginning with the assumption that Creation began, not from the act of God, but from the emanation of God, due to his voluntary self-withdrawal in order that the universe might be created. "When the Holy Aged, the concealed of all concealed," says the Zohar, "assumed a form, he produced everything in the form of male and female, for Wisdom expanded, and Intelligence, the third Sephirah, proceeded from it, and thus were obtained male and female, viz., Wisdom the father, and Intelligence the mother, from whose union other pairs of Sephiroth successively emanated." The first Triad, then, which is represented, is Hochma or Wisdom, Binah, or Intelligence, and Cheter the Crown or the equilibrising force. These three in one are the Balance of forces, otherwise the Reason of the Universe. This Reason is not represented separately. It is held to be inherent in the relation existing between and in the first group of three.

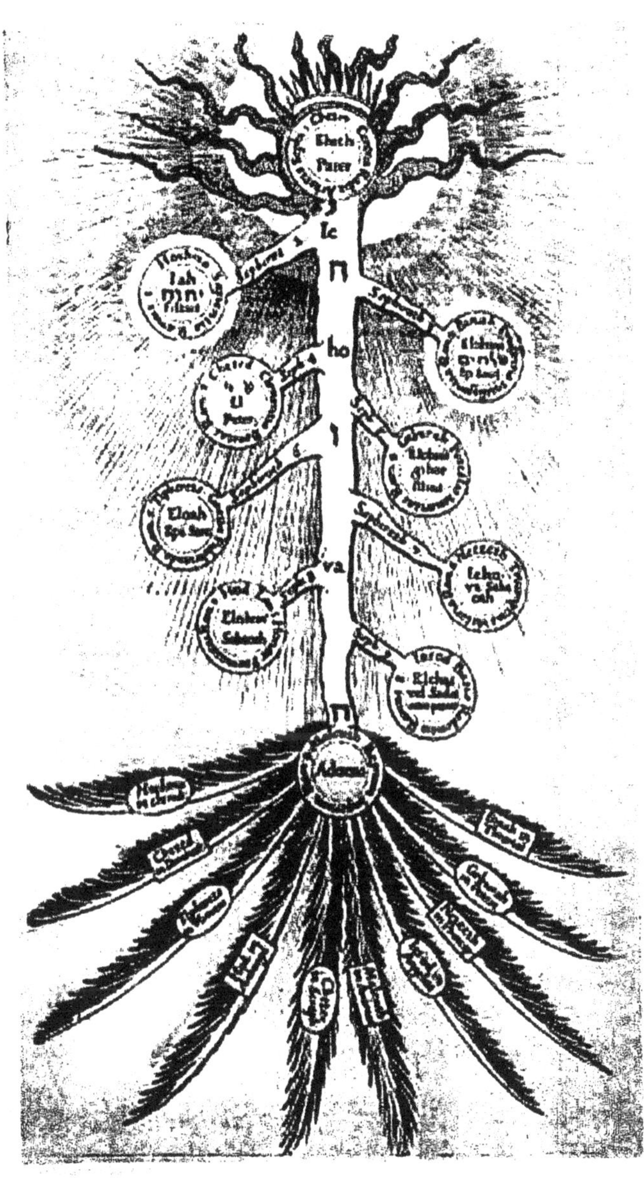

PLATE XXI. ARBER SEPHIROTHECA
(From Utriusque Cosmi; Robert Fludd, 1621. Vol. II)

Then, from this first group of three forces, or its result, Reason, came the second group of three, Chesed or Mercy, the father, Geburah or Justice, the mother, which together produce Tipherets, or Beauty. This sixth again represents Balance or equilibrium in forms about to be materialised, the mediator between the Crown or Creator and the Kingdom or Creation.

The third triad consists of Netzeth or Victory, the father (explained sometimes as the eternal triumph of Intelligence and Justice, the two mothers), Hod or Glory, the mother, from which two springs Iesod, the Foundation, the Absolute.

The three triads, three forms each of the intellectual, the spiritual, and the material qualities, combine to form the tenth Sephirah, Malcuth or the Kingdom--or Sovereignty over the Kingdom or universe, manifested in the ten branching leaves. These branching leaves manifest, in turn, the direct relation existing between the ten Sephiroth and Adam Kadmon, the primordial, heavenly, incorruptible man, created in this way only "in the image of God." Adam Kadmon is the branching fruit of the Tree of Knowledge, and holds the middle place between the En Soph or All in All and the ten emanations; holds, that is, the point of Balance or equilibrium. In this sense Adam Kadmon here, as in Plate IV, is regarded as the supporter and upholder of the universe. Nothing could be at first sight more unlike than these two images of the three worlds, but there are enormous likenesses between them.

Another way of expressing this interrelation between the ten emanations is that the first Sephirah, by virtue of its equilibrising power, unites the second and third--Wisdom and Intelligence; that the sixth Sephirah, Beauty, by the same virtue, unites the fourth and fifth--Mercy and Justice; that the ninth Sephirah, Foundation or Absolute, unites the seventh and eighth--Victory and Glory, and by union with all, sends forth the tenth Sephirah, the Kingdom or the Universe. Again, the first three Sephiroth form the world of Reason; the second three, the world of Spirit; the last four, the world of the Body.

A tree must have a soil in which to grow; soul and spirit must have a body; moving energy must take a form. And a very beautiful and subtle interpretation of the World Tree myth may be found in an old black-figured kylix by Exekias, dating from the sixth century B.C. It is called "Dionysos in the Ship," and its reading depends entirely on an understanding of what the story of Dionysos meant to the Greeks and all the peoples who came under their influence (Plate XXII).

The story of Dionysos is always the story of Dionysos-and-Apollo. There is not such a thing as even half of this story; one without the other does not exist. It veiled one of the greatest of the Greek mysteries, this conflict between these two gods, and the final reconciling of their struggle. It symbolised the conflict between light and darkness, between spirit and form--quite literally, the conflict between spirit and body. It was a mythological drama based on the old cry of man, "I feel two natures struggling within me." The first impulse of antagonism is to defeat, even to destroy; it seldom occurs to two opponents that there is a middle point, an equilibrium or balance, where peace abides. The story of Dionysos-Apollo is not one of destruction, but of final reconcilement between two opposing forces. Neither was to be rightly judged on the basis of "good" or of "evil," but on the basis of incompleteness only. Each needed the complementary force of the other; without the other neither was whole. It was not Dionysos alone, nor Apollo alone, but the two reconciled and united that solved the struggle. In this kylix, Dionysos-Apollo floats on the aethereal ocean. The body or boat--a great fish--carries the unified god. The two are one, and from them united spring two great vines laden with fruit and leaves. About the living boat seven dolphins, "spies of the sea," keep guard to forecast storms and to warn the pilot. In this Dionysian vine picture the myth-cycle of the World Tree rounds upon itself. The Tree, given by the gods to mortal man, is itself re-born through man reconciled and made immortal, and is given back to heaven as a celestial vine. Dionysos-Apollo had escaped the Wheel of Fate, and could forever mediate between the remnants of man still bound to it, and the Olympian gods.

The mystery of the relation between Darkness and Light, which is the mystery of Dionysos-Apollo, had another representation in the seventeenth century, when Robert Fludd based the whole scheme of Creation upon it (Plate XXIII). It will be interesting to compare this drawing with some Chinese conceptions of the primal causal cosmic struggle between Light and Darkness (pp. 147-150).

PLATE XXII. DIONYSOS IN THE SHIP
A black-figured kylix by Exekias (6th cen. B.C.). in Munich (Furtwängler-Reichhold; Griechische Vasenmalerei, No. 42).
(From Mythology of All Races, 1927. Vol. I, Plate XLIX)

"At the top of the figure," says Fludd, "is expressed the Head, or the Root, of all things, both in the simplicity of His unity and the duality of His universal attributes, namely, One God, One Supreme Being, One Essence or Divine Mind, whether willing or non-willing. In the negative aspect it withdraws within itself, and refrains from sending Itself forth from Itself.

"B. is the effect of the divine potency, or non-willing, in which state all things were formless and in potency only, before the beginning of the world. B., in other words, is a hieroglyphic Image of God thus far altogether non-willing; in which stage God is in His true Essence, shining within Himself, but not sending Himself forth from Himself. Such was the primal Chaos, from the bowels of which the materials of the Universe were originally drawn forth.

"Just as B. was the hieroglyph of the latent God, so C. is the representation of His glorious Emanation for the Creation of the World. This Emanation is the Word of God.

"From the union of these two comes one World [D. E.] in the Image of One Who participates in it both in His positive and negative aspects. That is to say, from the two opposites the World is born in the Image of its Creator. The World is in God, which means that the World is partly created and partly uncreated. Created, if we consider the material World, but uncreated if we consider its Maker.

"According to the mystical theology of Orpheus, Hesiod, Euripides, and Æschylus (who involved the divine mysteries in allegory), the Sun is taken in Archetype, as that divine source from which all ornament and beauty, embracing a multiple harmony of life, is derived. In His right hand is pity and benevolence, in His left, severity and punishment [F. G.]."

One aspect of this divine mystery of the Sun visible and the Sun invisible, they concealed, he says, under the name of Apollo, god of Day and of Light, the other under the name of Dionysos, god of Night and of Darkness. Each was but half of the other; only the two are one; yet each one, though separate, had within him the seeds of Darkness and Light. Hence, they argued that God is both destruction and creation, corruption and generation, author and actor; that "just as he composes by the number 7, so he destroys by the number 7, for the sacred number 7 is attributed to the God of life." Night in its darkness, or Dionysos, symbolised God in His negative aspect of withdrawal within Himself, and Day in its light, or Apollo, symbolised God in his positive aspect of giving forth by emanation from himself.

THE FAMOUS ROSE TREE of the Rosicrucians has a Dionysian connection, for the Rose as well as the Vine was sacred to this god. It has also a Peruvian connection; the Peruvian Eve--there is a native drawing of her later on--sinned not by eating the apple, but by picking roses, which were, in the Peruvian tradition, the fruit of the Tree." The bee is almost as much a part of this drawing (Plate XXIV) as the Rose Tree--here are a few odd myths of this marvellous being. According to Porphyrios, the Moon was called a bee; according to Virgil, the bee alone of all animate things descended from Paradise, is a part of the mind of God, never perishes, and alone of all animate things, ascends alive into heaven. Dionysos is sometimes identified with the Moon, and is said in some traditions to have been born again as a bee. Again, the wax of bees produces light, hence bees are those that feed on fire. As for the rose, its bud resembles the acuminated or pointed sphere that symbolises ether in the ancient Stupa (Fig. 1), and the opened rose, to the Rosicrucians, symbolised the Universe spread out like a book, which he who could might read.

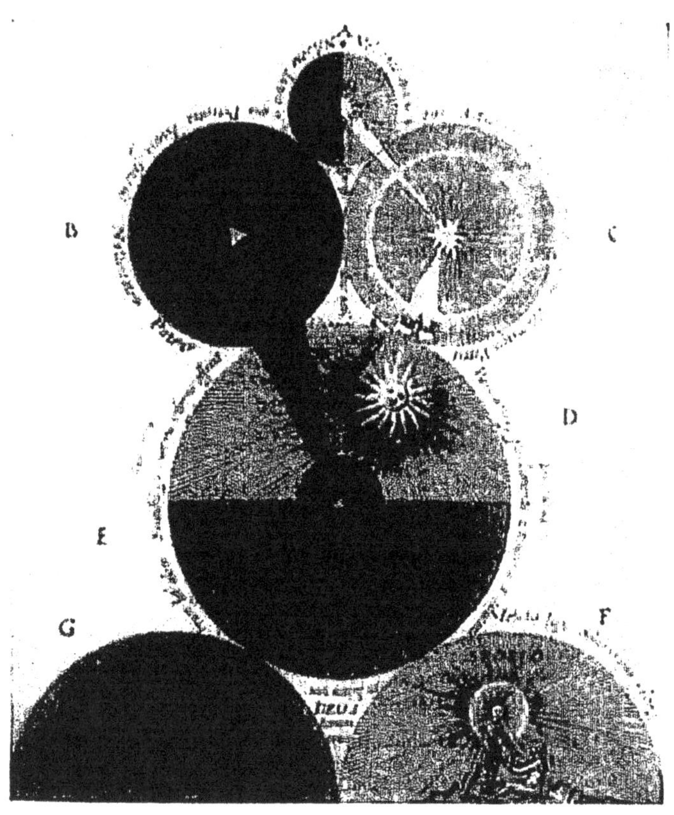

PLATE XXIII. "And God said, Let there be Light, and there was Light."
(From Medicina Catholica; Robert Fludd, 1629)

This representation of the universe by a rose appears to be a later development of a very ancient figuration of the universe by an onion--also a plant sacred to the old gods. Rather, the universe was represented by the layers of the onion--the Egyptians and the Hebrews and the Tibetans have used this over and over again. The core, to which the layers cling, may be the axis of the world, or the polar mountain of the world. In the Tibetan universe the onion's core is Mount Meru, surrounded by fifteen opaque, semi-transparent layers of oceans and mountains and oceans again until the outer skin is reached, which is the wall of iron about the universe. And all the heavens are one above the other, like the layers of an onion," says the Kabbala. ". . . And our companions who live in the South, have seen in the First Book and in the Book of Adam, that all these earths which are Below, are like the firmaments Above, that upon that, and this upon this, and between each earth, a heaven (firmament) is spread out between each other (like the fine skin of the layers on the onion)."

MOUNTAINS OF THE WORLD

IN MANY OF THESE WORLD TREE PICTURES we have seem World Mountains as well, but northern ones mostly. Yet the concept of the antipodal polar mountains of Earth is very old. They stand opposed to each other in the Babylonian Universe (Plate VIII). They are inherent in the very idea of an Underworld to this Over-world, whether the idea is carried to its logical conclusion or not. As above, so below. If the World Mountain of the North was the abode of gods, the abode of demons was--the World Mountain of the South. Fig. 53 illustrates not only the antipodal mountains of a spherical Earth, but also the "four quarters of the Earth," the abode of gods, of living men, of dead men, and of demons, beginning with the northern mountain and descending to the south.

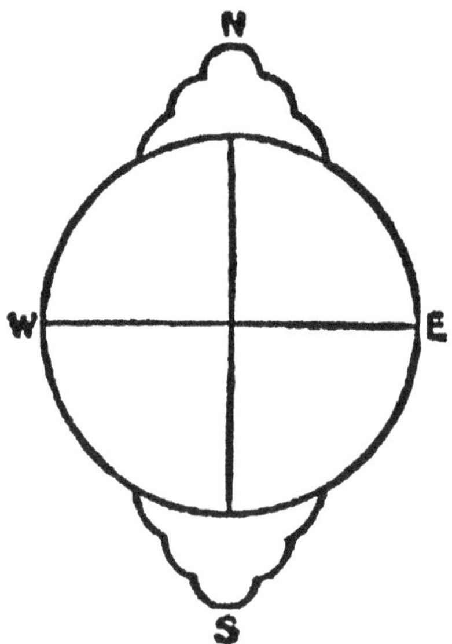

FIGURE 53. The Antipodal Polar Mountains.
(From Paradise Found; William Fairfield Warren, 1885.)

PLATE XXIV. THE ROSE TREE OF THE ROSICRUCIANS
(Frontispiece, Summum Bonum; Robert Fludd, 1629)

It may be it is only because the popular concept of the figure of Earth swung more or less uniformly to that of a sphere after the western world was discovered, and all the continents of the Earth were mapped out, that we are apt to think the spherical concept is a modern one. As a matter of historical fact the Greeks established it in the minds of philosophers by at least 500 B.C., and it is certain that the idea did not originate with them. Its origin, like the origin of most of these concepts, is trackless, if for no other reason than that the concept of Earth as the Mundane Egg--a spheroid form--goes back into untraceable antiquity. More and more it seems that, in order to explain any of these recurrences, we must take almost literally Fechner's conception of a great reservoir in which lie pooled the memories of all of the Earth's vanished inhabitants, which now and then "opens," to let a little spill out into the minds of a few living men. For more and more it begins to appear as if always, somewhere on the Earth, all of these figures of Earth have existed in the minds of some of its people. Perhaps it may mean that the Earth has been all of these things, at different stages of its development, that it is constantly changing, never the same; that its changes are its life, and that, far from being a disintegrating, dying planet, it is a continuously evolving one, always undergoing the mysterious process of creation. But this is only a guess.

Certainly, thanks to the symmetrical speculations of the Pythagorean and Platonian Greeks, the theory of the antipodal region and the antipodal race of beings was so much a part of the science of the day, that it seemed necessary to St. Augustine, a thousand years later (fifth century A.D.) to establish some sort of a theory of the figure of the Earth, which, although retaining its supposed spherical form, should nevertheless cast the theory of the antipodes into everlasting disrepute. The theory of two centres," or the theory that the Earth was composed of two spheres, one of land, and one of water, contained one within the other, but not concentric, solved the problem exactly of retaining the sphere and rejecting the antipodes. The terrestrial globe rose a little from the watery sphere, and it was, of course, the northern part of the Earth which so rose. When it was objected to, by some, on the ground that only lighter elements rise to the surface of water, and the denser irresistibly sink, the two-centre theorists promptly replied that the terrestrial sphere rose only a little from the water, as an egg, plunged into a water-filled basin, would rise a little to the surface; and they asserted farther that these two spheres signified the true meaning of the "separation" of land from water. But Strabo, several hundred years before, facing the problem of the density of the elements, accounted for it much more simply. It was true, he said, that by nature the water was higher in situation than the Earth, and in the beginning of things compassed it all about like a sphere. But since Providence designed to create animals and chiefly man, a creature not belonging to the water, God therefore "raised the Earth," and caused it to dwell in diverse places; and in others he sunk it and made it hollow, that the waters might lie hid, and that dry land might appear over it and thus afford a seat for man and other animals of the land.

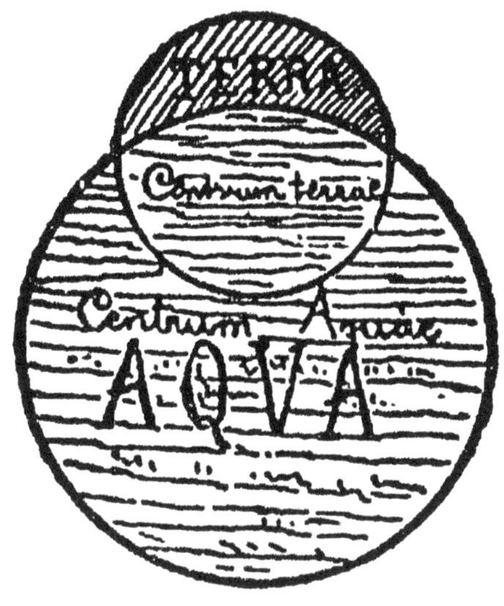

FIGURE 54. The Theory of Two Centres. Spherical Earth with no Antipodes. (After Rainaud.)
(From The Siege of the South Pole; H. R. Mill, 1905.)

What made the Early Church combat the idea of a southern habitable hemisphere was not so much the difficulty of explaining how men could stand "feet to feet," as the difficulty of explaining why races of men, all sons of Adam, should be utterly cut off and separated from each other by the impassable belt of fire that circled the Earth. There seemed no reason or purpose in this that could be called divine; this was the heresy. But it was also true that the literal mechanics of an inhabited antipodal region, without the convenient theory of gravitation to explain everything, was too much for reasonable man to accept without an admirable struggle.

"What are they," said Lactantius, a fourth-century Father of the African Church, "that think there are Antipodes, such as walk with their Feet against ours? do they speak with any likelihood; or is there any one so foolish as to believe that there are Men whose Heels are higher than their Heads? that things which with us do lie on the Ground, do hang there? that the Plants and Trees grow downwards, that the Hail, and Rain, and Snow fall upwards to the Earth? and do we admire the hanging Orchards among the Seven Wonders; whereas here the Philosophers have made the Fields and Seas, the Cities and Mountains hanging? What shall we think, that Men do cling to that Place like Worms, or hang by their Claws as Cats? or if we suppose a Man a little beyond the Center, to be digging with a Spade, is it likely (as it must be according to this Opinion) that the Earth which he loosened, should of itself ascend upwards? Or else suppose two Men with their Middles about the Center, the Feet of one being placed where the Head of the other is, and so two other Men cross them, yet all these Men thus situated, according to this Opinion should stand upright; and many other gross Consequences would follow, which a false Imagination is not able to fancy as possible."

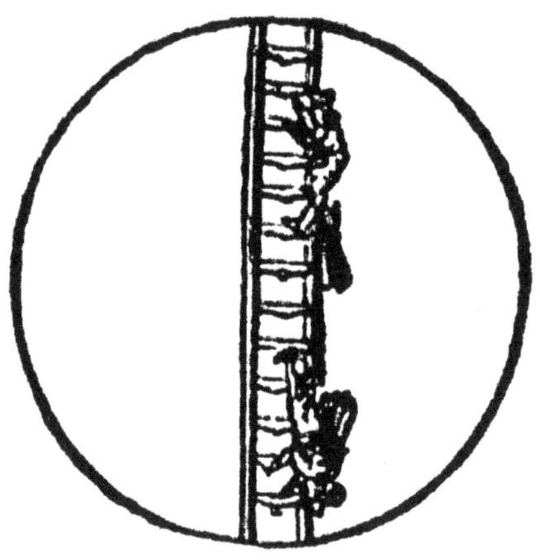

FIGURE 55. "Feet to Feet."
(From Physiologia Kircheriana Experimentalis, 1680.)

IN THE Universe of the Lamas (Plate XXV) we come upon the very greatest of the Mountains of the World, Mount Meru, the universal hub, the support of all the worlds. Meru is also the "Garden of the Tree of Life," for the Jambu or Rose Apple World Tree springs from it. This Tibetan Universe is not only a beautiful but a complex universe as well, and it is going to be difficult to describe its many divisions simply and directly. [1]

But first of all, say the Lamas of Tibet, this world of ours is merely one of a series, which all together form a universe or Chiliocosm of which again

[1] L. Austine Waddell's reading of this picture is followed here, as given in his Buddhism, or The Lamas of Tibet, pp. 77-121.

there are many. Each universe is set like a jewel in illimitable space, upon a warp or woof of "blue air" or wind. Crossed thunder-bolts are the symbols of this "blue air," which is hard and indestructible, like a diamond. Upon this "warp" or "woof" is set "the body of the waters," and upon this is a foundation of pure gold, on which is set the Earth. From the Earth's axis soars Mount Meru, crown of the world, which rises to a height of 84,000 miles before it is surrounded by the heavens. It is likened to "the handle of a millstone," and half way up its southern side is the Jambu, or Rose Apple Tree, the object of combat between the gods and the Titans. From its root four inexhaustible rivers take their source. It bears an immortal fruit, like gold, which falls into the rivers, and from its scattered pips comes the golden seed which is carried down to the sea, and is, sometimes, washed up again on its shores.

In the ocean about Mount Meru lie the four continents, each with two attending "satellites," and all with bases of solid gold in the form of a tortoise. But the continents are separated from the sacred Meru by seven "stages" or golden mountains, between which flow seven oceans of seven substances: fragrant milk which is churned by the gods, curds, butter, blood or sugar-cane juice, poisons or wine, fresh water, and salt water. Encircling all these divisions is a double iron wall which shuts off the light of the Sun and the Moon of each universe from all the space which intervenes between it and the succeeding universe. No ray of light illumines the void between the "thousand-thousand" universes. This is the "outer darkness."

The orbit of the Sun or "glazed fire," and of the Moon or "glazed water," is the summit of the innermost ring of mountains, called "The Yoke." Between these two heavenly bodies hang the jewelled umbrella of the kings and the banner of Victory--these are shown in the figure. In their realm of air, on this same plane, live the eight angelic "mothers."

The "four continents" are placed exactly in each of the four directions, and they are of four different shapes, corresponding to the four forms of the four elements (Fig. 1). To the north lies the cube or earth-shaped body; to the west the sphere or water-shaped body; to the south the triangle or fire-shaped body, and to the east the crescent or air-shaped body. Of the four continents, they say that all except Jambudvipa (F) are fabulous, but they are described as follows:

PLATE XXV. THE UNIVERSE OF THE LAMAS
(From The Buddhism of Tibet, or. Lamaism; L. Austine Waddell, 1899)
The following image was scanned directly from the original book, and is higher resolution than the previous.

The Universe of the Lamas

THE UNIVERSE OF THE LAMAS
(From The Buddhism of Tibet, or. Lamaism; L. Austine Waddell, 1899, p.78)

"On the East is Videha, or 'vast body' (P). This is shaped like the crescent moon, and is white in colour. It is 9,000 miles in diameter, and the inhabitants are described as tranquil and mild, and of excellent conduct, and with faces of the same shape as this continent, i.e., crescentic, like the moon.

"On the South is Jambudvipa (F), or our own world, and its centre is the Bodhi-tree at Budh Gaya. It is shaped like the shoulder-blade of a sheep . . . is blue in colour; and it is the smallest of all, being only 7,000 miles in diameter. Here abound riches and sin as well as virtue. The inhabitants have faces of similar shape to that of their continent, i.e., somewhat triangular.

"On the West is Godhanya, or 'wealth of oxen' (I), which in shape is like the sun and red in colour. It is 8,000 miles in diameter. Its inhabitants are extremely powerful and (as the name literally means cow + ox + action) they are believed to be specially addicted to eating cattle, and their faces are round like the sun.

"On the North is Uttara-Kuru, or 'northern Kuru'--tribe (M), of square shape and green in colour, and the largest of all the continents, being 10,000 miles in diameter. Its inhabitants are extremely fierce and noisy. They have square faces like horses; and live on trees, which supply all their wants. They become tree-spirits on their death; and these trees afterwards emit 'bad sounds.'

"The satellite continents resemble their parent continent in shape, and each is half its size. The left satellite of Jambudvip, namely, 'The ox-tail-whisk continent,' is the fabulous continent of the Rakshas, to which Padmasambhava is believed to have gone and to be still reigning there. And each of the latter presents towards Mount Meru one of the following divine objects respectively, viz., on the east (? south) the mountain of jewels, named Amolikha, shaped like an elephant's head, and on the south, the wish-granting tree, on the west the wish-granting cow, and on the north the self-sprung crops."

As for Mount Meru--some say that these four gifts of the left satellites are situated on the sides of Meru itself--which has square sides of gold and of jewels. Its eastern face is crystal or silver, like the colour of the eastern continent. The southern face is sapphire or lapis lazuli. The west side is of ruby, and the north side is gold. Mount Meru is always covered with fragrant flowers and herbs.

It has four lower compartments under the heavens. The lowest is inhabited by the Yaksha genii holding wooden plates. Above live the "wreath-holders." Above these dwell the "Eternally exalted ones," and above them the Titans, the race of beings who contend always with the gods for the Jambu or Rose Apple Tree. Originally gods, the Titans were, like Satan, thrown out of heaven, and their place in the Tibetan system is intermediate between heaven and Earth.

Above the Titans, at a distance of 168,000 miles, are the realms of the gods. In the lowest compartment are the "four great guardian kings of the quarters," the white guardian of the East, the green guardian of the South, the red guardian of the West, and the yellow guardian of the North, who forever guard the heavens against attacks of outer demons. The eight great classes of supernatural beings are subjects of these kings, and these guardians of the four quarters are aided by the ten Lokpals who watch the ten directions, that is, the eight points of the compass, and above, and below.

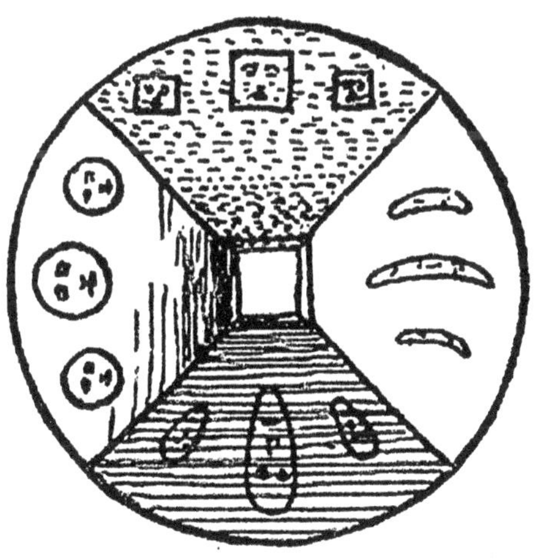

FIGURE 56. A Kalmuck World-picture.
(From Mythology of All Races, Vol. IV, 1927.)

A Kalmuck World-picture (Fig. 56) is quite worth comparing with this. Universe of the Lamas, for the Kalmucks, now of Russia, primitively inhabited China. They arrived on the shores of the Caspian Sea about 1600, but they brought with them their own conception of the world, with its colours and shapes. This drawing shows Mount Su-meru in the centre of the world, through whose centre the World Tree springs. Sometimes they will say that each of the four mountain sides bears a tree. Su-meru is shaped, they believe, like a truncated pyramid, and around it are seven mountains and seven seas not represented in this drawing. The nearer a mountain ring is to the central mountain, the higher it is, they believe; and the higher the mountain rings, the farther they are from each other. The Kalmucks say also that the distance of each from the central mountain is the same as its height.

The colours of the four sides of the truncated Su-meru are like those of the Tibetan Meru, and the Kalmucks also place four continents in the four quarters, each of a different shape, and each accompanied by two smaller "islands" of like shape; so that again the total number of islands surrounding the centre of the world is the zodiacal twelve. The Tibetan Jambudvip--the southern continent--which was "shaped like the shoulder-blade of a sheep," and whose inhabitants had faces shaped similarly, "somewhat triangular," is slightly modified in the Kalmuck picture to an oval continent inhabited by an oval or "egg-faced" race. But it is almost the same; an "oval" such as this is hardly more than an expanded or expanding triangle and the egg-shaped islands and faces may be called with a fair accuracy "somewhat triangular."

No claim for particular beauty and certainly no claim for any antiquity is made for the Chinese hemisphere shown in Fig. 57, drawn, says Dr. Du Bose, by a monk in Soochow, who perceived that times were changing, that the new geography was of a spherical Earth and not of a "World Mountain," but who realised that the North Pole is permanent--if anything is. He therefore drew a conventional modern hemisphere with its lines of latitude and longitude, over which he traced Europe-Asia-Africa; and then, upon the top of the world, raised his World Mountain, peerless Su-meru, spine and marrow of "the thirty-three heavens," and situated in the very centre of the world. Its shape is ordinarily that of an inverted cone, whose medial line is cut by the Earth's surface, whose base is above, and whose apex penetrates the Earth to a distance equalling the distance of its base from the Earth. Or, as the Chinese explain it, "Its depth in the sea is equal to its altitude (in the air)." In the undersea division are the countless hells. The unknown monk of Soochow made his Sacred Mountain resemble a pagoda more than a cone when he compromised with a new age, but a simple projection of the pagoda lines will result in a figure quite cone-like.

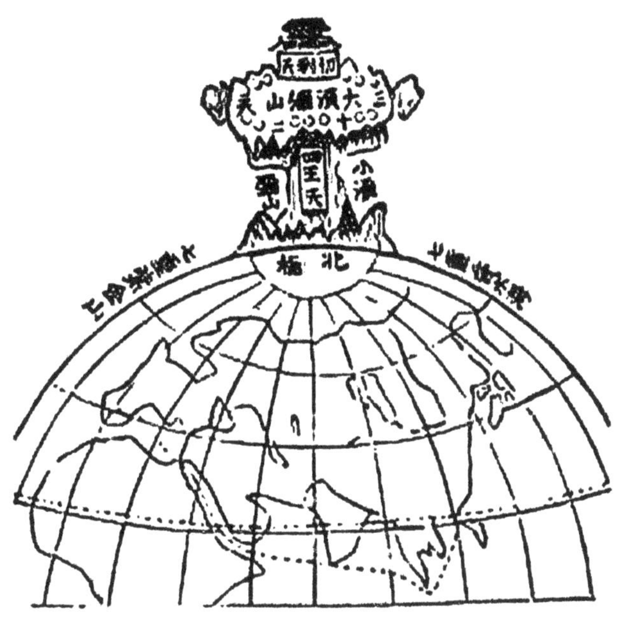

FIGURE 57. Mount Su-Meru of the Chinese.
(From Dragon, Image and Demon; H. C. Du Bose, 1887.)

THE WHEEL OF LIFE

CLOSELY ASSOCIATED with the World Mountains are the many Wheels of Life, by which the ancients sought to picture the relations of parts of the universe to each other and to the whole. There is a hint of this in the Tibetan world-picture, with Mount Meru the axis or hub of the world about which are placed like spokes in a wheel the four quarters of the Earth, with their three islands each, making the sum of twelve radii from the centre. The Wheel of the Zodiac was of course the great original for all such figures, particularly for the Wheels of Life. For uncounted centuries man knew the geography of the heavens better than the geography of the Earth, and whatever life on Earth meant to him, the unfailing procession of the great star-groups of the Zodiac meant certainty, law, order. There were zones written in the heavens long before man stretched his imaginary lines of the terrestrial zones over the Earth--"The circle called the Zodiac," said Plutarch, "is placed under the three that are in the midst, and lies obliquely, gently touching them all." And it is not hard to see how this great circle came to seem to man a mirror of the Earth, a storehouse of its history, its constant Watcher in the sky, and the unerring prophet of its future. The Greeks named this oblique ring of star-groups just behind the Sun when it sets or just before it when it rises, the Zodiac or Path of Animals, because the names and configurations of the groups were mostly those of animals, and by that name we know it. But no one knows how long before the days of the Greeks far earlier astronomers first linked the single groups of stars into the twelve great signs of the Star-bearing Circle.

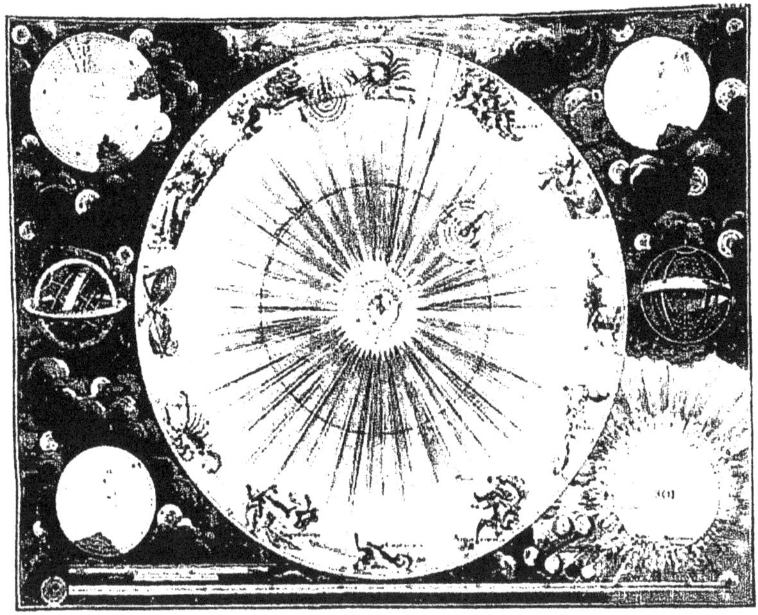

PLATE XXVI. CREATIO UNIVERSI
(From Physica Sacra; Johann Jacob Scheuchzer, 1731, Vol. q, Plate I).

Physica Sacra is an early eighteenth-century Bible illustrated almost text for text, and Plate XXVI is its first illustration, for the first verse of the first chapter of the first book: "In the beginning God created the heaven and the Earth." Outside the Zodiacal Wheel are clouds upon clouds bearing a multitude of spheres, and, in addition, seven numbered diagrams. Fig. I in this Plate illustrates the system of the "eleven heavens," with the Earth the centre of the universe. Fig. II is the Tychonian system; Fig. III, what is known as the semi-Tychonian system; Fig IV, the blazing and effulgent Sun, containing within himself his seven children, Earth and Moon and the five great planets; Fig. V, a group of the heavenly bodies; Fig. VI, an armillary sphere; Fig. VII, an Astrolabe, which is almost to say, "the handle of the stars," and which was called by the old astronomers "the Mathematical jewel."

The Northern and Southern hemispheres of the heavens (Figs. 58 and 59) are merely supplementary to Scheuchzer's Creatio Universi. They are taken from an Arabic celestial globe, made of brass, in 1275 A.D., which was deposited in the Museum of the Royal Asiatic Society of Great Britain and Ireland. Near the South Pole is an inscription in Cufic characters, stating that it was "Made by the most humble in the supreme God, Mohammed ben Helah, the astronomer of Monsul, in the year of the Hegira 674." The Zodiac was known to the Arabs, not as The Path of Animals," but as The Girdle of the Castles," and contained, with one or two variations in name, the same signs we have to-day: Aries, Taurus and Gemini, Cancer, Leo, Virgo (this the Arabs called the Ear), Balance or Libra, Scorpio, Sagittarius, Capricornus, Aquarius, and Pisces.

FIGURE 58. An ancient Arabic Celestial Sphere. Northern Hemisphere.
(From Transactions of the Royal AsiaticSociety of Great Britain and Ireland, 1830, Vol. II, Plate A.)

There are altogether, including the signs of the Zodiac, forty-seven constellations on these Arabic celestial hemi- spheres. The ones inscribed on the Northern hemisphere are: Little Bear; Greater Bear; The Dragon; Cepheus; Boötes; the Northern Crown; The Kneeling Hercules; The Lyre; The Hen, or Swan; The Lady in her Chair, or Cassiopeia; The Bearer of Medusa's Head, i.e., Perseus; The Charioteer; The Charmer of Serpents, or Serpentarius; The Arrow, or Sagittarius; The Flying Eagle, or Aquila; The Dolphin; Part of the Horse (the horse's head); The Greater Horse, Pegasus; The Chain, or Andromeda; The Triangle.

FIGURE 59. An ancient Arabic Celestial Sphere. Southern Hemisphere.
(From Transactions of the Royal Asiatic Society of Great Britain and Ireland, 1830, Vol. II, Plate B.)

The constellations inscribed on the Southern hemisphere are: Ketos, the Whale; The Giant, or Orion; The River, or Acarnar; The Hare, or Lepus; the Greater Dog, or Canis; The Dog, or Procyon; The Ship, or Argo; The Hydra; The Flaggon, or Crater; The Crow, or Corvus; The Centaur, or Centaurus; The Beast, or Fera; The Censer; The Southern Crown; The Southern Fish.

OF THE TWO WHEELS OF LIFE (or Fate or Law) to be given here, we begin with the one that seems the simpler. This Chinese Wheel (Plate XXVII) is almost a Zodiac or "path of animals," of itself. (The Chinese Zodiac, or "Yellow Path of the Sun," differed materially in its signs from the Greek-Arabic one just given; it contained twelve animals: the Mouse, the Cow, the Tiger, the Rabbit, the Dragon, the Serpent, the Horse, the Ram, the Ape, the Hen, the Dog, and the Pig.) Six of the twelve divisions are separating paths or currents, through or over which the traveller passes to the next stage. Four of the remaining divisions are the abodes of beasts, of insects, of fish, and of birds. The other two, separated from each other by one of the spiral-like rivers, are inhabited by Poor Men and Rich Men, or by Mandarins and Tillers of the Soil.

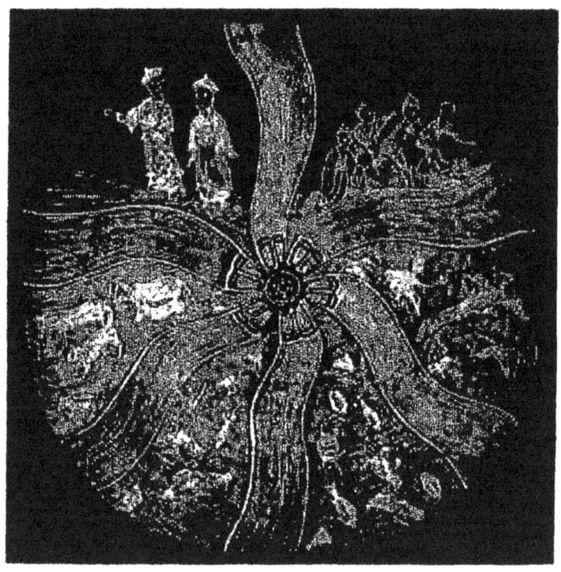

PLATE XXVII. THE WHEEL OF LIFE
(From Dragon, Image, and Demon; H. C. Du Bose, 1887)

The second of these wheels is the one elaborately developed in the Tibetan Wheel of Life (Plate XXVIII) to which is an almost necessary Key. It is a Tibetan version of an Indian painting in one of the abandoned cave-temples of Ajanta, which L. Austine Waddell holds to be "a complete authentic account of human life from the absolute standpoint of the earliest Buddhist philosophy."

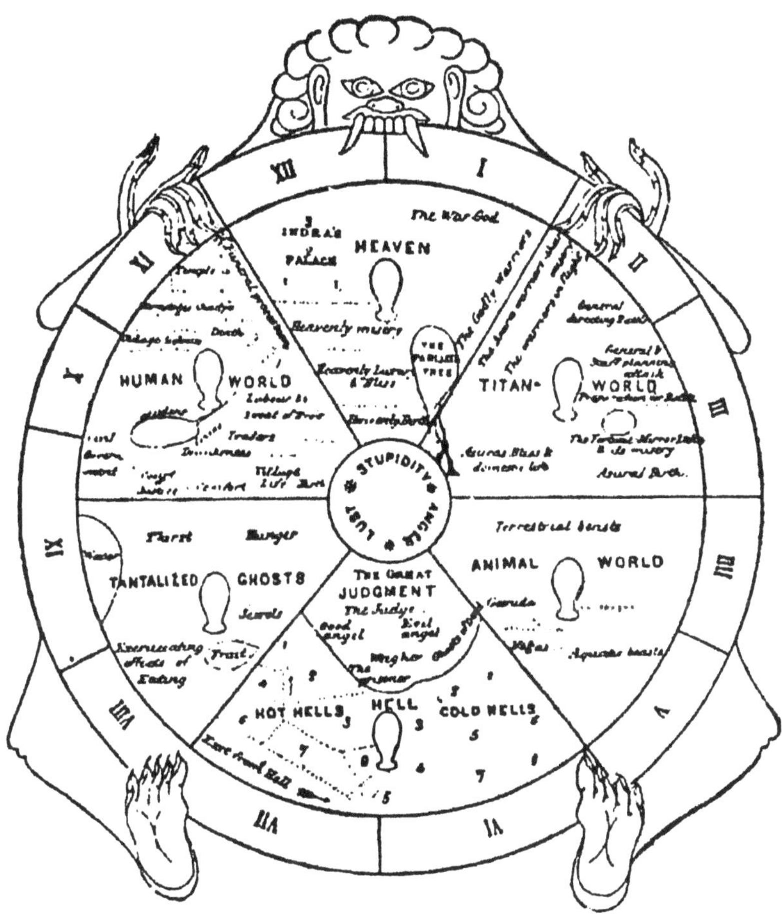

FIGURE 60. Key to the Tibetan Wheel of Life.
(From The Buddhism of Tibet, or Lamaism; L. Austine Waddell, 1899.)

The Lamas of Tibet say that Buddha himself originated the Wheel of Life, forming it on the Earth with grains of rice from a "rice-field school room." According to the old story, while tarrying for a while at the Squirrels' Feeding Ground in the Venuvana forest near Rajagriha, Buddha instructed his disciple Ananda, to make a Wheel, for the sake of illustrating what another disciple had seen when he visited other spheres. This Wheel was to have five spokes, between which were to be shown the several hells, animals, ghosts, gods and men. In the middle a dove, a serpent, and a hog were to symbolise lust, hatred, and ignorance. Around the outer rim was to wind "the twelve-fold circle of causation," in regular and inverse order. Beings were to be shown "as being born in a supernatural way as by the machinery of a water-wheel falling from one state and being produced in another." Buddha himself, as an "Enlightened One," liberated from the fate of recurrence on the Wheel, was to be outside of it--one who had escaped. This diagram, made first of rice-grains, was later filled in (second century A.D.) with pictures by the Indian monk Nagarjuna, but these pictures are said to be not his own inventions, but the visual images of Buddha's own parables and allegories.

The Key to the Tibetan Wheel of Life will be found an aid in following the interpretation of it, which is Waddell's, and is given here much abridged. [1]

The disc, symbolising the endless cycle of life, is held in the grasp of a monster who represents the horrors of Attachment, the wretchedness of Clinging-to-Life.

The broad tire of the Wheel is filled with the twelve-linked closed chain called the Causal Nexus, or "the twelve-fold circle of causation," i.e., the causes of life and of misery. At the centre or nave lie the three vices or delusions, "the Daughters of Desire," symbolising lust, ill-will, and stupidity, which lie at the core of re-birth, and are here given in the forms of a dove, a serpent, and a pig, coloured respectively red, green, and black. The body of the Wheel, filled with varied pictures, is supposed to be constantly revolving, thereby producing "The Whirling on the Wheel" of Life.

The way of escape is indicated by the twelve "links," and the first link is the connecting link between the old life and the new. It might be denominated Unconscious Will to escape. The links in the causal chain are:

---

[1] Buddhism, or The Lamas of Tibet; L. Austine Waddell, pp. 105-121.

I. A blind she-camel (ignorant unconscious will) led by a driver (Karma). In this picture, however, the first link is represented by a blind old woman led by a man, with its meaning the same. II. A potter modelling clay on his wheel (Conformations and impressions of and on formless clay). III. A monkey (the beginning of Consciousness; the new man is approaching to the human, but is still an unreasoning automaton). IV. A man being ferried across an Ocean (Self-consciousness--the Individual crossing the Ocean of Life). V. An empty house (Understanding achieved through "the empty house of the senses"). VI. The Kiss (or contact with the outside world). VII. An arrow entering a man's eye (Feeling or perception). VIII. A man drinking wine (Desire--or thirst). IX. A man gathering fruit and storing it in baskets (Greed, or the satisfying of Desire). X. A married woman--wife of him whose life is here traced (fuller life, Being, Becoming, even Re-birth and the continuance of Being for another existence). XI. Parent and child (Birth--of an heir). XII. A corpse being carried off to burial (Decay and Death), which leads to I, Unconscious Will for re-birth--and the cycle of the Wheel is begun again.

The ways of "life" or "re-birth" are, from highest to lowest, 1. Gods--the Sura. 2. Titans--the Asura. 3. Man--Nara, or Mi. 4. Beasts--the Du-do or "best goers." 5. Tantalised Ghosts--Pretas. 6. Hell--Naraka or Nal-k'am.

To live in the first three worlds is superior; to live in the last three is inferior--the highest world being Heaven, and the lowest Hell.

In Heaven, above the Titans, on the aethereal summit of Mount Meru, dwell the gods (Plate XXV). In the lowest regions of the heavens dwell the "guardian kings of the four quarters"; Dritarashtra, the white guardian of the East; Virudhaka, the green guardian of the South; Virupaksha, the red guardian of the West; and Vaisravana, the yellow guardian of the North.

In the upper right-hand section of the Wheel of Life the Titans (the Asura or not-gods) have their abode. Since their chief characteristic is pride, this is the world of re-birth for the "proud." The Titans correspond to Satan and his hosts, having been, like Satan, and for like cause, cast out from Heaven. Living at the foot of Mount Meru, they hover forever between Heaven and Earth. The life of the Titans is much longer than the life of men; but it is the fate of every Titan to die warring against the gods for the fruits of the heavenly Parijata tree, whose branches are in Heaven, but whose roots are in their country--"the tree of the concentrated essence of Earth's products." The Jambu tree is, in reality, according to this reading, the "climber" which encircles the aethereal tree, and through it the quintessence of Jambudvip, or the Jambu continent" of Earth is instilled into the Parijata Tree.

PLATE XXVIII. THE WHEEL OF LIFE
(From The Buddhism of Tibet, or, Lamaism; L. Austine Waddell, 1899)

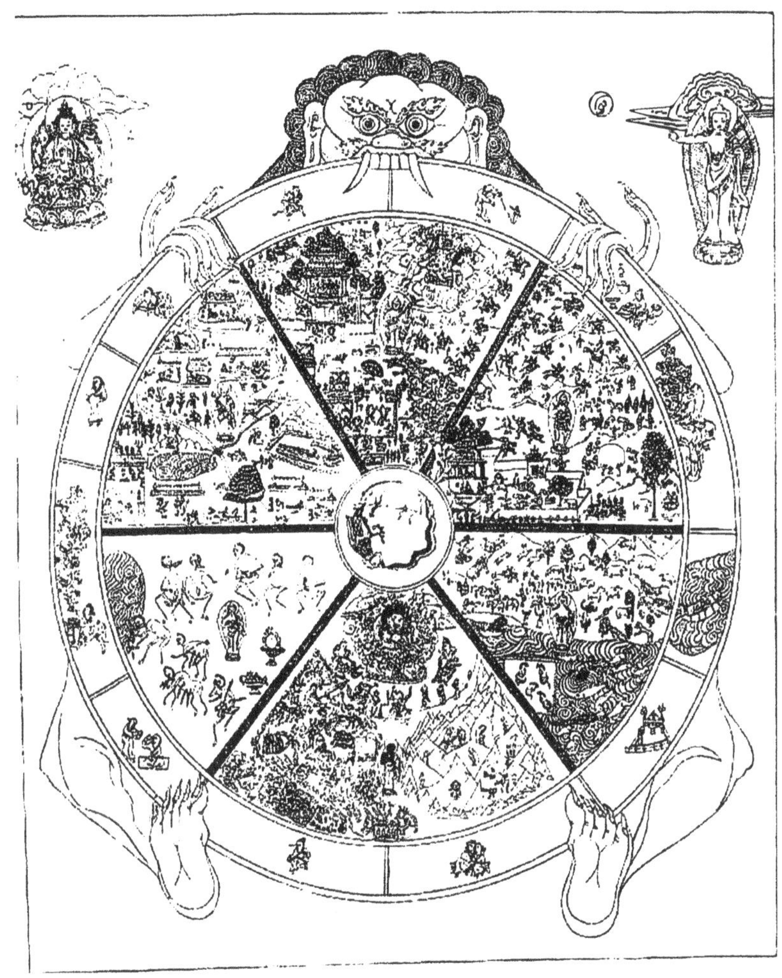

THE WHEEL OF LIFE
(From The Buddhism of Tibet, or, Lamaism; L. Austine Waddell, 1899), p. 108

Man--Nara or Mi--lives in the upper left-hand region, constantly confronting the eight miseries--birth, old age, sickness, death, ungratified wishes and struggle for existence, misfortune and punishment for law-breaking, separation from relatives and cherished objects, offensive objects and sensations. Of all these and other phases of ordinary existence pictures abound within the Wheel--birth in a cottage; children at play; village scenes--people drinking wine under a tree; a flute player; women spinning and weaving; a borrower; two traders; a drunken man; workers tilling a field or gathering fuel in a forest or bent under heavy loads; the accidents of life--a man and a horse falling into a river; crime--two men fighting--another on trial--another suffering punishment; government--a king and his ministers; old age, disease--a doctor feeling a sick man's pulse; death--a corpse and funeral ceremonies; religion--a temple placed above all the other objects within the Wheel--that is, Indra's Palace.

Beasts--lower right-hand quarter--are more miserable than man. They are shown consuming each other and being consumed; hunted by men, overburdened with loads, and filled with fear. Far beneath the waters of this animal world is the region of the Nagas or Mermen (great snakes), their home preyed upon by Garuda, Lord of birds, seeking here the serpents of the deep for food.

The region of the Tantalised Ghosts--lower left-hand quarter, is situated above Hell, and hunger and thirst torture the inhabitants. Always before their eyes there are food and drink and jewels in abundance, but the Pretas have mouths no larger than the size of a needle's eye, throats no wider than a hair's diameter, and through these openings they can never satisfy their huge bodily appetites. Add to this that, when food is taken, it is changed into knives or molten metal, and their hunger and thirst can be realised as incessant and never to be appeased. The little pictures within the Wheel show flames pouring from their mouths--if they touch water, it changes to liquid fire. The great Maudgalyayana once descended to the Tibetan purgatory to relieve his mother's distress, but even he could not aid her, and the rice he offered her turned to fiery ashes as she touched it.

Hell, the lowest region, is "situated in the bowels of the human Earth," and is ruled over by Yama, king and judge of the dead, who must himself every day swallow molten metal. His domain is divided into many compartments, each with its special form of punishment for the expiation of different sins. In the upper part of Hell sits Yama with his good and evil angels, ghosts of the dead, the Weigher, and the Prisoner. Below are the Hot Hells, and the Cold Hells, to each of which the damned are assigned according to their sins. The Hot Hells are sunk in the Earth, beginning at a depth of 11,900 miles, and they reach to a depth of 40,000 miles. They are of deepest black, although each is surrounded by a wall of fire. The Cold Hells are at the very edge of the Universe, circled by icy mountains and supplied with glacier water in which the victims are constantly immersed, until chilblains appear and become great sores and ulcers.

There is an exit from Hell, through a sort of borderland Hell called "the near (to re-birth) cycle." This has four divisions; the first filled with hot ashes and dead bodies and offal; the second a quagmire or "sinking sands," beyond which is a forest of spears, which must be crossed--like the razor-bridge of Mohammed, the Bi-frost of Yggdrasil, the slippery fir-tree of the American Indians, or the wide river of The Pilgrim's Progress. After--if--the bridge is crossed, there comes a river of freezing water whose farther shore is thickly set with tree stumps bearing three spiked leaves which impale the pilgrim. What is left to man after this pilgrimage is called "The Surviving Thing."

EARTH THE MUNDANE EGG

THE GREAT MONAD, or the Great Beginning, or the Great Extreme, or the Great Vacuum, or Yin and Yang, or "Heaven," is one of the old, mysterious figures of Earth. It represents all the pairs of opposites that we know--Light and Darkness, life and death, death and re-birth, heat and cold, good and evil, subtle and gross, male-female in Nature, or the great principles Yin and Yang. It is One yet All Things, the great hermaphrodite--"the indivisible monad, of itself generating itself, and out of this were formed all things." It looks like a shell, it looks like an ear; it looks like a tadpole, an embryo, a whirlpool, a claw, a comma, two eyes, strange Moon upon the Sun. It looks perhaps like the Universe itself before the creation of Heaven and Earth. It is the epitome of all the "egg-shaped" figures of Earth. It is animated Chaos, primordial Air dividing into two Airs to generate a multiplied cosmos, for they have the power to make and transmute all things. It is the Ovum Mundi--Egg of the World.

FIGURE 61. The Great Monad.
(From Dragon, Image and Demon; H. C. Du Bose, 1887.)

It is never a life or a birth symbol merely; it is always associated with the idea of primal causal cosmic energy. The Japanese mitsu tomoe is a variation of the Great Monad of the Chinese; instead of the two-comma-shaped figure, its "commas" are three.

"The Great Extreme," says the Chinese philosopher Choo-tzse, writing of this ancient symbol, "moved and generated the Light; having moved to the utmost, it rested, and resting, generated the Darkness. . . .

"The Great Extreme resembles a root which sprouts upwards, and divides into branches, and which also divides and produces blossoms and leaves, generating unceasingly. When the fruit is formed, then, it contains inside, the seed of endless generations, which generates and springs forth. This is the Infinite Great Extreme, which never ceases altogether, but only when the fruit is perfected it ceases to generate for a while. . . .

FIGURE 62. The Mitsu Tomoe of the Japanese.
(From Internationales Archiv für Ethnographie; Bd. IX (1896), S. 265.)

"In the beginning Heaven and Earth were just Light and Dark Air. This one Air revolved grinding round and round. When it ground quickly much sediment was compressed, which, having no means of exit, coagulated and formed the Earth in the centre. The subtle portion of the Air then became Heaven, and the Sun, Moon, and Stars which unceasingly revolve on the outside. The Earth is in the centre, and is motionless, it is not below the centre.

The Earth is the sediment of the Air; and hence it is said that the light and pure Air became Heaven; the heavy and muddy Air became Earth." [1]

Here is a series of Chinese diagrams (Fig. 63) illustrating the process of the Creation of the universe from the beginning--the whole infinite mass of Primordial Air when in Chaos. This is represented by the black disc (e), the Ovum Mundi or "Mind" of the universe, inherent in which, even in its mingled state, is the Divine Reason. In (f) is shown the separation of the Primordial Air into two Airs, the division of Subtile from Gross, of Light from Darkness. This is the beginning of all things, from which sprang the First God, All Light (a), called Reason, Fate, the Immovable Mover, or the Infinite. From this First God came the Second God, or Light, and the Demon-god or Darkness (b), which, say the Chinese, represent Mind or the two-fold Soul, contained within the body of the visible world (c). To represent the complete being of the animated cosmos the three circles or globes are placed like three bodies, one within the other (d); this is sometimes called the Three-fold Air. The Great Extreme is represented in another form in the upper half of the lower right-hand figure, whose inner circle represents the First God inherent in all things, with the Light and Dark Airs alternating unceasingly. From this ceaseless alternation are generated the Five Elements whose Chinese terms differ considerably from those we have been using--namely, earth, water, fire, air, and ether. For the first one, they say, is termed water, and by some is called black. The second is fire, and by some is termed red. The third is called wood and is therefore termed green. The fourth is called metal and is white. The fifth is called earth, and is presumed to be yellow.

---

[1] Confucian Cosmogony. Thomas M'Clatchie, Shanghai, 1874.

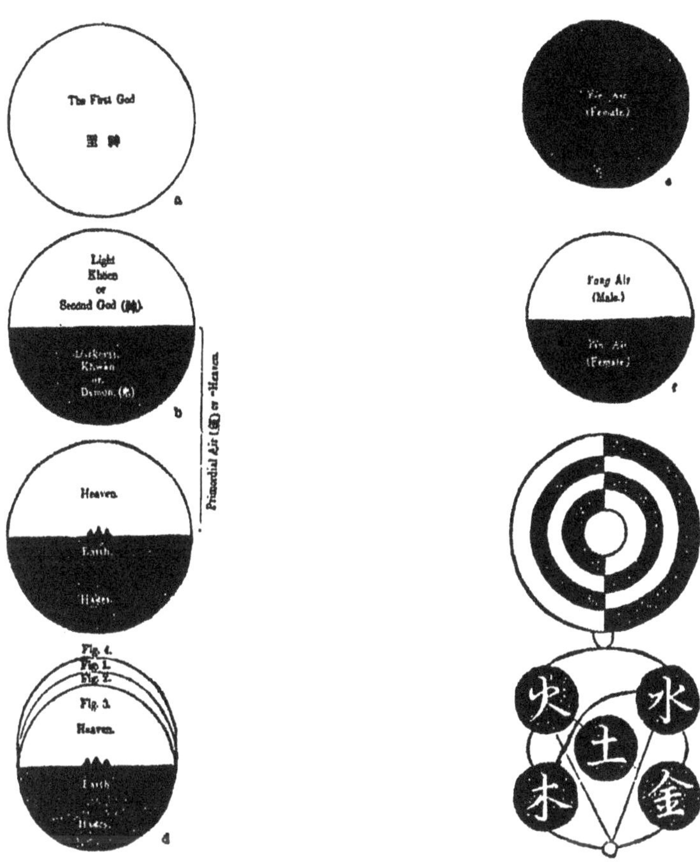

FIGURE 63. Chinese Conception of the Creation.
(From Confucian Cosmogony; Thomas M'Clatchie, Shanghai, 1874.)

Besides the Great Monad and its associated diagrams, the Chinese had yet another series of diagrams by which, they asserted, it was possible to account for all the changes and transmutations within the forces of Nature. These are the Eight Diagrams of Fuh-he, which, according to him and his disciples, manifest the Mind of Heaven and Earth, whose only purpose is to generate--that is, to change and to transmute. "That which proceeds gradually," they said, "is transmutation [like the growth of a tree]. That which is united in one and is incomprehensible is God. Transmutation is each thing succeeding in order." They tried to explain this further by saying: "That which when at Rest cannot Move, and when in Motion cannot Rest is Matter;. that which Moves yet moves not, Rests yet rests not, is God." They said, too, that the "thirty-six palaces"--the number of units that make up the Eight Diagrams--are no more than merely the strokes of the Light and the Darkness.

Each set of three lines (Fig. 64) represents the three powers, Heaven, Earth, and Man, and represents also the exact force exerted by each one in each of the eight combinations. The three undivided lines, for instance, indicate the tireless strength of Heaven, the three divided lines, the divided Earth. Beginning at the top and going to the left, the triads are supposed to read: river or running water, Heaven, wind, Earth, Sun, lake or dormant water, mountain, thunder. The centre of this mirror is said to represent the Sun, surrounded by four constellations, which are in turn encircled by the Eight Diagrams, and these again by the Chinese Zodiac, or Yellow Path of the Sun, with its twelve animal signs--the Mouse, Cow, Tiger, Rabbit, Dragon, Serpent, Horse, Ram, Ape, Hen, Dog, and Pig.

FIGURE 64. The Chinese Zodiac. From a Mirror of the Tang Dynasty.
(From Journal of the Royal Asiatic Society of Great Britain and Ireland, 1835, Vol. II.)

THE FIVE FIGURES OF EARTH as the Mundane Egg, given in Plates XXIX, pl30, and XXXI, are all of them different, yet all of them the same, and they range in time and region from ancient Egypt to seventeenth-century England. The idea of the "Ophis et Ovum Mundanum" (PlateXXIX, B) is not to be traced to its source; it is found everywhere, in the open or secret traditions of all races--this concept of the great World Serpent warming, guarding, hatching, sometimes feasting on the Earth Egg. The "Deus Luna" () is one of the old attempts, in varying forms and with more interpretations, to link the great triad of heavenly bodies, Sun, Moon, and Earth, into a figure symbolic of the whole universe. Here the Mundane Egg is held in its fiery vase very much as an acorn is held in its cup. It is guarded by the Moon, which, as a "great white bird," was supposed to rest at night upon the Earth; "like a goose," said the Egyptians, "brooding over her egg."

The third figure (Plate XXIX, C), as much a World Mountain as a World Egg, is asserted by Flammarion to represent the world-concept of Edrisi, an Arabian geographer of the eleventh century, "who, with many others, considered the Earth to be like an egg with one-half plunged into the water." This is identical with the figure illustrating the "Theory of Two Centres" (Fig. 54). It is also a modern religious rendering of the Northern hemisphere, with Jerusalem and Palestine at the apex of the world.

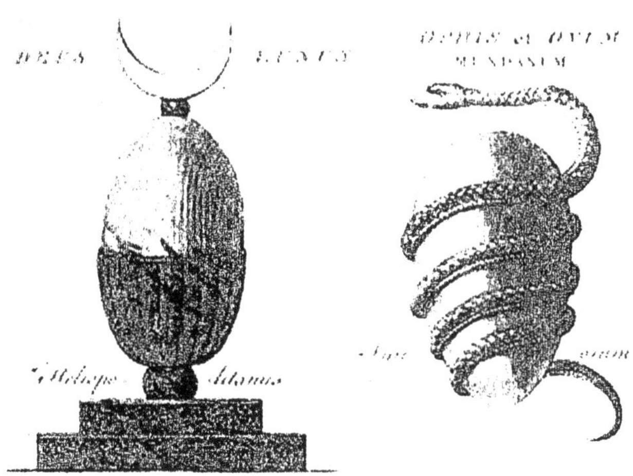

PLATE XXIX. A. Deus Lunus. B. Ophis et Ovum Mundanum.
(From Ancient Mythology; Jacob Bryant, 1774, Vol. II)

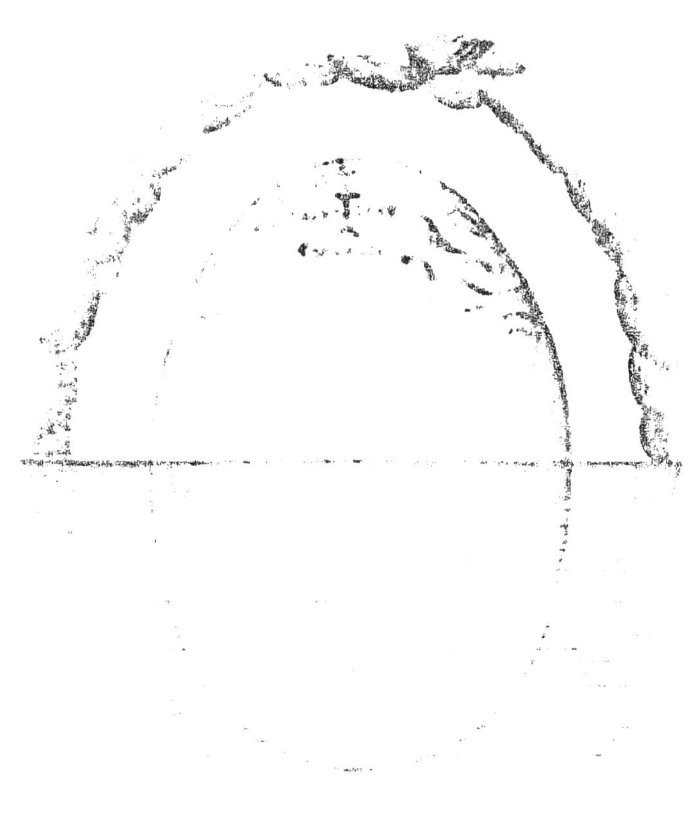

PLATE XXIX. C. Earth as a floating Egg.
(From Flammarion's Astronomical Myths. 1877)

The last two figures bring us back again to Thomas Burnet and his Theory of the Earth, which emphatically was the theory that it is almost literally, certainly by every analogy, the Mundane Egg.

"There is another thing in Antiquity," said this great English Platonist, "relating to the form and construction of the Earth, which is very remarkable, and hath obtained throughout all learned Nations and Ages. And that is the comparison or resemblance of the Earth to an Egg. And this is not so much for its external figure, though that be true too, as for the inward composition of it; consisting of several Orbs, one including another, and in that order, as to answer the several elementary Regions on which the new-made Earth was constituted. For if we admit for the Yolk a Central fire . . . and suppose the Figure of the Earth Oval, and a little extended towards the Poles . . . those two bodies do very naturally represent one another, as in this Scheme, which represents the interiour faces of both, a divided Egg, or Earth. Where, as the two inmost Regions (A. B.) represent the Yolk and the Membrane that lies next above it; so the Exteriour Region of the Earth (D.) is as the Shell of the Egg, and the Abysse (C.) under it as the White that lies under the Shell. And considering that this notion of the Mundane Egg, or that the World was Oviform, hath been the sence and language of all Antiquity, Latins, Greeks, Persians, Egyptians, and others, I thought it worthy our notice in this place."

The unknown author of De Imago Mundi had, it happens, compared not the Earth but the Universe itself to a ball, or an Egg. In his scheme, the shell corresponded to the upper heavens; the white to the upper air; the yolk to the lower air; and the pinguidinis gutta, or drop of grease in the centre, to the Earth. And, even earlier than these, the Venerable Bede had written (in the sixth century A.D.): "The Earth is an element placed in the middle of the world, as the yolk in the middle of an egg; around it is the water, like the white surrounding the yolk; outside that is the air, like the membrane of the egg; and around all is the fire, which closes it in as the shell does. . . . The ocean, which surrounds it by its waves as far as the horizon, divides it into two parts, the upper of which is inhabited by us, while the lower is inhabited by our antipodes; although not one of them can come to us, nor one of us to them." These three analogies are developed differently, but Burnet's figure of the "divided egg" will serve to illustrate all of them (Plate XXX).

Having divided his Earth-egg to show the order of arrangement of its inner parts, Burnet then closed it up, to represent it entire, with only a reminder of the great abyss under it (Plate XXXI), on which his whole theory of the Deluge and the dissolution of the Earth rested. Either the great abyss opened (which he doubted), "or the frame of the Earth broke and fell down into the Great Abysse." In the latter case, there would be two effects. This "smooth Earth" in which were the first scenes of the world and the first generations of mankind, which had the beauty of youth and not a wrinkle, scar or fracture in all its body, no Rocks or Mountains, no hollow Caves nor gaping Chanels," would be first submerged during the agitation of the abyss by the violent fall of the Earth into it. Then, when the flood had subsided, "you would see," said he, "the true image of the present Earth in the ruines of the first" (Fig. 34 and Plate XIV). He compared his "smooth" or primal Earth to an Æolipile or hollow sphere filled with water, which the heat of fire rarefies and turns into vapours and winds. "The Sun here is as the Fire," he said, "and the exteriour Earth is as the Shell of the Æolipile, and the Abysse as the Water within it. . . . So we see all Vapours and Exhalations enclos'd within the Earth, and agitated there, strive to break out, and often shake the ground with their attempts to get loose. And in the comparison we used of an Æolipile, if the mouth of it be stopt that gives the vent, the Water rarefied will burst the Vessel with its force. And the resemblance of the Earth to an Egg, which we used before, holds also in this respect, for when it heats before the Fire, the moisture and Air within being rarefied, makes it often burst the Shell. And I do the more willingly mention this last comparison, because I observe that some of the Ancients, when they speak of the doctrine of the Mundane Egg, say that after a certain period of time it was broken."

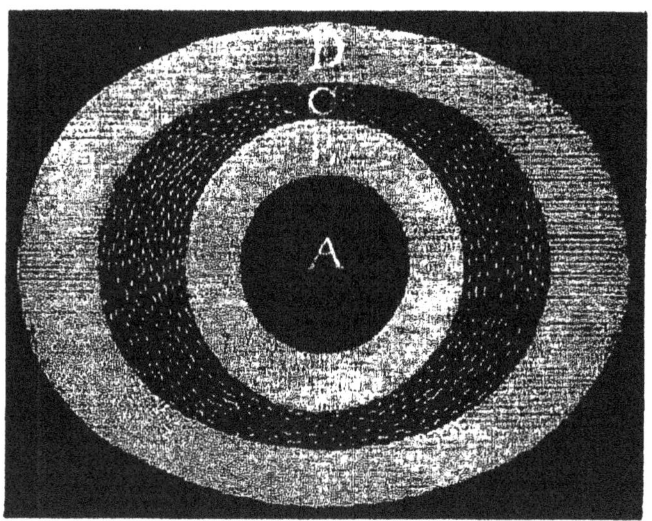

PLATE XXX. "A DIVIDED EGG, OR EARTH."
(From The Theory of the Earth; Thomas Burnet, 1697)

Another cosmogony worked out along this same analogy is that of the Gnostics, a group that flourished during the first two centuries of the Christian era, who are said to be the descendants in wisdom of other groups far removed. But the Gnostic group was really an aggregation of groups who combined the Christian teachings with a gnosis or higher knowledge through which the inner meaning of Christianity was revealed. Their doctrines were akin to those of Pythagoras, the higher Egyptian, Indian and Chinese teachers, and to those of the Essenes who for centuries before the Christian era had dwelt apart on the shores of the Dead Sea. They strove after the knowledge of God; wisdom was their goal, and the life of man on Earth their study. For gnosis, in the words of Theodotus, is the knowledge of what we were, what we have become, where we were, into what place we have been thrown; whither we are hastening, whence we are redeemed; what is birth, and what is re-birth." Their scheme of the universe has come down to us through "the diagram of Celsus," who called it the diagram of the Ophites, a sect of the Gnostics, with whose beliefs he was most familiar.

In the beginning, said the Gnostics, was the Trinity, Light, Spirit, and Darkness, all intermingled; and from the striving of the Darkness to retain the Light and Spirit, and so to imprison life sparks in matter, and from the striving of Light and Spirit against the power of Darkness, the first great form was produced, Heaven and Earth, symbolised by the World Egg in the womb of the universe. This World Egg was represented as a circle with a serpent twined several times around it, signifying the mysterious force which first set into separating, light-producing motion the mingled Light and Darkness of the Great Monad. The great serpent, they believed, was not the Great Tempter, but the form through which Divine Will and Divine Reason incessantly moved and manifested.

The diagram itself is divided into two great regions, the upper and the lower, separated from each other by the thick black line called Gehenna or Tartarus. The upper region belonged to the supreme Intelligences; it was the world of the Æons, or the Pleroma of the Gnostics--the World of Light. Here was perfect harmony, the state of ideal fulness or perfection.

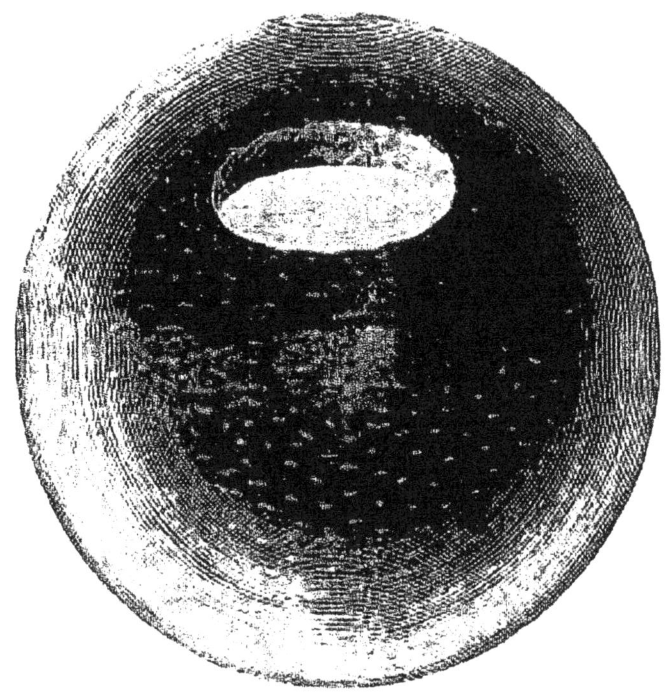

PLATE XXXI. "THE WHOLE EARTH IS AN EGG"
(From The Theory of the Earth; Thomas Burnet, 1697)

The lower region is divided into two groups, one of ten, the other of seven, spheres, each group of spheres being enclosed within a sphere, and the two separated from each other by the band of Lower Air. The circle enclosing the seven spheres is labelled Leviathan, and represents the Soul of the World, as the body represents the spirit that dwells in it. For it chanced that, one day, the Universal Mother, brooding over the Waters, let a "Drop of Light" fall downwards into chaotic matter, and this was called Sophia, or Wisdom, the World Mother. The waters of the Æther being then set in motion, formed a body for Sophia, called the Heaven-sphere. Whereupon Sophia, freeing herself, rose upwards to the Middle Region, below her Mother who was herself the bounding line of the Ideal Universe. Sophia had herself produced Ialdabaoth (child of Chaos, and also identified with Saturn), who in his turn produced a son, and so on, until there were seven in all, the Formative powers of the phenomenal world.

The second group of spheres within a sphere is labelled Behemoth--it is the terrestrial world. Its lower seven spheres carry within them the signatures of seven great animals, and, without, the names of seven angels. The higher three spheres bear only interrogation marks, but they are supposed to belong to Ialdabaoth, the ruler of terrestrial affairs, or perhaps to Sophia herself.

Concerning the signatures of animals inscribed within the seven lower spheres and their relation to the seven angels named outside, Celsus says that the first, a goat, "was shaped like a lion," and was a part of Michael the Lion-like. The second in descending order was a bull--or Suriel, the Bull-like; the third was "an amphibious sort of animal and one that hissed frightfully"--Raphael the Serpent-like; the fourth had the form of an eagle--Gabriel, the Eagle-like; the fifth had the countenance of a bear--Thauthabaoth, the Bear-like; the sixth had the face of, a dog--or Erataoth; "the seventh had the countenance of an ass and was named Thaphabaoth or Onoel."

Might any soul succeed in escaping through these seven spheres and the three empty globes or circles, he must then pass "the fence of wickedness," or "gates" subjected to the world of ruling spirits called Leviathan. Beginning with the lowest, he passed to what was called Ialdabaoth, then to Iao, to Sabaoth, to Astaphæus ruler of the third gate, to Alœus governor of the second, and to Horæus, keeper of the first. Celsus calls this world of Leviathan "circles upon circles."

The Gnostics are famous for their strange symbolic figures. They believed in a Watcher of the World, a Mind that perceived, and they often represented this See-er of the World as a human body pierced with eyes. The extraordinary frontispiece to Riccioli's Almagestum Novum (Plate XXXII) is by no means a Gnostic picture, but its left-hand figure is a perfect delineation of the myriad-eyed Watcher of the universe.

Almagestum Novum appeared at just the time when the whole universe had been turned, so to say, inside out half inside out, at least. For the Ptolemaic system of the universe, by which we know that theory which places the Earth at the centre, with the rest of the heavenly bodies revolving about it, had but lately fallen. Copernicus, after many years of hesitancy, had at last dared, in 1543, to publish his De revolutionibus, which declared the Sun to be at the centre of our world. Eighteen years later Riccioli's Almagestum Novum was published; and this little time-scheme lends even more interest to its remarkable frontispiece. For between the "'Watcher of the World" and the "Starry One," the two great systems of the universe hang in the balance, one with the Earth, the other with the Sun, in the centre of Space. The first disc is inscribed with the new Copernican system; the second with the ancient Egyptian. At the goddess's feet lies the system known as Ptolemy's. In one hand she holds the Balance, in the other an armillary sphere. In the upper left-hand corner winged beings float, bearing orbs associated with Light; in the upper right-hand corner move the bearers of those heavenly bodies which bring Light into Darkness--the Moon, Saturn, Jupiter, and the flying serpent of the skies.

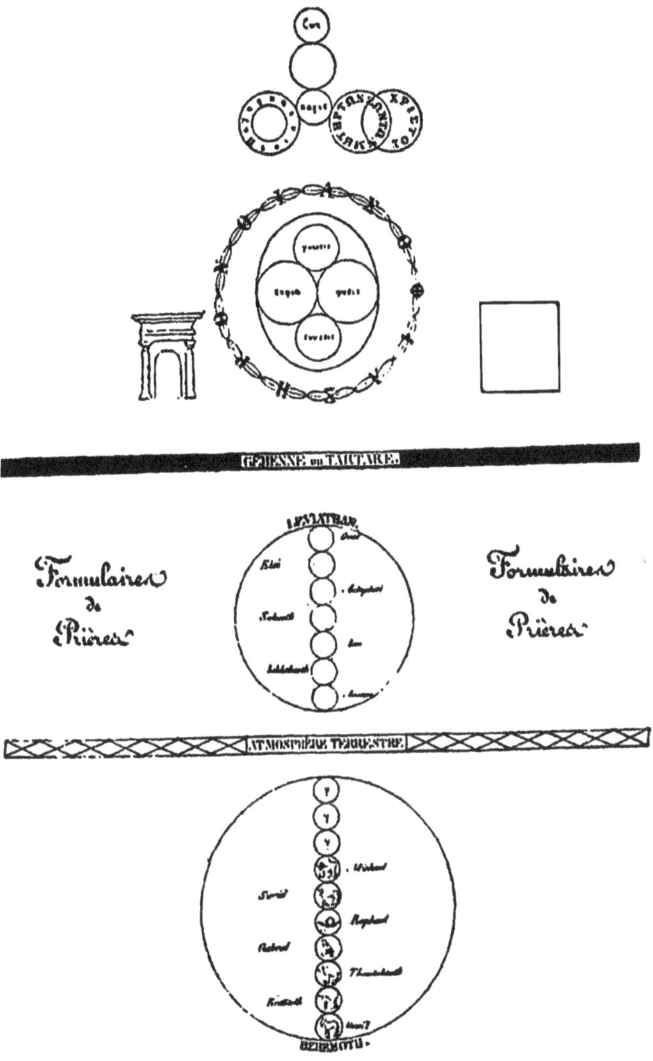

FIGURE 65. Gnostic Diagram of the Universe.
(From Histoire critique du Gnosticisme; Jacques Matter, 1826, Vol. III, Plate I, D.)

SYSTEMS OF THE UNIVERSE

WHEN THE GREEKS IN THE SIXTH CENTURY B.C. took up the study of the universe, its systems multiplied. The order of the orbits of the heavenly bodies, above all, their disorder, fascinated the Greek mind. Eclipses occurred, but how? A Comet fled through the sky, and did not collide with a sister body--why? How were the Earth, Sun, Moon, and all the stars supported in space? What are the relative distances of the spaces between them? Which were the larger bodies? the smaller? What were the divisions of Space? What were the major combinations of the great elements? How were these combinations effected--and a hundred other questions.

PLATE XXXII. (Frontispiece to Almagestum Novum; Ioannes Riccioli, 1561)

Homer was the first poet of the Greek universe, but Thales was its first philosopher (640-572 B.C.). He believed the Earth was a disc floating "like a piece of wood or something of that kind," on the waters which were the origin of all things, including fire and air as well as Earth; and his interest in eclipses led him into a protracted study of the movements of the Sun and the Moon and their relation to the Earth.

Anaximander (c. 611-545 B.C.) was his contemporary. He gave up the idea that the water was the origin of everything, any more than any other substance known to man. Everything originated "from the nature of the infinite," and to it returned. Hence it followed that this world was not eternal, but merely one of a procession of worlds. He described the figure of Earth as either flat or convex on the surface, but much more like a cylinder or stone column than the thin disc of Thales. Eventually he called it cylindrical, with a height equal to one-third of its breadth. This cylinder, being in the centre of the universe, was stable, in equilibrium, since it had the same relation to every part of- the universe. Above it were a series of heavens, the first of air, the second of all the stars, the third of the Moon, above that the heaven of the Sun and above all the heaven of the heavenly fire. He had an extremely complicated theory to account for a motionless heaven and moving bodies; he appears to have imagined the Sun, for instance, to be an enormous wheel filled with fire, its rim pierced by a single hole the size of the Earth.

So, too, the Moon and stars rolled through their heavens; eclipses came from the holes in the Sun-wheel's rim and that of the Moon being partially or wholly stopped up. Quite exactly, his Sun and Moon were vessels filled with fire.

Of course only the upper surface of Anaximander's Earth was habitable; below it the heavenly bodies had their underworld course; for the rest, the horizon marked the limits of the known and the knowable.

He seems to have held too the curious idea that the series of worlds which come out of the infinite and go back into it may be also called gods, since, like gods, they are created, they live, they die, and are again created.

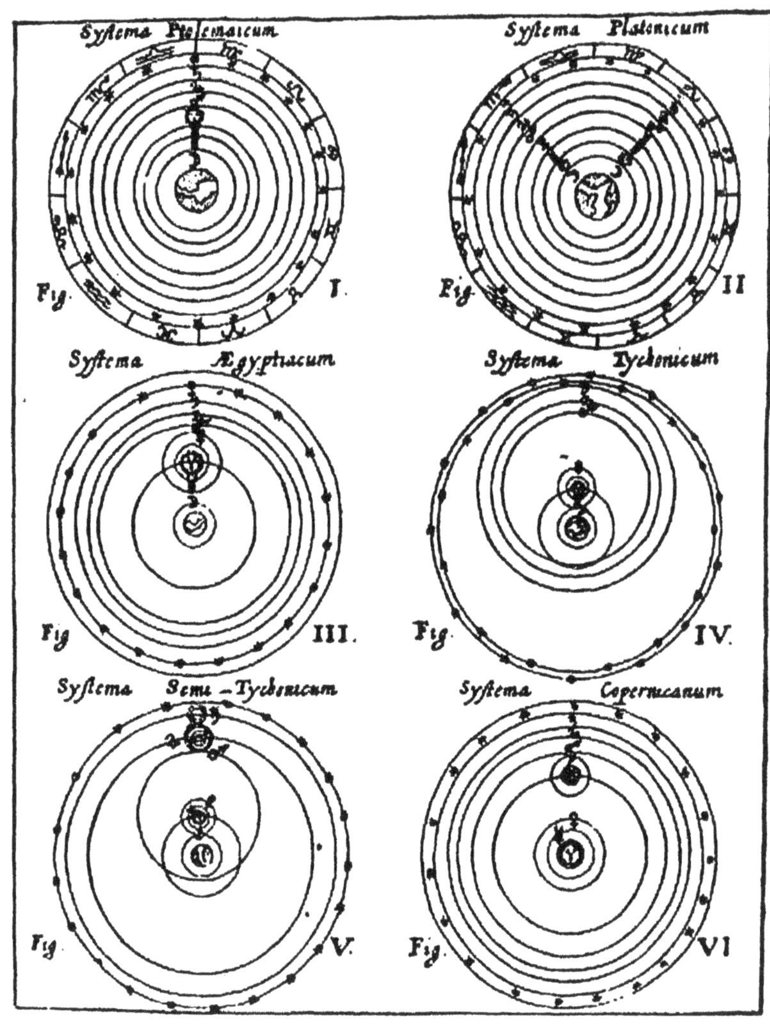

FIGURE 66. The Systems of the Universe.
(From Iter exstaticum cæleste; Athanasius Kircher, 1660, Plate II.)

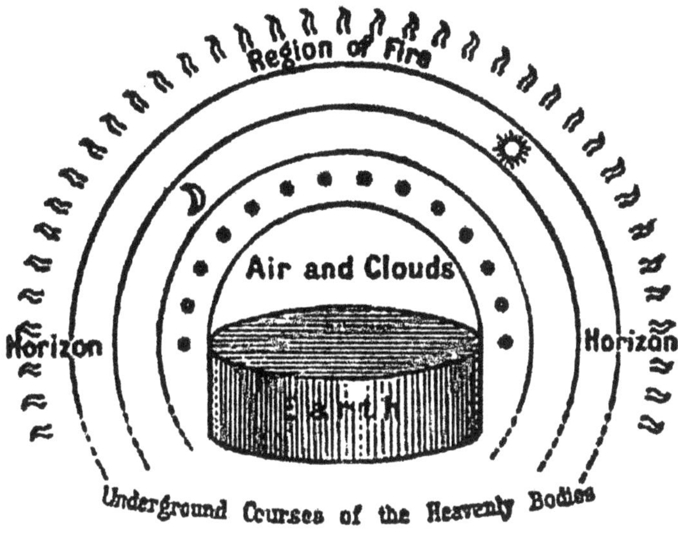

FIGURE 67. The Universe according to Anaximander
(c. 611-545 B.C.)
(From Dante and the Early Astronomers; M. A. Orr (Mrs. John Evershed), 1913.)

For a hundred years following Anaximander's death, the Greeks were still asking how the Earth was held in balance, and why the heavenly bodies did not fall from their places in the sky and destroy the Earth. Empedocles and Anaxagoras offered this explanation--that a great whirl-wind swept continuously round the Earth, serving the double end of holding the heavenly bodies aloft and of driving them across the sky. Anaxagoras believed that this same whirlwind was responsible for the stars themselves; that they were fragments of the Earth, torn off by the violence of the whirlwind, and that their light came from no more than the heat produced by friction. He also believed that the "heaven of the stars" was far beyond that of the Sun.

As for Empedocles, he re-asserted that everything consists of the four elements, Earth, air, fire, and water, either in a pure, or a combined, or a mixed state merely; and he said further that all these combinations and mixings were brought about by two forces alone, one attracting, and one repulsing, one Harmony, the other Disharmony, one Cord, the other

Discord. He had also a very individual idea of the Moon and the Sun; the Moon is air rolled together with fire--it is flat like a disc and gets its light from the Sun. But the Sun, he said, is a reflection of the fire surrounding the Earth; it is not itself of a fiery nature, but merely a reflection of fire, "like that which is produced in water."

Leucippus (c. 450 B.C.) changed Anaximander's figure of the universe considerably. He still held that the Earth's flat upper surface was its only habitable area, but he gave the whole mass of the Earth the shape of a tympanum or kettle drum, flat, with a slightly raised rim--according to this idea man was living on the flat top of the southern hemisphere. Above the hemisphere of Earth was the hemisphere of air, the two surrounded by the crystal sphere which held the Moon. Above the Moon's sphere was the planetary sphere; above this the sphere of the Sun, with the star-zone last, "perhaps outside." He accounted for the inclination of the axis to the horizon by saying that the Earth had sunk towards the south, which is merely the other half of the ancient saying that the Earth is raised towards the north.

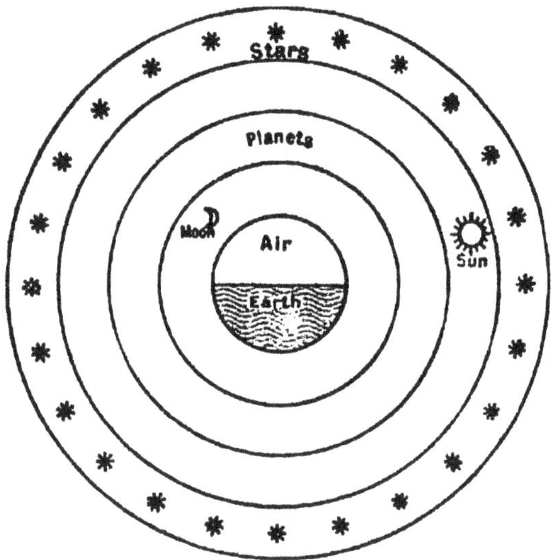

FIGURE 68. The Universe of Leucippus (c. 450 B.C.)
(From Dante and the Early Astronomers; M. A. Orr (Mrs. John Evershed), 1913.)

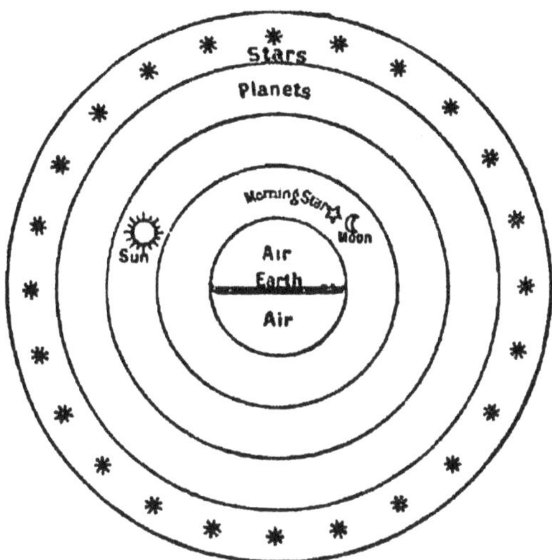

FIGURE 69. The Universe of Democritus (c. 430 B.C.)
(From Dante and the Early Astronomers; M. A. Orr (Mrs. John Evershed), 1913.)

Leucippus had a disciple, Democritus (c. 430 B.C.), who retained the thin Earth-disc of Thales, but added to it the surrounding rim of his master's Earth-drum. He changed Leucippus's Air-Earth sphere into a sphere of Air, divided horizontally through its centre by the Earth-disc. Thus, like the cylindrical Earth of Anaximander, it rested on nothing but air. Next the Air sphere he placed the Moon and the Morning Star, then the spheres of the Sun, the planets and the fixed stars.

The Sun, he said, was ignited stone or iron, and the Sun and Moon, each a large solid mass, were none the less smaller than the Earth. Originally, he said, the Sun and the Moon had been two Earths, like this of ours, and each of them, like ours, at the core and centre of a world. But these two worlds had encountered our world, which had absorbed them both, and had taken possession of the "Earth" of each. Comets, he said, are caused by two planets approaching each other closely. The Moon was not only a solid body, but, having once been the "Earth" of another world, it still has mountains and plains and chasms, which cause the markings on its face. Anaxagoras however had said this before him, and had also asserted that the Moon was still inhabited. Democritus also taught that the light of the Milky Way was caused by a great multitude of very faint stars. Later it was said that the Milky Way was a former path of the Sun, which for some obscure reason had changed its course.

It was Pythagoras who numbered and measured and named for the Greeks the five great planets of our system, and who gave them places in the heavens equal in importance to the greater heavenly bodies. And it was Pythagoras who taught that the Earth was a perfect sphere, hanging, if not moving, freely in space, with its whole surface habitable, and with men moving freely on all its sides. For the Earth, he said, balanced in the centre of the world, cannot fall, nor can it let anything which belongs to any part of it fall. There is no below, there is no above, for our North is South to the men of the antipodes; there is nothing but the Centre, where we are, and it is illusion to believe otherwise.

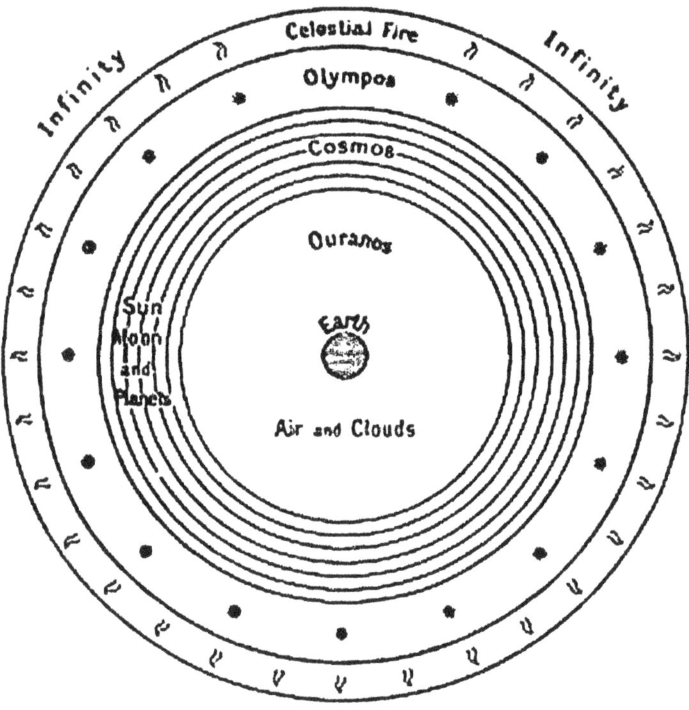

FIGURE 70. The Universe of Pythagoras (c. 540 B.C.)
(From Dante and the Early Astronomers; M. A. Orr (Mrs. John Evershed), 1913.)

Number played the principal part in the universe of the Pythagoreans, for, said they, everything in nature is governed by number, since number is the beginning and the end of all relations. There are cosmic principles, they declared, and these cosmic principles are mathematical principles, which are living principles; numbers are the essence of the universe, the very substance of things, the cause and effect of all that is in nature.

Pythagoras separated the planets and affirmed that their distances are in exact proportion to the intervals between musical notes. Combined with the Sun and Moon into a running scale, they make up the sacred number seven, and these seven notes of the cosmic scale constitute, with the mysterious star-sphere, the cosmic octave. As each of the heavenly bodies moves in its path, different to, yet harmonious with all the others, it sounds its own individual note in the great octave that is "the music of the spheres." This music, said the Pythagoreans, is all about us and has been since our infancy, but we live beside it "as one lives beside the cataracts of the Nile"--we never know we hear it.

According to Aristotle, the Pythagorean universe was divided thus:
The Earth was, first of all, a sphere situated in the centre of the universe, and was surrounded by many spheres.

Ouranos or Sky stretched between the Earth and the Moon. It was the region of illusion and change, always filled with whorls of air and shifting clouds.

Cosmos was the region of "the celestial octave," the appointed place for the Sun, the Moon, and the planets. It consisted of seven concentric rings or spheres, in which these heavenly bodies, or "divine beings," lived their conscious, joyous lives.

Olympos was the Star-sphere, the pure-elemental region which completed the cosmic octave.

Beyond Olympos stretched the region of celestial fire.

Beyond the region of celestial fire was Apeiron, Infinite Air, Infinite Space, from which and into which the Cosmos breathes, and through which and by which only it lives.

The Pythagoreans did not fail to take into account the five great elements, from which they believed all things were fashioned. They fitted these five "Causal Beings" into the five regular solids (Figs. 2-6 and), to whose forms, they said, the component particles of the different elements correspond. The component particle of Earth, for instance, corresponds to the cube; of water, to the icosahedron; of air, to the octahedron; of fire, to the tetrahedron; of ether, to the dodecahedron--the form which had been God's model for the whole universe.

FIGURE 75. The Five Great Elements.
(From Sphæra Mundi; Orantius Fineus, 1542.)

"A Figure of the Whole World" (Fig. 72) is the Pythagorean-Ptolemaic system, much elaborated. It begins by taking into account the "foure Elements," but it extends the number of the imaginable heavens beyond the "cristaline" to two--this was an invention of the mediæval astronomers. These two additional heavens were the Primum Mobile, or the "First Movable," and "The empyreal heaven, the habitation of the blesed." This last was the Heaven of Heavens, motionless, incorruptible, the place of the eternal mysteries. None of these spheres consisted, of course, of any materially palpable substance; they were great spherical zones of aethereal space, arranged one within the other, which circled about the motionless Earth at differing rates of speed. Perhaps, instead of "spheres," or "shells," or "zones," these moving regions are better expressed by the term "velocities."

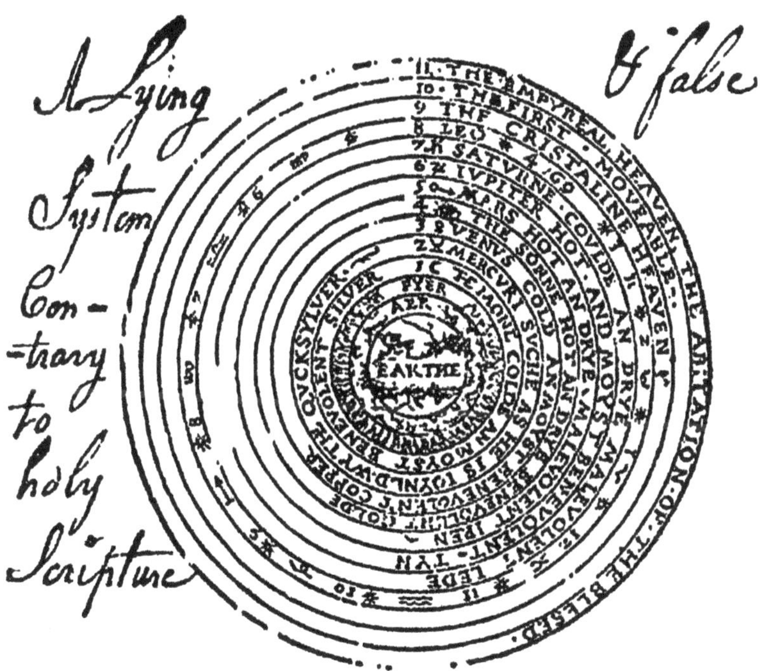

FIGURE 72. "A Figure of the whole world, wherein are set forth the two essentiall Parts, the eleven heavens, and the foure Elements.

Fig. 73 represents again the same system, even more elaborately inscribed with "correspondences." By aid of these two guides through the "two essentiall Parts" of the whole world--that is to say the eleven heavens and the four elements, the six systems of the universe shown in Fig. 66 can be more or less easily followed.

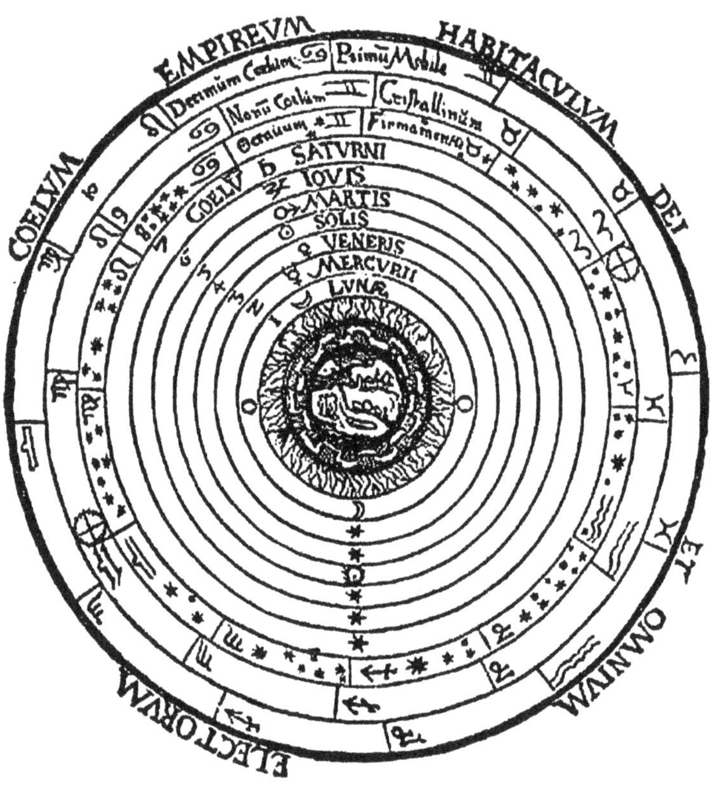

FIGURE 73. System of the diverse spheres.
(From Cosmographia; Petrus Apianus, 1660.)

ONE DEVELOPMENT OF THE PYTHAGOREAN SYSTEM might be mentioned here--the attempt of an otherwise unknown astronomer, Philolaus, to remove the motionless Earth from its place in the centre of the universe and give it an orbit of its own. His reasons, except that he hoped by this to account better for the seemingly contrary movements of the heavens, do not concern us here. But it is a transition-picture. For by moving the Earth from the centre and letting her move in Space, he may have solved one problem, but he raised two new ones. He had left the sacred place, the Centre of the World, empty, and he had disturbed the cosmic octave by adding to it another moving body. Heretofore the Earth had been mute because it was motionless; now movement gave it its own note in a disturbed scale. So in the sacred place he put the purest of the elements, Fire, forerunner of the Central Sun. Then, more to restore the harmony of number, quite likely, than to explain Night and Day, he created another moving heavenly body, the planet Antichthon, or Counter-Earth, and gave it an orbit between the Earth and the Central Fire with one of its faces turned always to the Fire. This gave nine moving bodies, and with the star-sphere as another, the number was increased from the sacred number seven to the sacred number ten. The Earth revolved with one face turned always away from the centre; Antichthon, the new planet, was therefore always invisible. After this rearrangement was completed, explanations purporting to reconcile a geocentric with an ignicentric system were invented plenteously, some of them very interesting ones. "Those who partook of a greater knowledge," wrote Simplicius, "called the fire in the middle the creating power, which from the middle gives life to the whole Earth and again warms that which has been cooled. . . . But they called the Earth a star because it also is an instrument of time, for it is the cause of days and nights, for it makes day to the part illumined by the Sun, but night to the part which is in the cone of the shadow." And he ends by saying that the moon was called the antichthon, because it is "an aethereal Earth."

Some modern students of this confusion have suggested that the Earth and the Counter-Earth or Antichthon might have been intended to be the two halves of a single sphere, cut through a meridian and separated very slightly, with the flat sides toward each other, but with the convex side of Antichthon turned always towards the Central Fire, and the convex side of the Earth turned always away from it. This may be so, but no one knows. For the Upper figure: Night on Earth. Only the side turned away from the centre is inhabited; consequently the Central Fire and Antichthon are invisible.

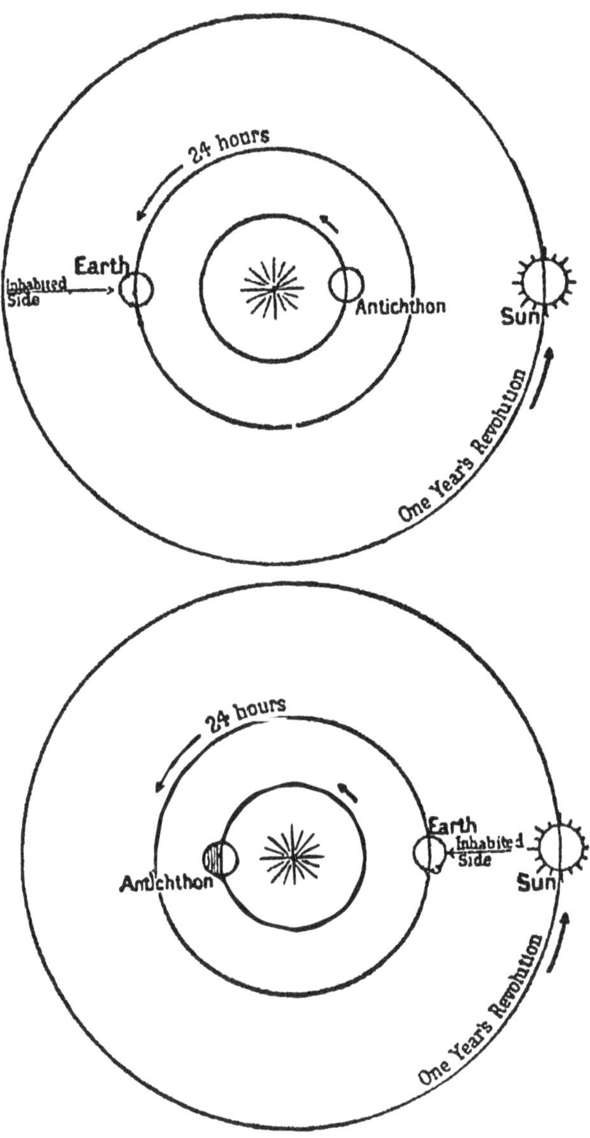

FIGURE 74. The System of Philolaus.
(From Dante and the Early Astronomers; M. A. Orr (Mrs. John Evershed), 1913.)

Lower figure: Twelve hours later; Day on Earth. Earth has made half a revolution, and her outer side is now lighted by the sun, which has only moved about half a degree forward in its yearly orbit. Antichthon has also made half a revolution, therefore remains invisible.

Pythagorean teachings were at the best obscure, and the Pythagorean text that has come down is scanty and corrupt. One Pythagorean, Hicatus of Syracuse, is said to have believed and taught that the heavens, the Sun, Moon, stars, and all the heavenly bodies are standing still, and that nothing in the universe is moving except the Earth, which, while it turns and twists itself with the greatest velocity round its axis, produces all the same phenomena as if the heavens were moving and the Earth were standing still."

As above, so below! Philolaus placed the planet Antichthon or Counter-Earth in the heavens, perhaps five hundred years before the Christian era. In the first century A.D. Pomponius Mela, a Latin cosmographer, convinced that a spherical Earth must have a more or less balanced distribution of land and water, drew the first map on which the mysterious continent of Earth appears in the unknown half of Earth--our antipodes. This continent he inscribed with the name Antichthones, the Unknown. His pen had leaped over the impassable equatorial zone, and had drawn below it a solid, bowl-shaped mass of land which no man had seen, and which no man might ever see. And yet it must be there! It had been long known through travellers that from Greece or from Italy the eastwardly land stretched much farther than the land to the west, and it was therefore quite possible, with no proof of the existence of a great western ocean, that the northern continent of Europe-Asia-Africa might wrap around the sphere until its eastern edge touched the western shore of the known Atlantic. But it was implicitly believed that the known land stopped at the equator; the balancing continent must be therefore at the antipodes. When Pomponius Mela dropped his second continent to the south, he was a mistaken man, but his Antichthones lingered in the imagination of men--lingered for nearly fifteen hundred years, until Columbus, sailing west--to India--came upon the West Indies and the Americas. The great astronomer and geographer, Claudius Ptolemy, lived in the century after Pomponius Mela. There is a legend that he was a descendant of the Egyptian kings, and knew their secret science of the heavens; certainly he brought about a revival of mathematical geography that had not been in the world since the great

Alexandrian period, and he drew his maps upon a form that was to be the model of the Earth up to and through the Middle Ages.

FIGURE 75. Pomponius Mela's Map of the World, with Antichthones (1st century A.D.)
(From De situ Orbis; Pomponius Mela, 1536.)

Ptolemy believed the Earth to be a globular body, but the form on which his maps were modelled was one slightly depressed at the north, and sharply cut off a little below the equatorial line by a supposedly continuous Southern Ocean which circled the equator and flowed below it. His historians do not seem to doubt that his knowledge of the regions of the Earth extended as far as the equator, and that he himself knew this fabled zone of fire was both habitable and inhabited. But he confined himself to a map-form that included neither the unknown Polar regions nor the hemisphere of Antichthones.

THE SQUARE EARTH OF COSMAS INDICOPLEUTES

ONE OF THE STRANGEST OF WORLDS is the Square Earth of Cosmas Indicopleustes, an Egyptian monk of the sixth century A.D., who expended an astonishing ingenuity upon the development of a theory of the universe that would eliminate the increasingly popular notion that the Earth was a sphere. He was filled with a holy hatred of the heresy of the "spherists" and the antipodists, and he evolved at last a figure of the universe modelled upon the design of the Tabernacle built by Moses in the wilderness, which, he pointed out, Moses himself had declared to be constructed upon the pattern of the visible world. His own explanation of it may be read in his Christian Topography.

Cosmas says that the Earth is a rectangular plane surface, whose long sides are twice the shorter ones. These are the measurements of the Tabernacle, and of the Table of Shew-bread. This Earth-table is divided into three parts: the habitable Earth, in the middle, the ocean which everywhere surrounds it, and beyond the ocean another surrounding continent, which is now altogether inaccessible to man, but which was once the seat of Paradise and the home of the human race up to the time of the Deluge, when the flood swept the Ark with its few saved men across to the "other Earth." It is true, says Cosmas, that after the Fall Paradise itself had been closed to Adam, but until the Deluge he and his descendants had dwelt on the coast edges of the First Continent of man.

Upon the edges of this outer inaccessible continent rest the four walls of heaven--four perpendicular planes joined hermetically to the edges of the trans-oceanic Earth, and cemented at the top by an enclosing roof, in form like half a cylinder. Its ends rest on the eastern and western sides of the world, and its sides on the north and south. These directions are determined by the Tabernacle Table, which was placed lengthwise from east to west. Here is a bit from Cosmas himself:

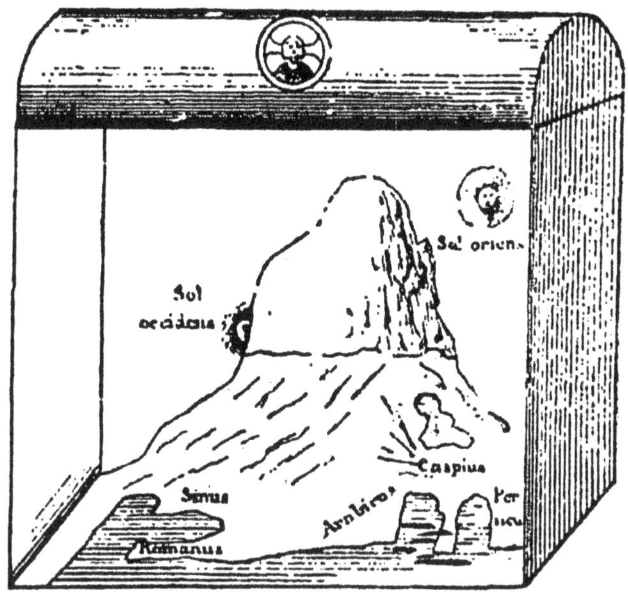

FIGURE 77. The Square Earth of Cosmas Indicopleustes (6th century A.D.)
(From Flammarion's Astronomical Myths, 1877.)

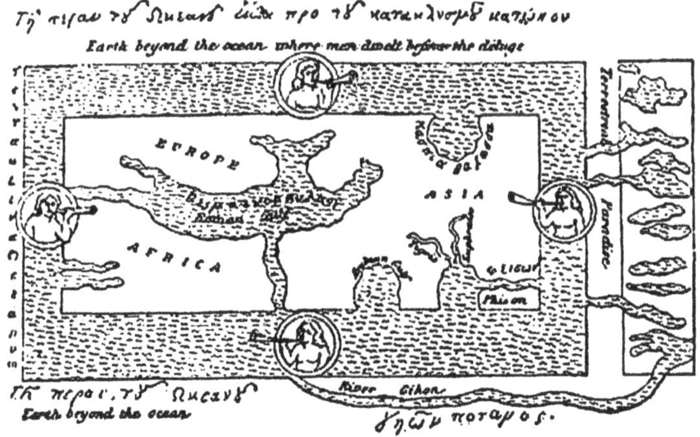

FIGURE 78. The Square Earth. Its habitable plane.
(From Flammarion's Astronomical Myths, 1877.)

"The Deity accordingly having founded the Earth, which is oblong, upon its own stability, bound together the extremities of the heaven with the extremities of the Earth, making the nether extremities of the heaven rest upon the four extremities of the Earth, while on high he formed it into a most lofty vault over-spanning the length of the Earth. Along the breadth again of the Earth he built a wall from the nethermost extremities of the heavens upwards to the summit, and having enclosed the place, made a house, as one might call it, of enormous size, like an oblong vapour bath. For, saith the Prophet Isaiah (xlix, 22), He who established heaven as a vault. With regard moreover to the glueing together of the heaven and the Earth, we find this written in Job: He has inclined heaven to earth, and it has been poured out as the dust of the earth. I have welded it as a square block of stone." [1]

The interior of this "oblong vaulted vapour bath" consists, like the Tabernacle, of two parts, the outer and the inner--the veil of the Tabernacle corresponding to the firmament which divides the universe into two parts, and which is the floor of the upper and the ceiling of the lower story. The first story reaches from the Earth-plane, "the footstool of the Lord," to the firmament, and is the abode of men and angels. The presence of angels is necessary in man's world, not only for the sake of their beneficent effect on him, but also because the Sun, Moon, and stars are carried in their courses, not by the firmament which is motionless, but by angels appointed to this work until the last day.

On the Earth-plane rises a high cone-shaped mountain, which makes possible, in this world-system, the rising and the setting of the Sun, day and night, climates, seasons, etc.

With the universe enclosed within a square box, it was no longer possible for the Sun to sink in western waters, swim under the Earth, and emerge again from the eastern sea. But forever circling the conical mountain of the world, in the arms of its carrying angel, it is hidden from a part of the world all of the time, and thus comes day and night. The length of the days and nights varies, says Cosmas, according as the Sun is close to or far from its mountain screen, and from this cause spring summer and winter, storms, eclipses, heat and cold, and such phenomena. "All the stars are created," he says, "to regulate the days and nights, the months and the years, and

---

[1] Christian Topography of Cosmas Indicopleustes: Hakluyt Soc. Pub. 1897, p. 30.

they move, not at all by the motion of the heaven itself, but by the action of certain divine Beings, or lampadophores. God made the angels for his service, and He has charged some of them with the motion of the air, others with that of the Sun, or the Moon, or the other stars, and others again with the collecting of clouds, and preparing the rain." Cosmas also says that men are mistaken when they say that the Sun is much larger than the Earth; that it is, in reality, very much smaller; and, by measuring its shadows at the different "climates" of Ptolemy, he concludes that the sun has the size of "two climates."

Above the firmament and beneath the upper vault live the Blessed. Along the outer side of this vault which terminates the world, rest the heavenly waters. The Mosaic account of the Tabernacle and its enclosed Ark, says Cosmas, gives all the measurements and hence all the secrets of the world, and by it alone man may reconstruct the universe within himself and look down upon it, as the Creator surveys his handiwork from the vaulted roof of Cosmas's "vapour bath."

Here are some of the correspondences which Cosmas drew between the pattern of the Tabernacle and that of the visible world.

In the first Tabernacle, "Moses placed in the south of it the candlesticks, with seven lamps, after the number of days in the week--these lamps being typical of the celestial luminaries--and shining on the table placed in the north of the Earth. On this table again he ordered to be placed daily twelve loaves of shew-bread, to typify the three months between each of the four tropics. He commanded also to be wreathed all around the rim of the table a waved moulding, to represent a multitude of waters, that is, the ocean; and further, in the circuit of the waved work, a crown to be set of the circumference of the palm of the hand, to represent the land beyond the ocean, and encircling it, where in the east lies Paradise, and where also the extremities of the heaven are bound to the extremities of the Earth. And from this description we not only learn concerning the luminaries and the stars that most of them, when they rise, run their course through the south, but from the same source we are taught that the Earth is surrounded by the ocean, and further that beyond the ocean there is another Earth by which the ocean is surrounded."

THE PERUVIAN UNIVERSE

THERE IS ANOTHER "SQUARE EARTH" shown in one of the rarer world-pictures in this collection--the Universe of the ancient Peruvians. Juan de Santa Cruz Pachacuti Yamqui Salcamayha, a native Peruvian, left the drawing in his Account of the Antiquities of Peru, written about 1620. His manuscript reached Spain, where it lay long forgotten among the treasures of the Biblioteca Nacional at Madrid. Salcamayha was not only a Peruvian, but he is credited with being one of the chosen recipients of the traditions of his people, and in close touch with the final glories of the Ynca empire; for his great-grandparents were living at the time of the Spanish conquest of Peru, and stories of the vanished days came to him almost from the lips of those who had witnessed them.

Salcamayha left no reading of this crudely sketched cosmos, and what follows is based largely on Beuchat's interpretation.

The World, says Beuchat,[1] was called Pacha. It was a square World, with a roof indicated, ridge-shaped, where dwelt the great God. The lowest plane was Earth, which gave support to the four quarters where dwelt the gods.

Outside the World, above it, to the left, is a small disc, so Beuchat calls it, but it far more resembles a figure of the Cosmic or Mundane Egg, surrounded, though not en-circled, by five stars. Within, in the centre of the pointed roof, this outer design appears again, much enlarged, slightly rearranged, and with the addition of a single star. In the rearrangement of the design, three of the stars have been connected along a thread, and from these three is suspended the oval figure of Huiracocha, the Creator of the World. On his left is the Sun or Inti; on his right the Moon or Quilla. The bright star below the Sun is Chasca or the planet Venus, and under Venus lies a star representing Catachillay, or the Milky Way. Between the Milky Way and Venus is a group of stars--thirteen--which are the constellations.

---

[1] Manuel d'Archeologie américaine: H. Beuchat, 1912, pp. 630-631.

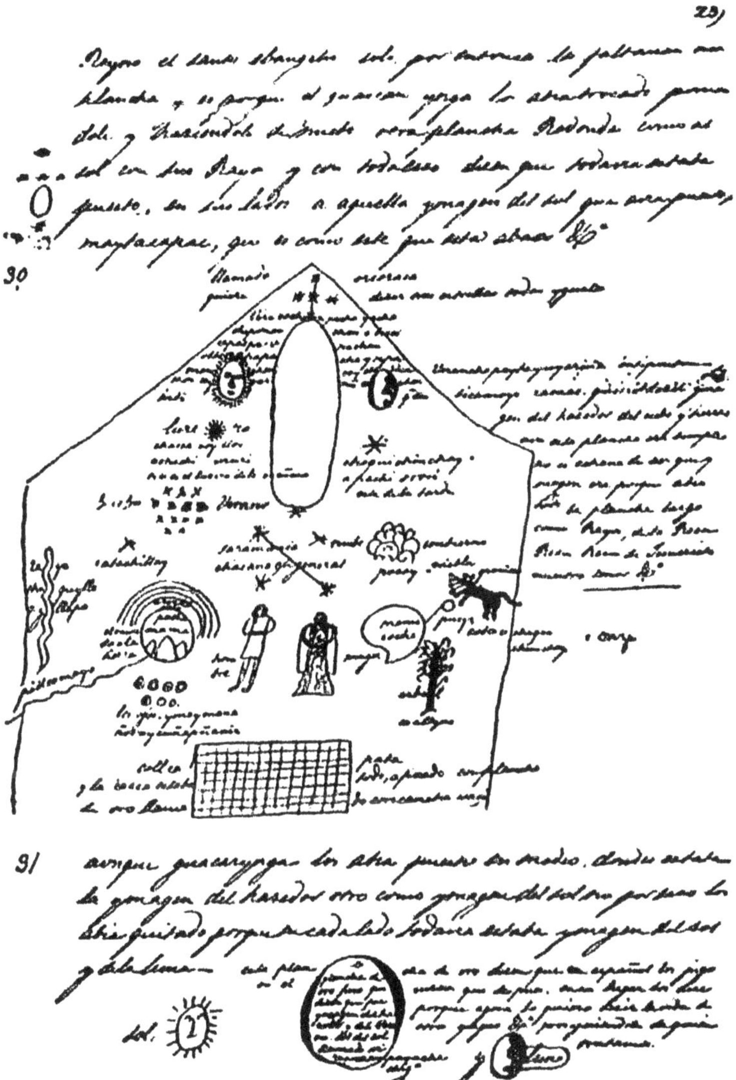

FIGURE 79. World-picture of the ancient Peruvians. In

Below Huiracocha are five stars, but arranged differently from the group above. One is separated entirely from the other four, but the four are united by crossed lines. Beuchat ventures to believe that these also represent constellations.

Beneath the Milky Way, Catachillay, are a number of concentric semi-circles, which signify the Rainbow; the two wave-lines at the left are Thunder, and below them is the River Pillcomayo. To the right of the river and immediately beneath the rainbowed circle are "eyes," "dont," says Beuchat, "on ne voit point clairmant la signification." Far to the right is an irregular figure labelled mamacocha--"the sea," says Beuchat, and a little above it a black puma. Below these two is mallqui, "a tree." At the bottom of the picture is a rectangle, which represents Coricancha, and above the figures of a man and a woman.

In his manuscript Salcamayha explains Coricancha, accompanying the text with another oval "creation" figure. A certain Ynca, he says, after he and his people had settled at Coricancha on whose site was reared the Temple of the Sun, "ordered the smiths to make a flat plate of fine gold, which signified that there was a Creator of Heaven and Earth, and that it was of this shape. He caused it to be fixed in a great house, called Couricancha pachaya-chachipac huasin," which is to say, "the golden place, the house of the teacher of the world."

Another reading of this world-picture gives some interesting literal translations of some of the old Indian and Spanish text. Outside of the diagram are two Indian words, Uamado and Orcorara, followed by a bit of Spanish commentary--"which is to say (quiere decir) three stars all equal." Inside the figure at the peak of the "roof," mingled with the Sun and Moon are many Indian words, with a Spanish translation outside: "Which is to say that this is the image, or pattern, of the maker of both heaven and earth; yet this plate was simply (or crudely) (made) and not to be perceived (easily by all), because there was a lack in all the tablet (or design) of the radiance of the resurrection of Jesus the Lord."

"Lucera" written about the star Chasca, beneath the Sun, and designated by Beuchat as Venus, is a Spanish word meaning "luminous stars," as differing from fixed stars, and is applied to Venus as the morning, and to "Lucifer" as the evening, star. Under Chasca are Indian words and, in Spanish, "This is the luminous star of the morning." To the right, the star beneath the Moon carries several Indian words and, in Spanish, "This is the Evening (star)."

The five stars below Huiracocha are designated by two Indian words, Saramania and Chacana, followed by "en general." "Perhaps they mean Cosmogony, but this is only a guess."

The group of thirteen stars signify "summer season." And the corresponding design at the right reads "Clouds in winter (season)." The two wave-lines at the extreme left are in this reading, "Lightning." To their right, the Rainbow, above "El mundo o la tierra"--"the world or the earth."

The seven "eyes" under the "world" are said here to be Indian words.
The "black puma" above the Tree of Life is said to signify hail, "and since hail is bad for crops, they represent it by a little animal."

THE AZTEC UNIVERSE

THE AZTEC WORLD-PICTURE (Plate XXXIII) is the first sheet of the "Night Side" of the Codex Ferjérváry-Mayer, an old Mexican painted book now in the Free Public Museums at Liverpool. The foundation for the series of paintings is a sort of parchment made of deerskin covered on both sides with a thin coating of an extremely adhesive paste on which the paintings were executed in the usual way--the outlines in deep black and the spaces filled in with colours. It consists of twenty-two folded shapes 17½ cm. square. One side Dr. Eduard Seler, its interpreter, calls the "Night Side," the other the "Day Side."

This first sheet is the most interesting and the most famous of the entire manuscript. It represents the Five Regions of the Aztec world and their tutelary deities, spread out like a cross, all their spaces filled with figures of trees, gods, birds, rivers, and symbols of the cosmos, both of its objects and its attributes.

In the Middle Place, says Seler, [1] is the Fire deity, Xiuhtecutli, "the Mother, the Father of the gods, who dwells in the navel of the Earth." From his body four streams of blood flow towards the four cardinal points, and are continued beyond the square space enclosing the centre to the outer corners of the picture, where the signs acatl, "Reed," tecpatl, "Flint," calli, "House," and tochtli, "Rabbit," are seen on shields respectively borne by a quetzal bird, an arara, an eagle, and a green parrot. "These are the four signs by which the consecutive years are named with constant reiteration, because they are the signs which fall on the first days of those years, and therefore, since they are exhausted with the number four, have become symbols for the four cardinal points, East, North, West, and South."

The stream of blood pointing to the sign acatl (Reed), that is, to the East (left-hand above), terminates with a hand painted yellow--"the hand (ray) of the Sun god?" The stream pointing to the sign tecpatl (Flint) ends with the stump leg of the god of the North. The stream flowing towards the sign

[1] Codex Ferjérváry-Mayer, elucidated by Eduard Seler, 1901, pp. 5-24."

calli (House) or West (right-hand below) ends in a figure of a chest formed by the vertebrae and adjoining ribs of a skeleton. "For the West is the region of the setting (dead) Sun." The stream flowing towards the sign tochtli (Rabbit) or South ends in a head in whose hair is stuck a downy feather ball, which symbolizes the "warrior in the South" and at the same time, the "warrior in the North," the dual god of the two quarters.

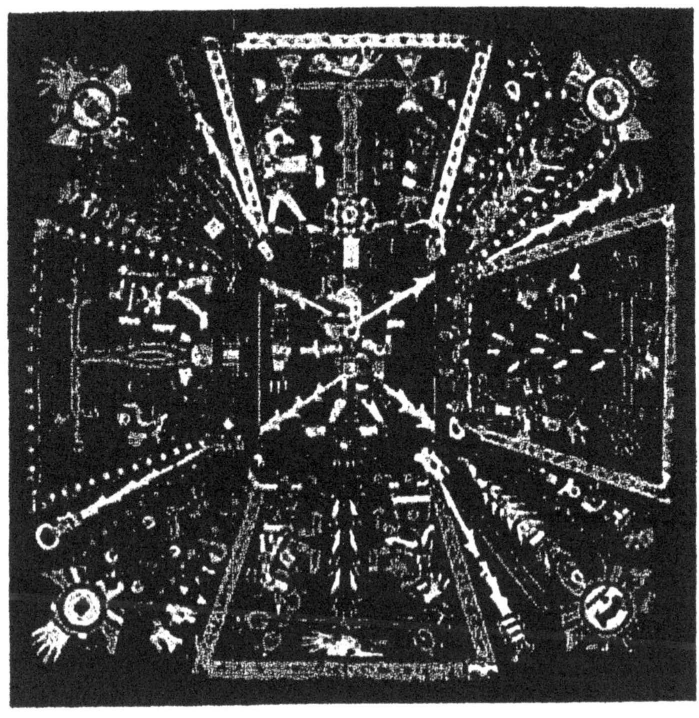

PLATE XXXIII. A WORLD-PICTURE OF THE AZTECS
First page of the Codex Ferjérváry-Mayer, representing the five regions of the world, and their tutelary deities.
(From Mythology of All Races, 1927, Vol. XI, Plate VI)

Above the upper side of the central square is a sort of platform with steps in the centre; that is to say, to the right of the corner which, owing to the shield with the sign acatl, "Reed," we have to regard as the East corner." At the level of the steps, which are painted red, is shown the image of the Sun. "This can obviously be nothing but the House of the Sun, the East."

Above the left side of the central square is a votive dish in which are a rubber ball, an agava-leaf thorn, and a bone dagger. They are the symbols of sacrifice, of blood-letting, of self-torture, voluntarily made in honour of the gods, but, says Scier, they belong to the gods of the South, and bringing them into the Northern quarter of the heavens means a reversion of the order, or an interchange of North and South."

Above the lower side of the central square is seen a monster descending from above, that is, here, from be-low. It would seem to be tolerably certain that this is intended to represent the Tzitzimimê, the demons which symbolise the realm of darkness, the eclipse of the Sun. I shall have more fully to explain farther on that the Tzitzimimê are originally images of the stars, which, merely because at the solar eclipses the stars become visible in broad daylight, have been made demons of darkness, symbols of the devouring gloom. In any case, here the figure denotes the West, the region of the setting Sun, of the light swallowed up by the Earth."

Above the fourth or right-hand side of the central square is seen "the wide open throat of a monster hieroglyph of the Earth, which in this form is obviously thought of as the taker of life, the mictlampa, the realm of death, i.e., the North."

The flowering tree rising above the picture of the Sun (upper East side) is surmounted by a quetzal bird and guarded by Itztli, the Stone-knife god (on the left), and Tonantiuh, the Sun god, all symbolising the Eastern quarter. This tree, like all in the four quarters, has the form of a cross.

The tree above the left side of the central square is a thorn tree surmounted by an eagle, and is guarded by Tlaloc, the Rain god, and Tepeyollotli, the Heart of the Mountains or the Voice of the Jaguar in the Mountains--symbols of the North.

The tree of the West, growing out of the forehead of the Tzitzimitl, or the dragon of the eclipse, has a stem set with huge upright thorns. Instead of flowers, it bears feather balls at the tips of its branches. "On it is perched doubtless a humming bird," which according to Aztec belief, dies with the dry and revives with the rainy season. The guardian deities are Chalchiuhtlicue, goddess of flowing water, and the Earth goddess Tlazolteotl.

Above the South side (right) is a tree growing out of the open jaws of the monster symbolising the Earth; "its stem is set with notches (or fruit pods?) turned downwards, while the branches bear a kind of star-shaped blossom like that of the tree of the North." On it is perched a parrot, and it is guarded by Cinteotl, the maize god, and Mictlantecutli, god of death.

The deities depicted about the four arms of the St. Andrew's Cross, that is, in the spaces enclosed by the trapezes above the four sides of the central square, are the eight gods of the four quarters. In the central square stands the Fire god; he belongs to the Centre or the Middle Place because he represents the hearth fire which burns in the middle of the house. These nine are the deities of the Five Regions and "Lords of the Night."

Like the Tibetan and Kalmuck worlds, the four quarters of the Aztec world have their four colours, and they are: East, red; North, yellow; West, blue; and South, green. These are the colours also of the years and of the days. The whole figure symbolises the orientation of the world-powers in Space and Time-years and Earth-realms and Sky-realms.

TARTAR-MONGOL WORLDS

IN Picture-Writing of the American Indians, Garrick Mallery has collected a delightful group of Tartar and Mongol magic drum tops, over which a little time will not be wasted just here. These drums were used--are used--by various Tartar and Mongol tribes in religious ceremonies, and their shamans believe that the sound of one design or figure painted on the stretched skin differs essentially from that of another pattern painted, and that therefore, one drum sounded may kill or torment, while another may heal. Many of these designs are little world-pictures purely.

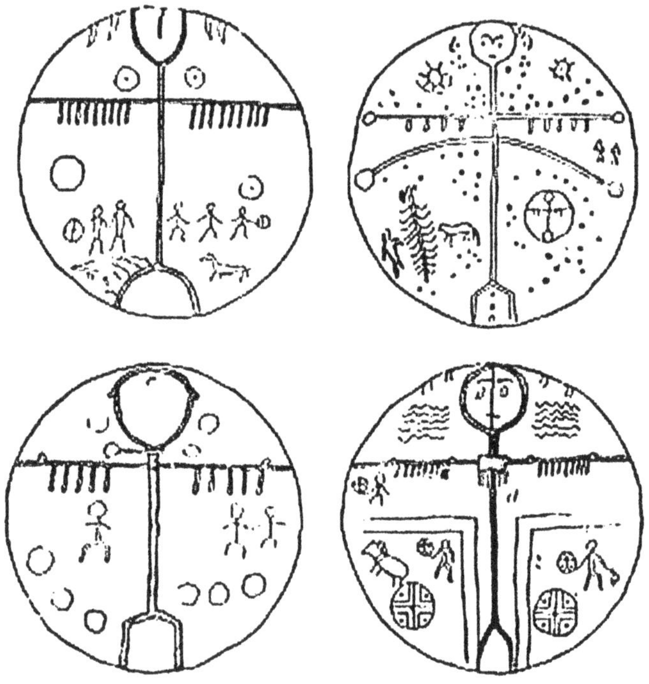

FIGURE 80. Painted Tartar and Mongol drums.
(From Picture-Writing of the America, Indians; Garrick Mallery, 1894, p. 515.)

The upper left-hand design in Fig. 80, for instance, suggests at first glance not only a two-storied division of heaven and Earth, but a World Mountain and a World Tree. According to Mallery, the two circles with inner dots above the cross-bar represent the Moon and Sun.

Two shamans or priests of magic are pictured on the left, and with them a wild goat and five serpents. On the right are three shamans and a deer.

The upper right-hand design (b) had the same four-quarter division, with a face indicated in the top loop of the axis or tree, and with the upper heavens spangled with stars, suns and moons. Below the cross-bar are a rainbow with stars beneath it, and, above the rainbow, two "heavenly maidens." This magic drum design represents "the bringing of the horse to sacrifice."

The lower left-hand design (c), says Mallery, "is the external delineation of a head without eyes and nose." The shamans who owned this drum said that the circles, two above the cross-bar and six below, all empty, are "representations of drums, and the three human figures are masters or spirits of localities."

The fourth design (d) was explained by the shaman no further than to say that the five wave-lines on either side of the face above the cross-bar are "serpents."

The upper left-hand design in Fig. 81 has above its dividing line two trees. "On each of them sits the bird karagush with the bill turned to the left." "On the left of the tree," Mallery goes on to say, "are two circles, one dark (the moon), the other light (the sun)." But the design as given shows but one. Below the horizontal lines are three animals, a frog, a lizard, and a serpent--all of them watery animals, who appear to be swimming in the waters under the tree-bearing Earth.

The upper right-hand design (b) "has on the upper half two circles, the sun and moon; on the left side four horsemen; and under them a bowman, also on horseback. The centre is occupied by a picture of a net and sieve for winnowing the nuts and seeds of the cedar tree. On the right side are two trees, beigamin (literally, the rich birch), over which two birds, the karagush, are floating. Under a division on the right and on the left side are oval objects with lattice-figures or scaly skin. These are two whales. In the middle, between them, are a frog and a deer, and below them a serpent. Above, toward the hoop of the drum, is fastened an owl's feather."

FIGURE 81. Painted Tartar and Mongol drums.
(From Picture-Writing of the American Indians; Garrick Mallery, 1894, p. 516.)

The lower left-hand design (c) has, in the upper half, seven figures "reminding one of horses, bura, going to heaven, i.e., their sacrifice." Above them are two light-giving circles, the sun and the moon; on the right of the horses are three trees; under a horizontal line on the left is a serpent, on the right a fish, "the kerbuleik, the whale according to Verbitski, literally the bay-fish."

The lower right-hand design (d) has its upper half divided into three layers, the first of which "is heaven, the second the rainbow, and in the lower stratum the stars." At the left and right are the sun and moon, below, a goat, and three trees." Mallery adds that underneath there was an undefined figure not given in this drawing which the interpreting shaman called "the bura. Some said that it meant a cloud; others that it meant heavenly horses."

The left-hand design in Fig. 82 is divided by four vertical and four horizontal lines. "The latter," says Mallery, "represent the rainbow; the vertical lines borsui. Circles with dots in the center are represented in three sections, and in the fourth one circle." Further than this, the shaman did not interpret.

The right-hand design shows in its upper section five human figures. "These, according to the shaman's own explanation, are heavenly maidens (in the original Turkish, tengriduing kuiz). Below, under a rainbow, which is represented by three arched lines, are portrayed two serpents, each having a cross inside. These are kurmos nuing tyungurey, i.e., the drums are kurmos's. Kurmos is the Altaic word for spirits, which the shamans summon."

The shamans of these tribes admit three worlds; the world of the Heavens (hallan jurda); the middle one of the Earth (onto-doidu); and the lower one of Hell (jedăn tiigara); the first the realm of light, the last the realm of darkness. The middle world, or Earth, has for a time been given over by the Creator (Jut-tas-olbohtah Jürdan-Ai-Tojan) to the will of the devil or tempter, and the souls of men at death, according to their merit, are sent either to the upper or the lower world. When, however, "the earth world has come to an end, the souls of the two realms will wage a war against each other, and victory must remain on the side of the good souls."

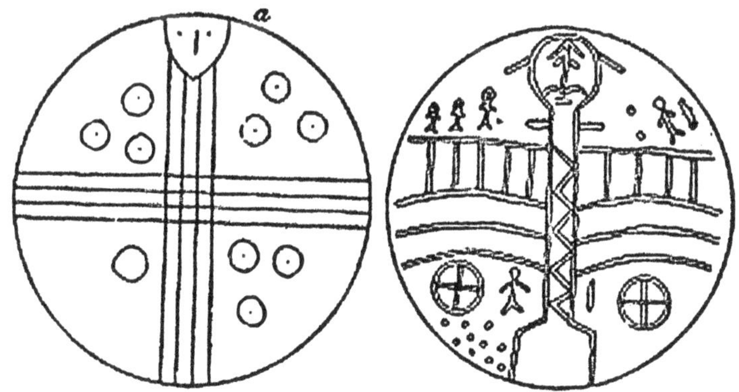

FIGURE 82. Painted Tartar and Mongol drums.
(From Picture-Writing of the American Indians; Garrick Mallery, 1894, p. 517.)

MAPS OF THE EARTH

THE SPANISH PRIEST BEATUS who in the year 798 died in a Benedictine convent in the Asturias, is recognised as the original draughtsman of a remarkable world-map lost except for "copies," ten of which are known to-day. This map-group is known as the Beatus Maps; they all appeared between the tenth and the thirteenth centuries, and obviously derive from one common source, but the source-map has disappeared completely.

It came out originally in Beatus's Commentary on the Apocalypse, about 776, and its aim was, probably, to portray the spread of the Christian faith over the Earth, after the analogy of the world and the kingdom of heaven to a field sown with seed. It was divided into parts or fields, each ruled over by one of the Apostles, whose locality was more or less fixed by tradition, and who was at once the sower of the seed, the tiller of the field, and the reaper of the harvest.

The Osma Beatus map (Plate XXXIV), although one of the latest (1203), is regarded as one which is in many of its important features most like its prototype. It gives, for instance, alone of all the copies, the pictures of the Twelve Apostles in the regions over which they ruled. It also gives a realistic picture of the inhabitants of the Southern continent or Antichthones, still unknown--those monstrous beings known as Skiapodes or Shadow-footed men, who must always lie or sit in such fashion that their great feet were as umbrellas shading them from the otherwise deadly Sun. There were other fabulous races of this austral land; one whose huge lips, instead of feet, protected them from the scorching fire of the Sun; another whose heads had sunk to a plane almost level with their shoulders; and still another whose heads had sunk quite below the shoulders and had become absorbed in the trunk of the body. There were Dog-headed men; Ape-headed men; men without ears; men without tongues; men without noses; men without mouths, or with mouths so small that they sucked their food with great difficulty through a reed. Some never walked at all, but crawled along the ground like serpents, and ate serpents. Of these monstrous races of the Antipodes there were fourteen, we are told.

FIGURE 83. Monsters of the Antipodes.
(From Margarita philosophica, 1517.)

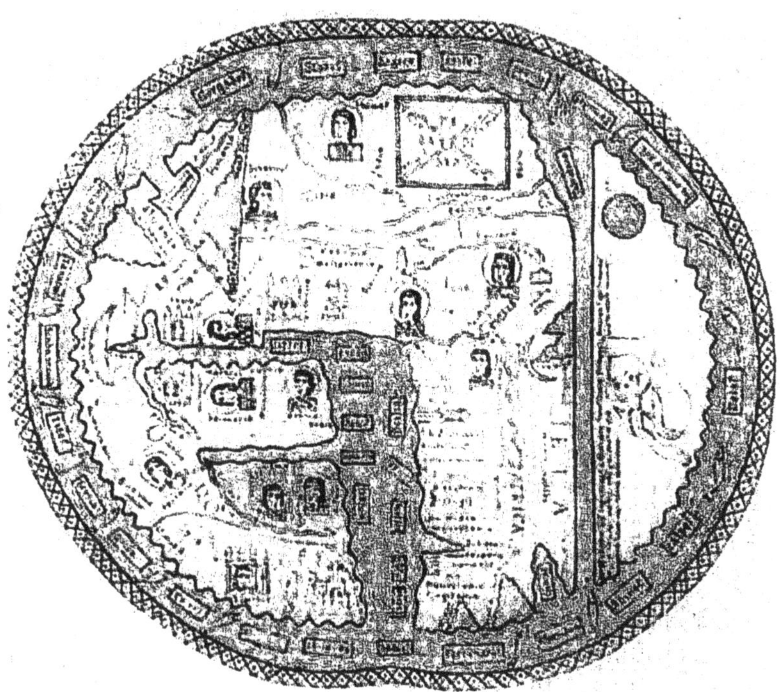

In portioning out the Earth to the Twelve Apostles, to Peter was given Rome; to Andrew, Greece or Achia; to Thomas, India; to James, Spain; to John, Asia; to Matthew, Macedonia; to Philip, Gaul; to Bartholomew, Lycaonia; to Simon Zelotes, Egypt; to Matthias, Judæa; to James the brother of the Lord, Jerusalem; and to Paul, the whole world. All these localities are indicated, and also the place of Paradise, this last by a rectangle from whose centre spring four rivers.

The division of the continents was usually that of the so-called T-O maps, with Asia filling the upper or eastern half (the tops of many of the mediæval maps were at the East); and with the lower half divided into Europe, on the left, and Africa, in the right-hand quarter. But in the Beatus maps shown here, Southern Asia and Africa were cut by a narrow strip of ocean, below which was supposed to lie the Austral continent, the Antipodes, or Antichthones, source of romance and fable run mad for hundreds of years.

Another of the Beatus maps is the famous one known as the Turin Beatus, of the twelfth century. Unlike the Osma Beatus, its shape is a pure circle--quite likely a departure from the form of the lost source-map, which is believed to have had the ovoid form. There is no attempt made here at any division of the world among the Twelve Apostles, but the Garden of Eden, the First Parents, the tempting serpent twined about the tree, and Mount Sinai are in evidence. The unknown continent is indicated, but its inhabitants are not shown. In many ways this copy deflects from the original; but the Turin Beatus is famous for its "Wind-blowers," seated on their inflated bags and keeping the universe to its course as they float through the aerial ocean.

FIGURE 85. The Turin Beatus World-map, c. 1150.
(From Santarem's Atlas, 1848, Plate IX.)

IN THE LIBRARY AT STOCKHOLM, among the manuscripts of Marco Polo, fantastic traveller and man of the world of the fourteenth century, lies his own mappa-mundi. It is a combination of the first-century world-map of Pomponius Mela (Fig. 75), where the continent of Antichthones was first shown, and the T-O maps of the Middle Ages, but with the odds in favour of Pomponius Mela's division, for Marco Polo gives rather more than half the land of the Earth to Antichthones. Strange to think of this as the travelling map of a tourist of the then known world! But Marco Polo's Travels, glorious romancing, glorious lying as much of it is, did more to popularise the notion that the whole world was habitable, including its unknown areas, than any writer since has succeeded in doing. For we still have unknown, impassable, uninhabitable areas of the Earth, and by what we think--perhaps rightly--of the Polar zones, we can gauge a little the opinions of the ancient world and even of the Middle Ages regarding Antichthones.

In any case, thanks to the Crusades, the habit of travel had laid strong hold of man, and a race of new adventurers sprang up over night. Marco Polo's contemporaries began to doubt the myths they had been bred on, and they hurried towards new ones, some of them Marco's own. His Travels paved the way for travel, and the new adventurers dared farther and farther the still impassable ocean that separated them from what they did not know, and brought back many tales, if not of continents, of groups of islands newly found, and the wildest rumours concerning the strange lands and races that lay beyond them. Less than two centuries after Marco Polo's map was drawn, Ptolemy's model of the Earth, which left out of account its unknown areas, was to be discarded for that of a "true sphere."

FIGURE 86. The World-map of Marco Polo. From one of his manuscripts in the Library at Stockholm.
(From Santarem's Atlas, 1849, Plate I, No. 3.)

For in 1509 a scrap of a book called Globus Mundi was printed at Strassburg by an author unknown--probably he will never be known. It was published in Latin and

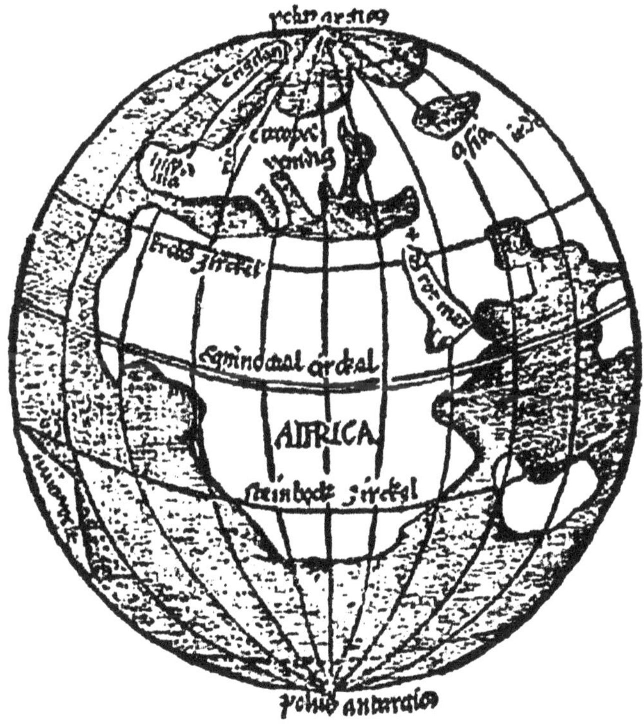

Globus mundi

Declaratio siue descriptio mundi et totius orbis terrarum, globulo rotundo comparati vt spera solida. Qua cuiuis etiam mediocriter docto ad oculum videre licet antipodes esse, quorum pedes nostris oppositi sunt. Et qualiter in vnaquaque orbis parte homines vitam agere queunt salutarem, sole singula terre loca illustrante: que tamen terra in vacuo aere pendere videtur: solo dei nutu sustentata, aliisque permultis de quarta orbis terrarum parte nuper ab Americo reperta.

FIGURE 87. Title-page of Globus Mundi, originally printed at Strassburg, 1509, showing a trace of the Americas.
(From Globus Mundi, reprinted at Milan (n.d.)

German, and it seems to have been no more than an expository pamphlet or tract to accompany or to be sold with a real globe. This is implied by its amplified title: The World Globe. Exposition or description of the world and of the terrestrial sphere constructed as a round globe like to a solid sphere, whereby every man even of moderate learning can see with his own eyes that there are antipodes whose feet are opposite ours. What makes this extremely interesting is that only seventeen years after Columbus discovered the Americas, a tiny bit of land to the south-west of Africa, labelled Nüe Welt, appeared on a spherical world-map. Another interesting thing about this map is the enormous size given to the African continent, under the lingering influence of the long-time belief in the impassable equatorial zone.

"This device proves the Earth to be a Globe" (Fig. 88) is a self-explanatory seventeenth-century attempt at popularising a scientific theory; no better but no worse than modern devices for popular education. The proof offered here is the outline of the shadow cast on an eclipsed Moon; if the Earth were an hexahedron, a tetrahedron, or a cube, its shadow on the Moon would not be circular in outline. But we know the shadow cast by the Earth is a circular one; therefore the Earth is a globe! That a cubical, tetrahedral, or hexahedral body rotating in Space at the Earth's supposed speed and in the diverse directions of its movements might tend to trace a curved line was not suggested.

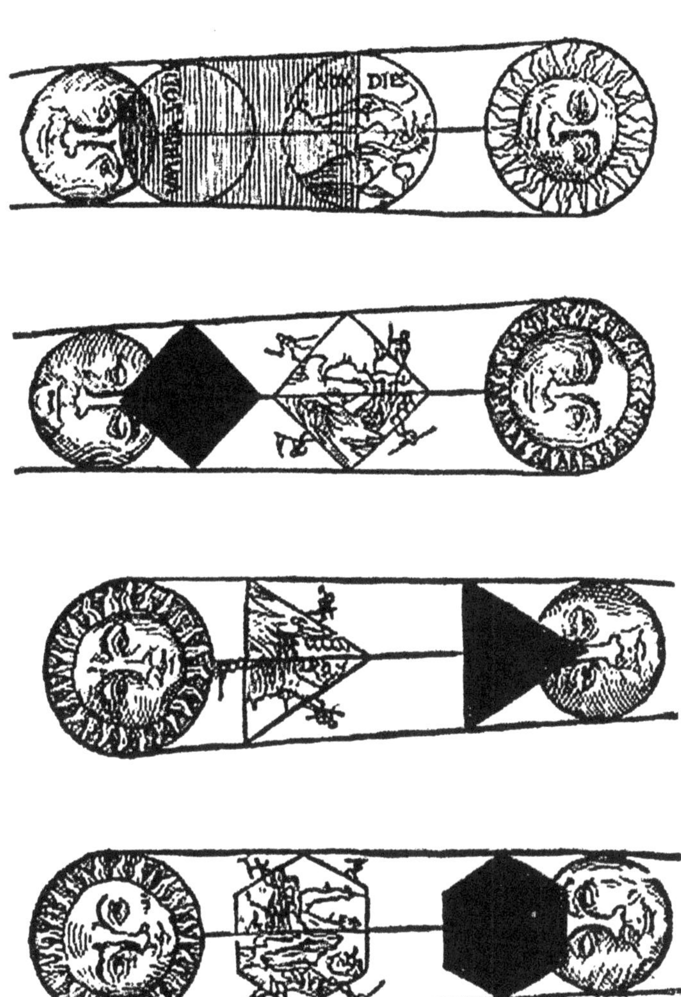

FIGURE 88. "This device proves the Earth to be a Globe."
(From Cosmographia; Petrus Apianus, 1640.)

THE EARTH OF COLUMBUS

IT IS ONE OF THE LITTLE IRONIES of life that the man who more than any other popularised the notion that the Earth was "shaped like a ball," himself believed it was shaped like a pear. Privately Columbus affirmed that the Earth was pear-shaped. We find this in his letters, and in the writings of his contemporaries. One of these latter, Pietro Martire, who accompanied Columbus on the voyage of 1498, in his Decades of the newe worlde published in 1555, said that "the Admirall" declared such things, "the which because they seeme contrarye to the oppinions of all the Astronomers, I wyll touche them but with a drye foote as sayeth the proverbe. . . . For he sayeth, that he . . . conjectured, that the earth is not perfectly rownde; But that when it was created, there was a certeyne heape reysed theron, much hygher than the other partes of the same. So that (as he saith), it is not rownde after the form of an apple or a bal (as others thynke) but rather lyke a peare as it hangeth on the tree. And that Paria is the Region which possesseth the super-eminente or hyghest parte thereof nerest unto heaven. In soo muche that he earnestly contendeth, the earthly Paradise to bee situate in the toppes of those three hylles, which wee sayde before, that the watche man sawe owte of the toppe castell of the shippe: And that the outragious streames of the freshe waters which soo violently issewe out of the sayde goulfes and stryve soo with the salte water, faule head-longe from the toppes of the sayde mountaynes."

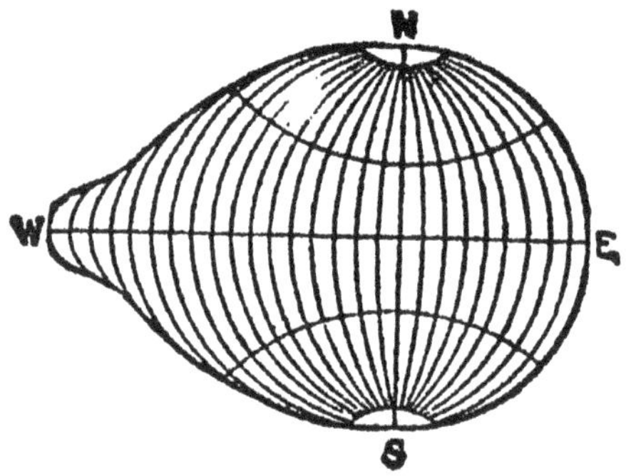

FIGURE 89. The pear-shaped Earth of Columbus.
(From Paradise Found; William Fairfield Warren, 1885.)

Columbus himself, in a letter to Ferdinand and Isabella regarding his third voyage, wrote: [1]

"I have always read that the world comprising the land and water was spherical, and the recorded experiences of Ptolemy and all the others have proved this by the eclipses of the moon and other observations made from East to West, as well as the elevation of the Pole from North to South. But as I have already described, I have now seen so much irregularity that I have come to another conclusion respecting the Earth, namely, that it is not round, as they describe, but of the form of a pear, which is very round except where the stalk grows, at which part it is most prominent; or like a round ball, upon part of which is a prominence like a woman's nipple, this protrusion being the highest and nearest the sky, situated under the equinoctial line, and at the eastern extremity of this sea. [He is in the Gulf of Paria, to the north or the north-west of the mouth of the Orinoco.] . . . Ptolemy and the other philosophers who have written upon the globe thought that it was spherical; . . . but this western half of the world, I maintain, is like half a very round pear, having a raised projection for the stalk, as I have already described."

When Columbus wrote this letter to his royal helpers, he supposed himself to be in Asia's easternmost waters, but he was really in the northern part of South America, which he himself went on to describe as the Paradise of the Earth or the Mountain of the World. But the World Mountain of Columbus had dropped from its northern quarter to the western.

[1] Select Letters of Columbus: Hakluyt Soc. Pub., and ed. pp. 134-138.

DANTE'S UNIVERSE

COLUMBUS WAS OF GENOA a century after Dante had died at Florence. Probably he had never read his countryman's Divina Commedia; even if he had, he might have seen little of value or significance in Dante's cosmology. Dante had one, however, and his scheme brought back into modern times, that most ancient of the figures of Earth, the hills of the gods, the antipodal mountains.

But, in Dante's Earth-figure also, as in Columbus's, the mountains have shifted. If Columbus, for some strange reason--and his reason is not at all clear--had put his mountain of Paradise at the western end of the Earth, Dante's two mountains give a still odder figure. In his Paradise Found, Dr. Warren has worked out this construction of Dante's Earth, showing that the Mountain of Paradise has slipped all of 30° below the equator. He bases this construction mainly on a few lines regarding the location of the Mountain of Purgatory (Purgatorio, Canto iv, 67-70): "Zion stands with this mountain in such wise on the earth that both have a single horison and diverse hemispheres;" and he adds: ". . . no careful reader of the Divina Commedia can fail to see that its 'Mount Zion' and the Purgatorial Montagna malagevole altissima et cinta de mare are simply unrecognised 'survivals' of prehistoric thought--antipodal world-mountains once situate at the poles, but here relocated to suit the demands of sacred mediæval geography. They are the Su-Meru and Ku-Meru of India figuring in Christian poetry."

Another construction of Dante's universe is given (Fig. 91), from Studies in the History and Method of Science, edited by Charles Singer. It is Caetani's diagram of Dante's Hell, Purgatory, Earthly Paradise and the nine Heavens. Dante describes Hell as a funnel or inverted cone descending in nine diminishing whorls through the hemisphere until the centre is reached, which is also the centre of the universe, and is situated just under Jerusalem, the centre of the habitable Earth. Or, according to Caetani, he pictures it as a circular mountain, cone-like. Purgatory, Dante places at the antipodes, that is, on an island in the ocean of the uninhabitable Earth. From this island springs a mountain ascending in a series of stages up to the summit on which is Eden, the Earthly Paradise, home of the First Pair.

Paradise includes all the spheres of heaven, through all of which Dante ascends, finding himself always on the planet that governs each sphere, until at last the Empyrean Paradise is attained, which crowns the universe.

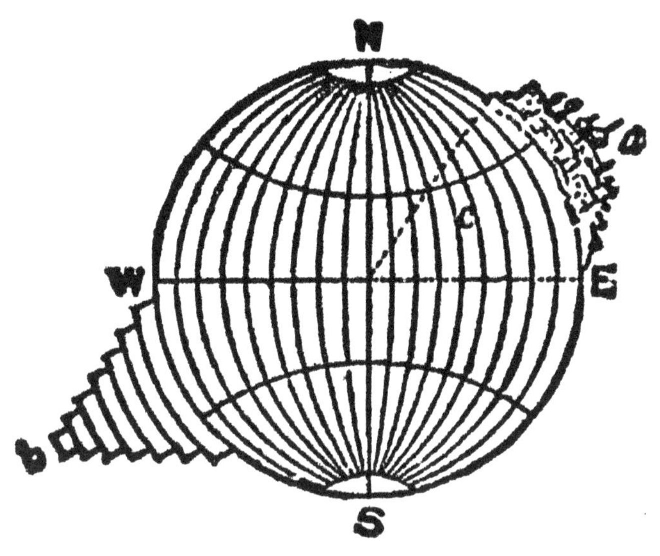

FIGURE 90. The Earth of Dante.
a. City of Jerusalem. b. Mountain of Purgatory. c. Inferno within the Earth.
(From Paradise Found; William Fairfield Warren, 1885.)

Two regions, of air and of fire, must be crossed before the sphere of the Moon, the first star, which bounds the region of fire, is reached; and on the lower right-hand quarter of Earth is the dark forest in which Dante spent a night before he began, or in which he began, his journey. At its end he is at the foot of a hill, confronting three great beasts, from whom he is rescued by Virgil, who is to be his guide through Hell and Purgatory. The poets enter the Inferno at twilight--a world of eternal night whose ruler is the Moon. They go through the ten Pits until in the very centre of the Earth they see Lucifer, its king, at this centre of gravity, encased in eternal ice.

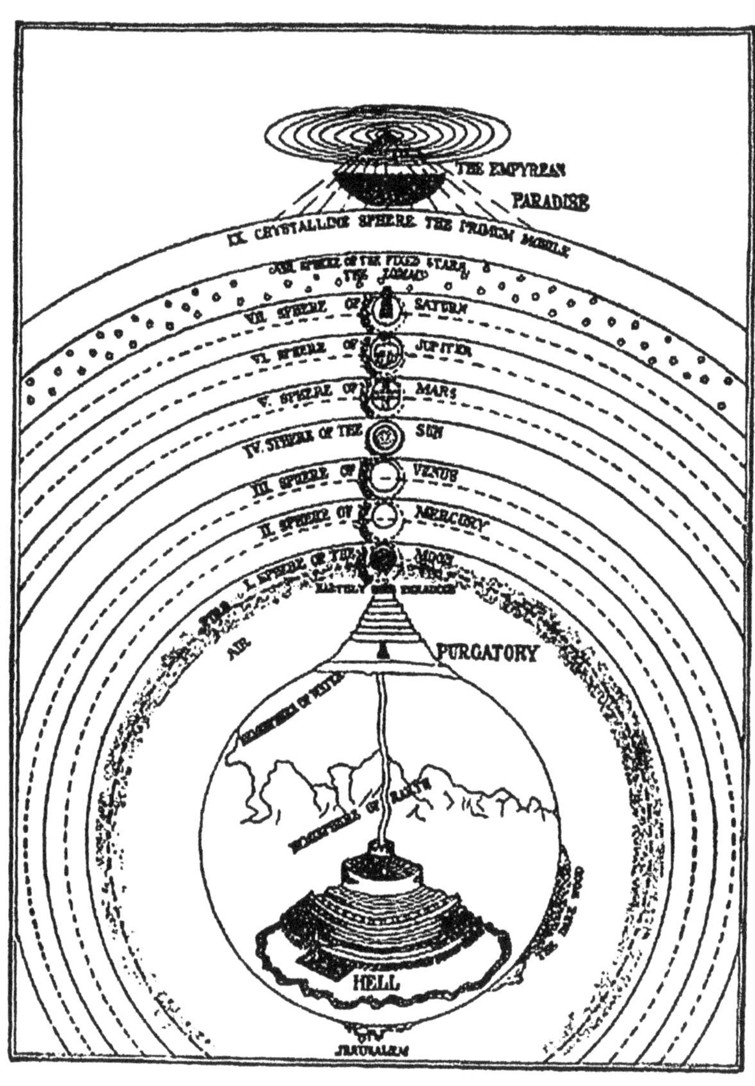

FIGURE 91. Dante's Scheme of the Universe.
Slightly modified from Michelangelo Caetani, duca di Sermoneta, La materia della Divina Commedia di Dante Alighieri dichiarata in Vi tavole, Monte Cassino, 1855.
(From Studies in the History and Method of Science, ed. by Charles Singer, 1917, Vol. I, Fig. 4.)

The passage through the centre of Earth is one of the greatest difficulty, and above it is ocean only, except for the Island of Purgatory. This division of land and water is explained to Dante thus: When Lucifer fell, all the land which existed in the mysterious hemisphere fell with him, and "fled for fear of him" escaping in what way it might around the globe, settling finally in the inhabited hemisphere. It is possible that the Earth in the interior fled also, but in the opposite direction, to form an island of land in the Purgatorial hemisphere. But, between land and land, there was left an empty space, and up this space they might climb to the island of refuge. Then comes the ascent of the stages of Purgatory to Paradise, and the flight through the heavenly spheres, until at last from the Heaven of the Stars the universe lies spread out under their feet, and Dante sees below him the purgatorial Earth, heart of the cosmos, "small and round as a threshing floor."

EARTH THE HEART OF THE COSMOS

THE COSMIC HEART--centre of life in the universe as man's tiny heart is his centre of life--meant to the ancient Aryans "Breath," the ceaselessly ascending and descending spiral which is the life-sustaining symbol of the universe. To the ancient Egyptians the cosmic heart was the Mind: "It is He (the Heart) who brings forth every issue, and it is the tongue that repeats the thoughts of the Heart." To the Chinese the heart of the universe was Buddha; it was also "the skilful workman," who made all the different conditions of existence in the ten regions of space; it was the "universal essence" from which everything in the universe came into being. Heaven and Earth, with this heart, they said, pervades everything. Man obtains it, and then it is the heart of man; when things obtain it, then it is the heart of things; when grass, trees, birds, and beasts obtain it, then it is the heart of each of these. And the heart of man, they said, is simply the inborn Buddha, which belongs to everything that has conscious existence, that infinitesimal particle of the divine that gives and sustains all. Somewhere, then, in the universe this divine heart of the cosmos pulsated, and if the Earth was the centre of the cosmos, then the Earth was its heart and its life.

Just as the unknown author of De Imago Mundi had worked out his scheme of the universe on the image of the Cosmic Egg, John Pordage, an Englishman of the seventeenth century, developed his mystical theory of the "Archtypous Globe" as the Cosmic Heart. Plate XXXV gives his drawing of the Eternal World, wherein the Holy Trinity do manifest themselves, as in a clear Chrystalline Glass or Mirrour." In it, he discerned three distinct places, the Outward Court, the Inward Court, or Holy Place, and "the Inmost Court, or the Abysmal Eye in the centre of the Heart of God, . . . which essential Eye of God, looking into it self, and finding nothing besides it self, by dilating it self, gives a beginning and an end to it self; which beginning and entring into, and joyning with one another do constitute and form the Globe of Eternity . . . for the Eye, turning it self inwards into it self, comes to know it self, and to see, feel, and taste it self; and if it look outward, it sees nothing but it self neither, because as the Eye is God, so is the Globe nothing but the dilation of the Eye . . . for the natural formation of a Globe or sphear is by the Centre's dilating and expanding of it self; a circumference being nothing else but a centre dilated, or a central emanation bounded by it self. . . . I am ashamed to present you such a dead lifeless figure of it; but no pen can decipher it on paper, it is only the Spirit of the Eye that can open it self, and give you the living and ravishing sight of its own essentiality without similitudes or figures, though I can express it outwardly no better than I have in the foregoing figure."

PLATE XXXV. THE EARTH OF THE MYSTICS--THE HEART OF GOD (From Theologia Mystica, or, The Archtypous Globe; John Pordage, 1683)

Pordage explains the tiny "figure in the Margent," as typifying the Holy Trinity. The Eye in the midst of the Heart represents the Father, the Generator of the Son who is the Heart of the Father; and the out flowing exit of powers, like a breath, represents the Holy Ghost proceeding from the Father, through the Heart of the Son. Thus the birth of the Holy Trinity is manifested in the opening of the Eye, to be a Trinity in Unity; the Eye is in the Heart, and the Heart is the Eye's Centre, and the Spirit is a proceeding Spirit from the Eye and Heart; and thus they are one in another, in one Essence, and undivided and inseparable; the Father is one with the Son, and the Son with the Father; and the Spirit proceeds from the union of these both, and abides one with them. Wheresoever the Eye is, there is the

Heart; and wheresoever the Eye and Heart are, there the outgoing of powers streams forth from them."

Map makers are not usually mystics, and certainly there is no indication that Petrus Apianus, distinguished German mathematician and astronomer of the sixteenth century, was proposing to do more than make an extraordinarily beautiful world-map according to a pattern he himself explains. On Ptolemy's figure of Earth, Apianus made his famous "cardiform projections" towards the poles, and obtained his heart-shaped map of the world. This is one of the earliest maps on which the just discovered western continents appear under the name of the Americas. (See Frontispiece Plate XXXVI.)

ST. HILDEGARD'S UNIVERSE

THERE IS ANOTHER UNIVERSE of the Middle Ages in which the Earth is like the heart." This is the Universe of Saint Hildegard of Bingen, who lived from 1096 to 1179 or 1180. Saint Hildegard would have been a remarkable woman in any age; in her own she had no parallel.

Abbess of a Benedictine convent near Bingen on the Rhine, she was the first of a great line of women mystics. She founded two convents, was the author of many letters and three books--possibly five--was for those days a physician in her own right, and wrote a long treatise on the nature and properties of herbs. She was interested in statecraft, was a musician and a poet, and over half a hundred hymns are credited to her. Her health was not good, but she governed her convent, wrote her books, healed her sick and ailing, corresponded with the wisest men of her age, and travelled hundreds of miles--in the twelfth century! And with all this, she led the contemplative life.

In that contemplative active life her curious system of the universe blossomed, and in her letters and her books she left the records of her mystical visions of its structure and meaning. These records usually begin with, "The Living Light sayeth . . ." It was her name for God, but it was in "The Shade of the Living Light" that she had her perceptions of the universe, and it is interesting to read her simple account of these "Lights." "From my infancy until now in the seventieth year of my age," she says, "my soul has always beheld this light, and in it my soul soars to the summit of the firmament and into different air. . . . The brightness which I see is not limited by space, and is more brilliant than the radiance around the Sun. . . . I cannot measure its height, length, breadth. Its name, which has been given me, is 'Shade of the Living Light.' . . . With that brightness I sometimes see another light for which the name Lux Vivens has been given me. When and how I see this I cannot tell; but sometimes when I see it all sadness and pain is lifted from me, and I seem a simple girl again, and an old woman no more."

In Hildegard's universe, the Earth was the centre, and spherical, around In Hildegard's universe, the Earth was the centre, and spherical, around which were arranged concentric shells or zones. The inner zones are spherical, the outer oval or egg-shaped, and the outermost (Fig. 92) so formed as to suggest the acuminated sphere that symbolises the fifth element, quintessence of the other four. This point that tapers into outer space is in the East, which is the top of the diagram. One of her drawings shows, says Singer, that she believed the antipodean surface of the Earth to be uninhabitable, "since it is either beneath the ocean, or in the mouth of the Dragon."

In the interior of the Earth, she believed, are two vast spaces shaped like truncated cones, where punishment was endured, and from whence great evil came forth. The Earth itself was composed of the four elements, which are represented, curiously unequal in proportion and shape. Their arrangement is not orderly, and this very disorder illustrates one of Hildegard's fundamental doctrines regarding the relation of this world to the universe. Before man's fall, the elements were united in an harmonious combination, and Earth was Paradise; after that catastrophe, the harmony of the universe was disturbed, with the centre of all the trouble on this planet which has ever since remained in its now familiar state of chaotic confusion or mistio, as Hildegard's age called it. This mistio she represents vigorously enough by the irregular distribution of the elements over the Earth. "Thus mingled will they remain until subjected to the melting pot of the Lord Judgment, when they will emerge in a new and eternal harmony, no longer mixed as matter, but separate and pure, parts of a new heaven and a new Earth."

Around this world, says Singer, [1] is spread the atmosphere, the aer lucidus or alba pellis, also circular. Through this alba pellis no Earth creature can penetrate. Later Hildegard seems to have divided this first zone of air into two, the aer tenuis or atmosphere whose outer part is the inner zone of the clouds, and the fortis et albus lucidusque aer, where certain fixed stars are placed.

Beyond this are four outer zones belonging to the four winds, indicated by the breath of supernatural beings.

---

[1] "The Scientific Views and Visions of Saint Hildegard;" Charles Singer: In Studies in the History and Method of Science, Vol. I, 1917, pp. 22-36.

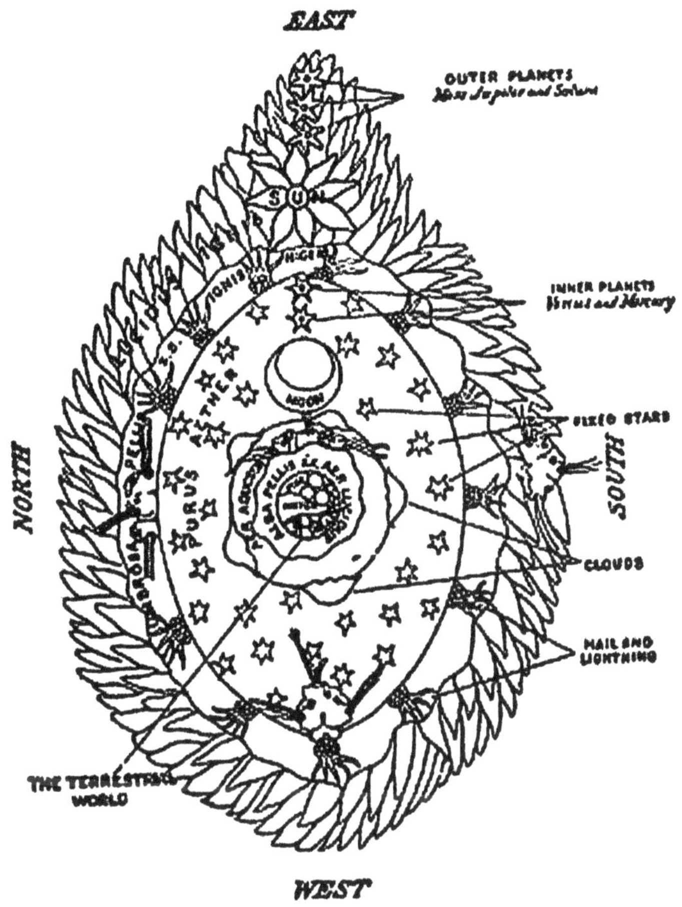

FIGURE 92. Hildegard's first scheme of the Universe. Slightly simplified from the Wiesbaden Codex B, folio 14 r.
(From "The Scientific Views and Visions of Saint Hildegard," by Charles Singer; in Studies in the History and Method of Science, ed. by Charles Singer, 1917. Vol. Fig. 2.)

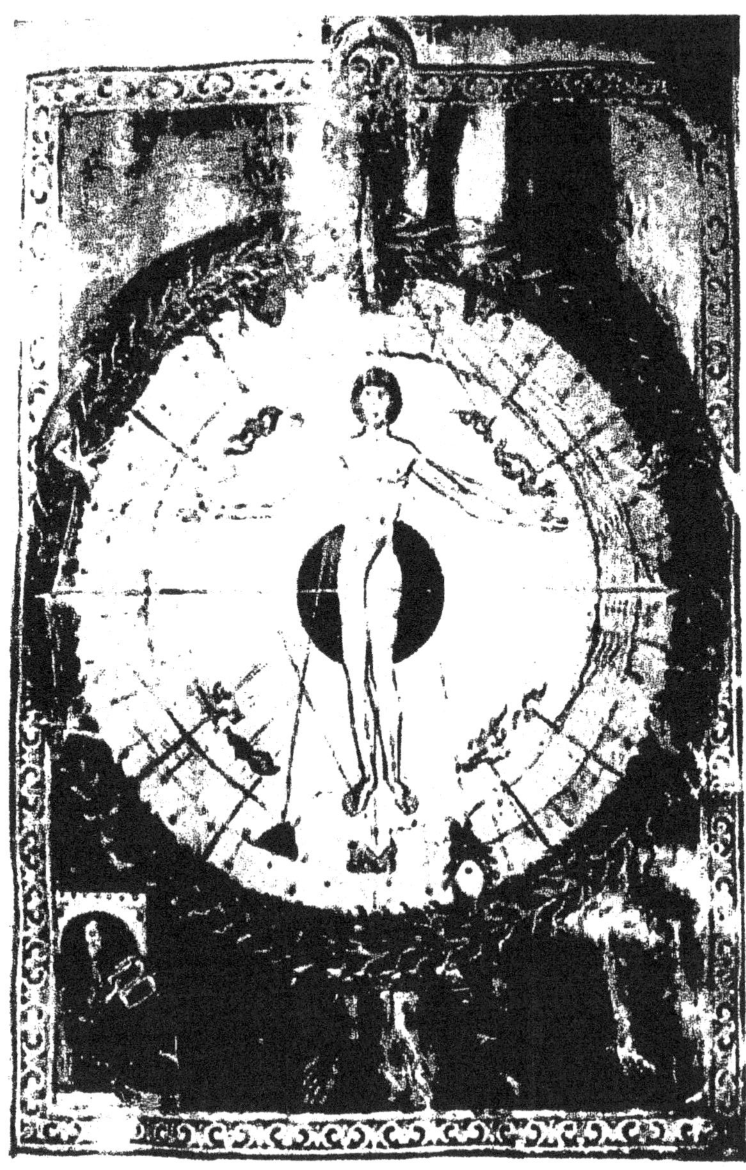

PLATE XXXVII. Nous pervaded by the Godhead embracing the Macrocosm with the Microcosm. From "The Scientific Views and Visions of Saint Hildegard," by Charles Singer. In Studies in the History and Method of Science, ed. by Charles Singer, 1917, Vol. I, Plate VII.

They also correspond confusedly to the four elements and to the four regions of the heavenly bodies.

The first is the aer aquosus, corresponding to water, and containing the east wind. In its outer part float clouds, expanding, contracting, and being blown this way and that, thus concealing or revealing the heavenly bodies.

Beyond the aer aquosus, or watery zone, is the purus aether, or zone of air, and containing the west wind. Of all the zones it is the widest, and the long axis of this zone and the remaining outer zones is from east to west, thus fixing the path of movement of the heavenly bodies. It carries in it the constellations of the fixed stars, the Moon, and the two interior planets, Mercury and Venus.

Beyond the zones of east wind and water and of west wind and air is the umbrosa pellis, or ignis niger, the zone of the "dry" and the "earthy," of the north wind, thunder, lightning, and storms. It is a dark, narrow shell which is the storehouse of "the treasures of the snow and of the hail."

The outermost shell is the lucidus ignis, zone of fire, of the south wind, and of the three outer planets, Mars, Jupiter and Saturn--also, in Hildegard's first scheme, of the Sun.

The movements of the four outer zones about each other, which carry the heavenly bodies, are caused by the four winds; and the elements peculiar to each zone are here comparatively pure. Each zone has also its own special mental character, and has a specific influence on the mind and the body of man. For, says Hildegard, "And again I heard the voice from heaven saying, 'God, who created all things, wrought also man in His own image and similitude, and in him He traced (signavit) all created things, and He held him in such love that He destined him for the place from which the fallen angel had been cast."

Plate XXXVII is an illustration from her Liber Divinorum representing her second vision, which shows Nous, the "world-spirit," animated and controlled by the God-head, with arms outstretched embracing the macrocosm with the microcosm. Only the head and the feet of Nous are visible, for the body is covered with the disc of the universe. In this picture of her universe, the zones are seven: they are, from without inwards, says Singer:

a. The lucidus ignis, containing the three outer planets, the sixteen principal fixed stars, and the south wind.

b. The ignis niger, containing the sun, the north wind, and the materials for thunder, lightning, and hail.

c. The purus aether, containing the west wind, the Moon, the two inner planets, and certain fixed stars.

d. The aer aquosus, containing the east wind.

e. The fortis et albus lucidusque aer where certain other fixed stars are placed.

f. The aer tenuis, or atmosphere, in the outer part of which is the zone of the clouds.

From all these zones with all their contents, elements, winds, Sun, Moon, planets, fixed stars, and the great animals or qualities of the heavens, are rained down influences upon the figure of the macrocosm.

Singer quotes a passage from Hildegard's Liber Divinorum to illustrate all this, and most of it can be followed in Plate XXXVII, and in Fig. 92.

"In the middle of the disk [of the universe] there appeared the form of a man, the crown of whose head and the soles of whose feet extended to the fortis et albus lucidusque aer, and his hands were outstretched right and left to the same circle. . . . Towards these parts there was an appearance of four heads, a leopard, a wolf, a lion, and a bear. Above the head of the figure, in the zone of the purus aether, I saw the head of the leopard emitting a blast from its mouth, and on the right side of the mouth the blast, curving itself somewhat backwards, was formed into a crab's head . . . while on the left side of the mouth a blast similarly curved ended in a stag's head. From the mouth of the crab's head, another blast went to the middle of the space between the leopard and the lion, and from the stag's head a similar blast to the middle of the space between the leopard and the bear . . . and all the heads were breathing towards the figure of the man. Under his feet in the aer aquosus there appeared as it were the head of a wolf, sending forth to the right a blast extending to the middle of the half space between its head and that of the bear, where it assumed the form of the stag's head; and from the stag's mouth there came as it were another breath which ended in the middle line. From the left of the wolf's mouth arose a breath which went to the middle of the half space between the wolf and the lion, where was depicted another crab's head . . . from whose mouth another breath ended in the same middle line . . . And the breath of all the heads extended sideways from one to another. . . . Moreover, on the right hand of the figure in the lucidus igni, from the head of the lion, issued a breath which passed laterally on the right into a serpent's head and on the left into a lamb's head . . . similarly on the figure's left in the ignis niger, there issued a breath from the bear's head ending on its right in the head of [another] lamb, and on its left in another serpent's head . . . And above the head of the figure the seven planets were ranged in order, three in the lucidus ignis, one projecting into the ignis niger, and three into the purus aether. . . . And in the circumference of the circle of the lucidus ignis there appeared the sixteen principal stars, four in each quadrant between the heads. . . . Also the purus aether and the fortis et albus lucidusque aer seemed to be full of stars which sent forth their rays towards the clouds, whence . . . tongues like rivers descended to the disk and towards the figure, which was thus surrounded and influenced by these signs."

In Hildegard's fourth vision--of the influence of the heavenly bodies and the pure elements on men, animals, and plants, she saw, from the upper fiery firmament, the lucidus ignis, ashes as it were cast to the Earth, which produced rashes and ulcers in men and animals and fruits. From the ignis niger she saw vapours (nebulæ) descending, which withered the plants and dried up the earth. Against these descending influences the purus aether struggled, seeking to hold back the plagues of disease and drought.

From the fortis et albus lucidusque aer she saw certain clouds descend to the Earth and infect men and beasts with a pestilence, but this plague the aer aquosus opposed, so that all were not destroyed. In the aer tenuis she saw its moisture as if it were boiling above the surface of the Earth, rousing the force of the Earth, and compelling it to bring forth its fruits by aid of the cosmic rays.

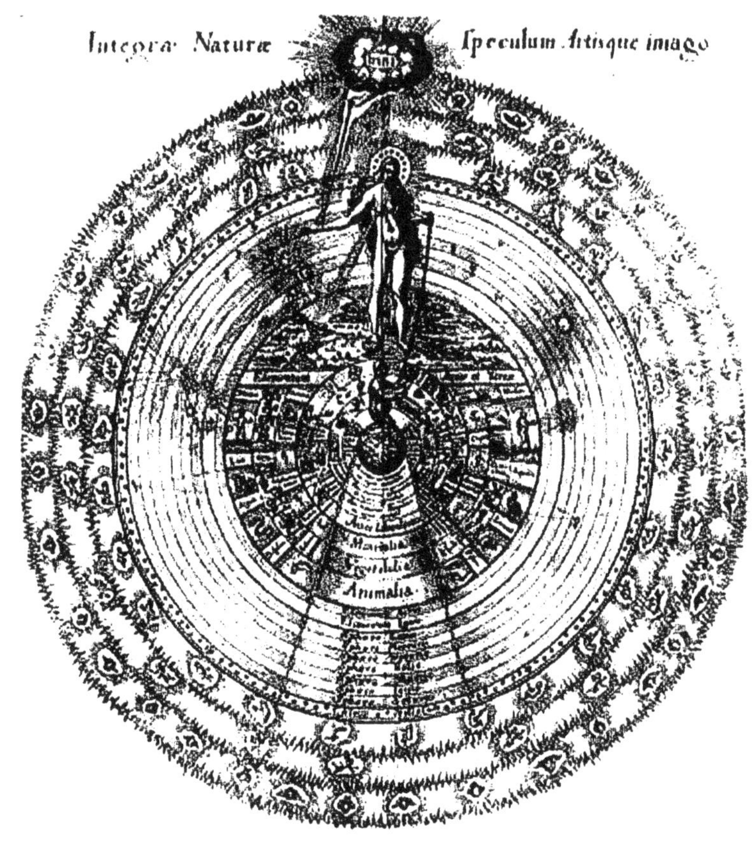

PLATE XXXVIII (From Uriusque Cosmi; Robert Fludd, 1621. Vol. I)

In the whole of her scheme of the universe, the winds are of prime importance. Were it not for the winds, which, she said, are the wings of God's power, the other three elements, the fires of the south, the waters of the west, and the great shadows of the north would burst over the Earth and destroy it. Or, were the four winds to move forward at once, the elements themselves would be split asunder, and the waters of the sea would be dried up. As man's body, she said, is held together by the soul, so the firmament is held together by the winds, which are, like the soul, invisible.

In developing her theory of the correspondence of the microcosm to the macrocosm, of man to the universe and God, she set down many of its details. The firmament corresponds to the head of man, in which, from the top of the cerebral cavity to "the last extremity of the forehead," are seven marked spaces all equal, which correspond to the seven planets, all of which, says Hildegard, are equally distant from each other in the heavens. The Sun, Moon, and stars she compares to his eyes; air is his hearing, the winds his smelling, the dew of heaven his tasting, and the sides of the world his arms and his touching. The Earth is like the heart of the cosmos, for it, like the heart of man, can be stirred by emotion; and, as the heart of man, moved by joy or sorrow, excites the brain to cause tears to flow, so the Earth, when the Moon begins to wax and wane, sends up her tears, the fogs of her oceans and seas.

THE EARTHS IN THE UNIVERSE

OF ALL THE MYSTICAL COSMOLOGISTS Emanuel Swedenborg wrote the longest scroll of correspondences between Man, Earth, and Heaven. His whole cosmology was founded on the Grand Man, who contained within himself the universe, and testified to the mystics's truth that "all things are created double, one against another"; that "there is no herb on earth to which a star does not correspond in heaven." But, unlike Hildegard, Swedenborg did not leave behind him his pictured conceptions of the cosmos, of the Grand Man, or of the multiplied Earths of the heavens. There is a little book of his, The Earths in the Universe, which reads like a fairy story, and should have had at least its frontispiece. His "Earths in the Universe" are the planets. He begins with the "Earth or planet" Mercury, following it with the Earth or planet Jupiter, and after these, in their order, come the Earths or planets Mars, Saturn, and Venus. Then he discourses on the spirits and inhabitants of the Moon, and the "five Earths of the starry heavens."

"That the universal heaven resembles one man," he says, "who is therefore called the GRAND MAN, and that all and singular the things appertaining to man, both his exteriors and interiors, correspond to that man or heaven, is an arcanum not as yet known to the world, but that it is so, has been abundantly proved. To constitute that Grand Man, there is need of spirits from several earths, those who come from our earth not being sufficient for this purpose, being respectively few; and it is provided of the Lord, that whensoever there is a deficiency in any place as to the quality or quantity of correspondence, a supply must be instantly made from another earth, to fill up the deficiency, so that the proportion may be preserved, and thus heaven be kept in due consistence."

The inhabitants of the Earth or planet Mercury, he says, have a relation, not to terrestrial objects, but to the memory of things abstracted from these objects. The spirits or angels who are from the Earth Jupiter, "in the GRAND MAN have relation to the IMAGINATIVE PART OF THOUGHT, and consequently to an active state of the interior parts; but die spirits of our earth have relation to the various functions of the exterior parts of the body, and when these are desirous to have dominion, the active or imaginative part of thought from the interior cannot flow in; hence come the oppositions between the spheres of the life of each." The beings of the Earth Mars have relation, in the Grand Man, to "the longitudinal sinus, which lies in the brain between the two hemispheres thereof, and is there in a quiet state, howsoever the brain be disturbed on each side." The inhabitants and spirits of the Earth Saturn have relation, in the Grand Man, to "the middle sense between the spiritual man and the natural man, but to that which recedes from the natural and accedes to the spiritual." The spirits of Venus have relation, in the Grand Man, to "the memory of things material, agreeing with the memory of things immaterial." The spirits and inhabitants of our Earth have relation, in the Grand Man, to "natural and external sense, which sense is the ultimate wherein the exteriors of life close, and rest as in their common basis."

WHEELS UPON WHEELS

BELOW IS A GROUP OF EIGHT FIGURES whose whole interest lies just in their association. With their science we have nothing to do here, since they are old attempts, most of them, to account for the observed aberrations of movement among the heavenly bodies. Wang Ch'ung, an old Chinese philosopher, expressed a part of this still unsolved problem very oddly and simply indeed. Writing of the complex movements of the Sun and the Moon in relation to the heavens, he said: That Heaven turns sideways to the left "like a millstone"; that the Sun and Moon move to the right, but are swept by Heaven to the left; that their real movement is towards the east, but they are carried by Heaven towards the west, where they "go down"; that they resemble ants creeping to the left side on a millstone turning to the right, but that the millstone, being much swifter than the ants, compels them to follow it to the right.

Old astronomers, however, employed two devices to aid them in their calculations; one to account for the seeming difference observed in the speed of the Sun's movement in its orbit; the other to account for the seeming alternation of direction in the movements of the planets.

The Sun, for instance, when describing a certain segment of its orbit, travelled at a greater speed--or so it seemed--than when it moved in the corresponding opposite quarter. To the Sun, therefore, was given a place in the heavens called the Excentric sphere--it was another theory of two centres. For it was assumed that all the heavenly spheres were not concentric, did not, that is, have the Earth's centre as a common centre; and that the centre of one sphere of revolution might be a point a little removed from the centre of the Earth. According to this theory, when the Sun was near the Earth, its speed would appear much greater than when it was moving at a distance farther away.

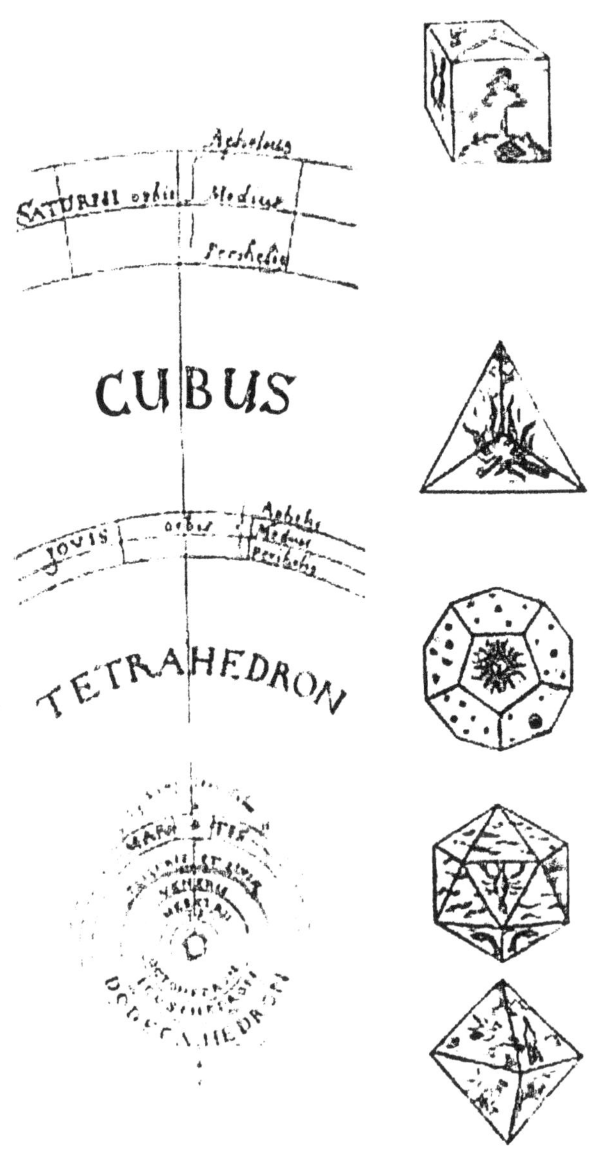

PLATE XXXIX. Kepler's diagram of The Law connecting the relative distances of the planets.

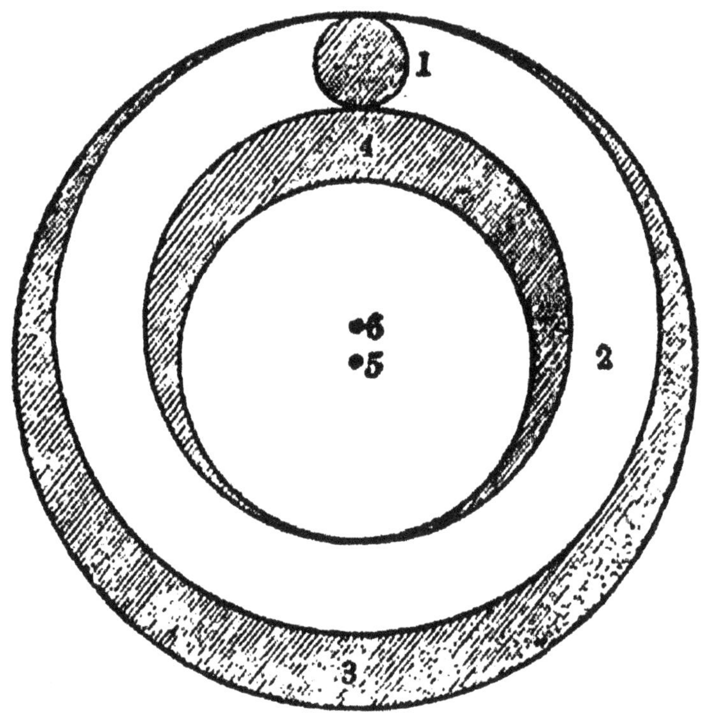

FIGURE 93. The excentric sphere of Mahmud ibn Muhammed ibn Omar al Jagmini (c. 13th century A.D.)
1. The Sun. 2. Excentric sphere. 3. Surrounding sphere. 4. Complement of the surrounding sphere. 5. Centre of the world. 6. Centre of the excentric sphere. (From The History of the Planetary Systems from Thales to Kepler; J. L. E. Dreyer, 1906.)

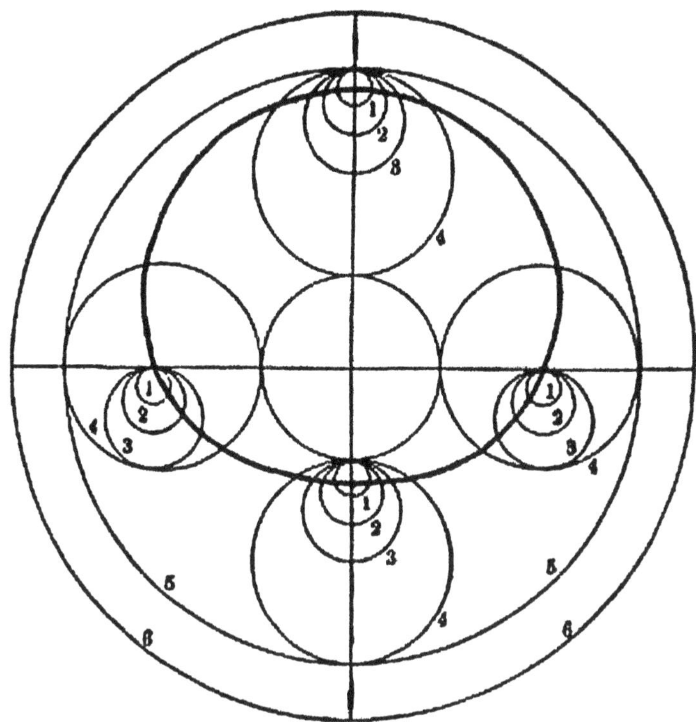

FIGURE 94. The "Guiding Spheres" of Nasir-Eddin Attûsi
(13th century A.D.)
(From The History of the Planetary Systems from Thales to Kepler; J. L. E. Dreyer, 1906, pp. 269-270.)

1. Epicycle of the Moon. 2. Surrounding sphere, destined to keep the diameter from apogee to perigee in its place, always coinciding with the diameter of the sphere (4); "Let us give it a suitable thickness, but not too great, so as not to take up too much space." 3. Sphere which corresponds to the smaller sphere, and the diameter of which is equal to the distance of the centre of the deferent in the Ptolemaic system from the centre of the Earth. 4. Sphere with a diameter twice as great as (3). 5. Carrying sphere concentric with the world and occupying the concavity of the sphere (6), the equator of which is in the plane of the lunar orbit.

(2) and (4) and (5) revolve in the same period, that in which the centre of the epicycle performs a revolution; (3) revolves in half that time, while (6)

revolves in the opposite direction with the same speed as the apogee of the excentric.

The figure now shows how the epicycle moves to and fro along the diameter of (4), and during the revolution of the circle (5) describes a closed curve, about which Nasir-Eddin justly says that it is somewhat like a circle but is not really one, for which reason it is not a perfect substitute for the excentric circle of Ptolemy.

To account for the seeming alternation of direction in the movements of the planets, the theory of the Epicycle was evolved. This meant, briefly, that a planet did not move directly in the circumference of its revolving sphere or cycle--as, for instance, the Sun moved in its excentric sphere, but in an epicycle or small circle that revolved around a fixed point in the larger circle and carried the planet with it; "fixed to its inner surface," says an old Arabian astronomer, "like a pearl on a ring, touching the surface in one point." For a time these devices of the excentric and the epicycle seemed to work fairly well; but after a while the astronomers found themselves entangled in such a maze of centrics and excentrics, cycles and epicycles, and spheres heaped upon spheres, that they never found their way out of the labyrinth they had themselves constructed, and eventually the system that was to account for all the mysteries of the heavenly movements fell of itself.

Dante's favorite description of the heavens was "wheels upon wheels," and Jagmini's diagram (Fig. 93) shows the "excentric wheel" of the Sun, itself a solid spherical body the edges of whose wheel touch two other surfaces, in the common centre of which is the Earth. But the centre of the excentric sphere is not "the centre of the world." For there were "pulls" in the heavens that resulted in constantly shifting centres. Nasir-Eddin Attûsi, great Arabian astronomer of Jagmini's century, attempted to account for the various lunacies of the heavens by, literally, "the spots on the moon." These spots, he assumed, are caused by other bodies moving in its epicycle and un-equally exposed to its light, and this phenomenon he calls "the anomaly of illumination." The movements of the five planets, particularly those of Mercury and Venus, required, he said, "the introducing of a system of guiding spheres," and this theory, when fully worked out (Fig. 94) gave him, for the path of Mercury, not the excentric circle of Ptolemy, nor a circle at all, but a curious closed curve with unequal radii which he described as "somewhat like a circle, but not really one."

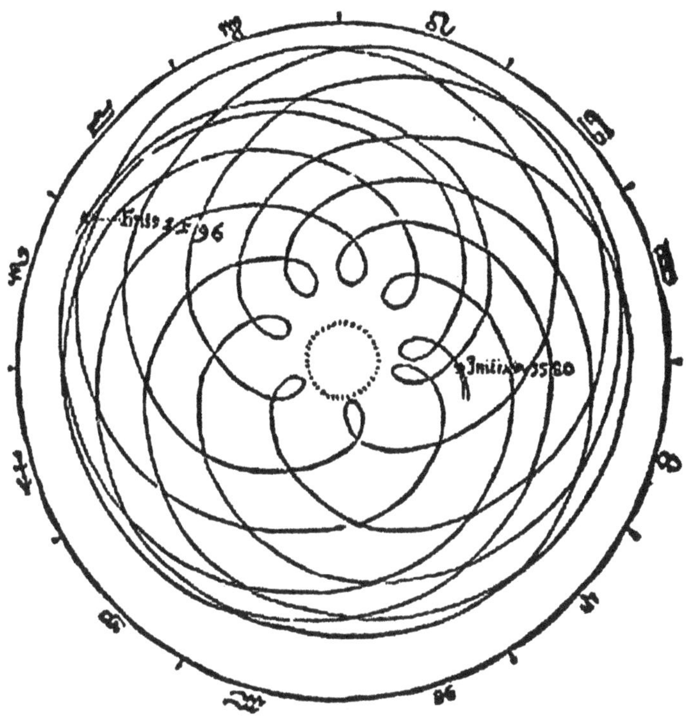

FIGURE 95. The movement described by Mars, 1580-1596.
(From Astronomia Nova; Johann Kepler, 1609.)

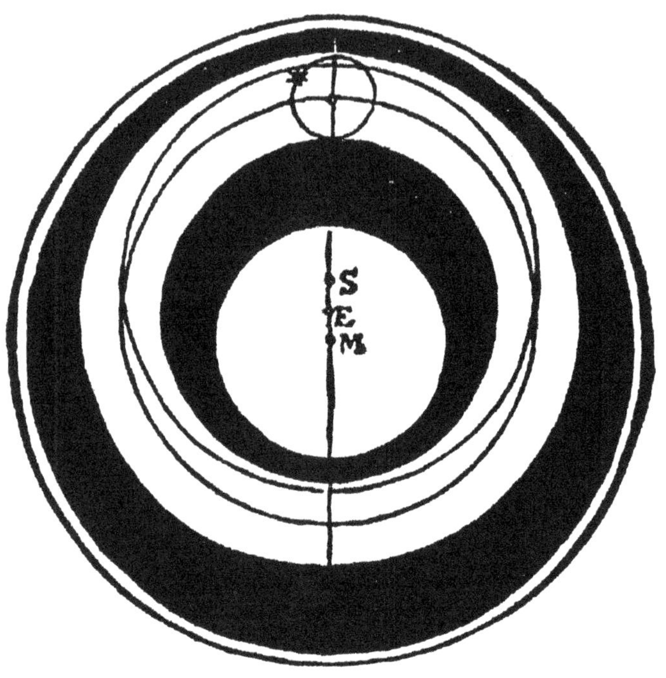

FIGURE 96. Theory of three centres and the movement of Venus.
M. Centre of the world. E. Centre of the excentric. S. Centre of the equant. The centre of the star-bearing circle at the top is the centre of the epicycle.
(From Theoricæ Novæ; Georg Peurbach, 1581.)

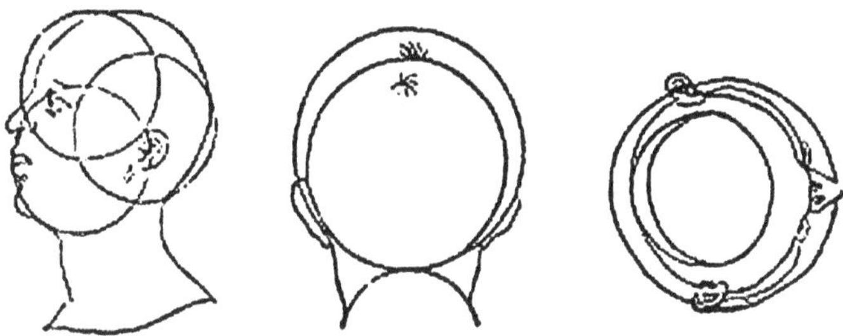

FIGURE 97. The relation of the harmony of the Microcosmos to the Macrocosmos.
(From Microcosmi Historia; Robert Fludd, 1621.)

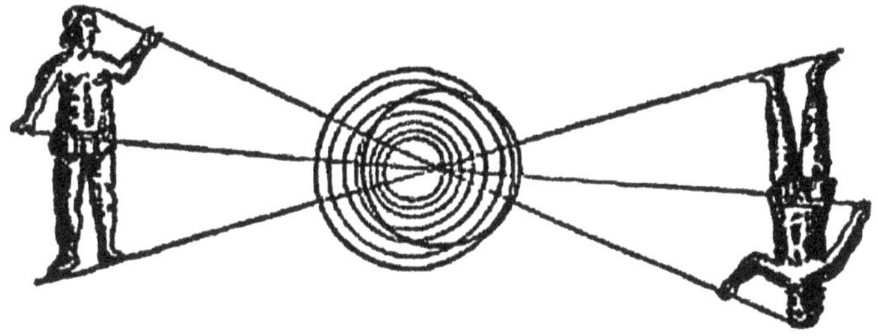

FIGURE 98. The Balance.
(From Mundus Subterraneus; Athanasius Kircher, 1678, Vol. II.)

THE WORLD OCTAVES

IT WAS HIS PROLONGED OBSERVATION of the movement of Mars (Fig. 95) that led Kepler to discover the true form of the planetary orbits, till then considered to be perfectly circular, and it was during the last year of his observations (1596) that he hit upon his beautiful "solution" of the "cosmographic mystery." He believed in the harmony of the spheres, and all his life he sought for some true and simple law binding the members of the solar system together. His first step was to discover the law connecting the relative distances of the planets, some simple ratio of distances that would do away with the complex and multiplied epicycles and excentrics with which Ptolemy and his successors had troubled, if not the heavens, the minds of men. By accident he was brought finally to seek this law of distances through simple geometry. A diagram he had drawn during a lecture, to illustrate the cycles of the great conjunctions of the planets, reminded him, in a sudden flash of illumination, of the "five regular solids," the "five mathematical bodies" (-6); and for the rest of his life he worked on the theory that these beautiful solids bore within themselves a proportion answering to the several distances of the planets from each other. That is, if we describe a circle around a cube and another inside it, or a circle about a tetrahedron and another within it, the distances between these circumscribed and inscribed circles will show the proportional distances of the planets each from the other between which these five solids fit.

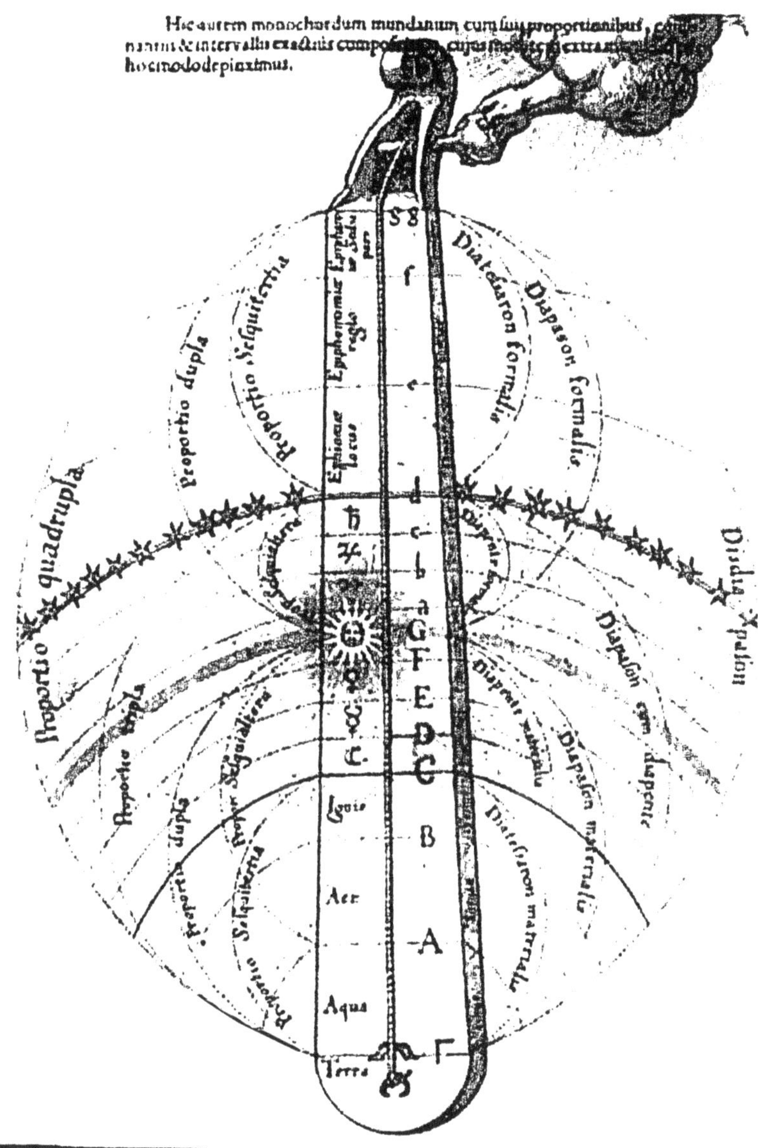

PLATE XL. THE MUNDANE MONOCHORD
(From Utriusque Cosmi: Robert Fludd, 1621. Vol. I)

Between the six planetary spheres there are five intervals, and Kepler placed the five solids between the spheres as follows:

Saturn
Cube
Jupiter
Tetrahedron
Mars
Dodecahedron
Earth
Icosahedron
Venus
Octahedron
Mercury

That is, the sphere of Jupiter is inscribed in a cube to which the sphere of Saturn is circumscribed; the sphere of Jupiter is circumscribed to a tetrahedron in which the sphere of Mars is inscribed, and so on. The rest is mathematics.

In Kepler's beautiful drawings of his solids (), which, more than plane figures, he said, must belong to Space, he assigned to each form that one of the great elements whose "component particle" corresponded. Within a crystalline cube he placed a mountain, a tree, a sprouted and leafing plant, and tools for tilling the Earth. Within the tetrahedron he placed fire; within the dodecahedron the firmament; within the icosahedron water and the inhabitants of water; within the octahedron "flying birds."

Kepler's "intervals" were not only spaces for the five mathematical bodies; they were also "notes" in an harmonic universal scale. His harmony of the spheres was not only the harmony of movement but the result of move-ment--sound. It was unimaginable that the grand revolutions of the spheres through Space were made in silence; unimaginable also that the ears of men could hear the prodigious concert of the whole universe in its rapid revolution. As they must close their eyes against the Sun, too bright to see, so must their ears be closed against a harmony too vibrant to endure.

Yet, if the ears of man may not hear the music of the spheres, his eyes may follow the paths of celestial sound, said Robert Fludd, and straightway began to "draw" the music of the spheres. "This," he wrote at the top of the first figure of his series of World Octaves, in his Musica Mundana (Plate XL), "is the world monochord, with its proportions, harmonies and intervals of its extra-mundane movement accurately spaced as herein depicted." Earth--the mute because motionless Earth of the Pythagoreans--plays its part through the division of the elements, Earth, Water, Air, and Fire. Only when the Earth's atmosphere reaches the zone of the Moon is the first note struck of the great C major scale. Beyond the seven zones of the Moon, the Sun, and the five planets, and above the firmament of the fixed stars, the divisions of the upper heavens correspond to those of the Earth below.

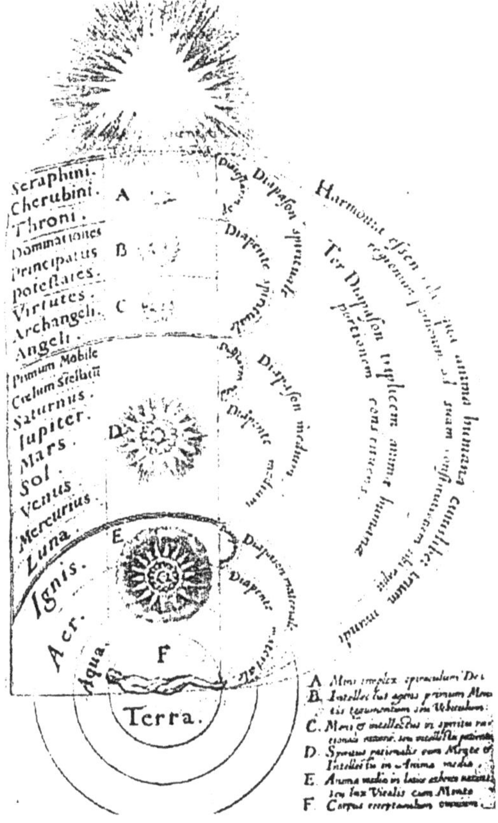

PLATE XLI. MAN AND THE WORLD OCTAVE
(From Utriusque Cosmi; Robert Fludd, 1621. Vol. I)

Plate XLI is the second of the series, taken up again in his Microcosmi Historia, in which man is shown as participator in the heavenly scale. Here is a single octave, instead of two, as in the preceding drawing; its scale given in terms of mind or reason, rather than in terms of the elements and the heavenly bodies. From A, the Absolute Mind or Essence of the Godhead, or Unity, or Spirit, it descends through B, the creative or active intellect, the first vehicle of the mind, to C, mind and intellect in the rational spirit (or the passive intellect), to D, the rational spirit together with mind and intellect in the median soul, to E, the median soul floating in the aethereal liquid (in other words, the Living Light combined with Mind), to F, the Body (or man), which is the receptacle of all things.

And then, having given the two-octaved universe--Heaven and Earth, and the one-octaved universe stretching from the Godhead to man, he drew a third figure (Plate XLII) of the three-octaved universe, with its three great scales of correspondences, rising one above the other, each corresponding exactly, note by note, to the other two, whether higher or lower. Sound, he says, is the connecting link between the three worlds; for sound is the language of the mind. Vibration is the secret of creation, and through it all secrets may be revealed, if the sleeping mind and memory of man is ever wakened through its power.

EARTH A HOLLOW SPHERE

WITH THE Symmes Theory of Concentric Spheres we take up, for the first time, a cosmogony of the nineteenth century. In this flight through worlds we have spanned not only the centuries but the oceans and continents of the Earth. We are in the year of our Lord, 1818, in America, and at St. Louis, Missouri, on the western bank of the mightiest river of the Earth. We are on the continent whose aboriginal inhabitants have, running through all their mythologies and traditions, the tradition and myth of a "hollow Earth," and we are about to consider, in their order, three modern American theories of the figure of Earth, all of them based on the assumption that this planet is a hollow sphere, habitable within.

A brief circular announced the first of these:

Light gives light to light discover--ad infinitum

St. Louis (Missouri Territory)
NORTH AMERICA, April 10, A.D., 1818

TO ALL THE WORLD:

I declare that the earth is hollow and habitable within; containing a number of solid concentric spheres, one within the other, and that it is open at the poles twelve or sixteen degrees. I pledge my life in support of this truth, and am ready to explore the hollow, if the world will support and aid me in this undertaking.

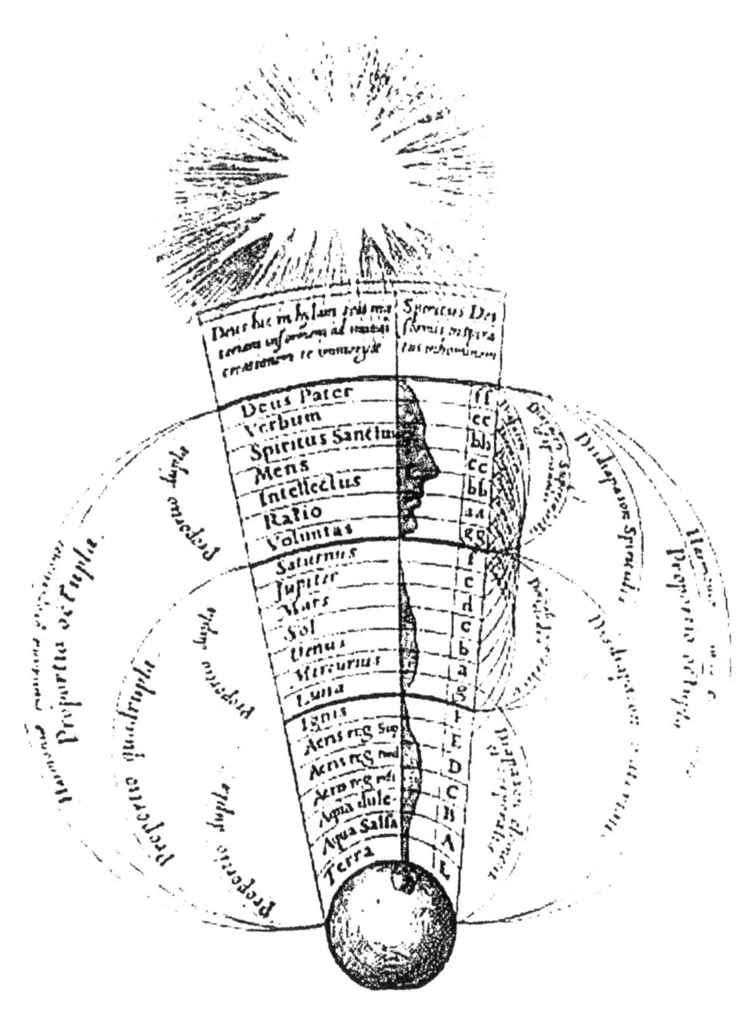

PLATE XLII. THE THREE WORLD OCTAVES
(From Utriusque Cosmi; Robert Fludd, 1621. Vol. I)

JNO. CLEVES SYMMES
Of Ohio, late Captain of Infantry.

N. B. I have ready for the press a Treatise on the Principles of the matter, wherein I show proofs of the above position, account for the various phenomena, and disclose Dr. Darwin's "Golden Secret."

I ask one hundred brave companions, well equipped, to start from Siberia in the fall season, with reindeer and sleighs, on the ice of the frozen sea; and I engage we find a warm and rich land, stocked with thrifty vegetables and animals, if not men, on reaching one degree northwest of latitude 62; we will return in the succeeding spring.

J. C. S.

Symmes never reached, nor even began his journey to reach, the "north polar Verge of the world," let pass its interior. In 1822 and again in 1823, he petitioned the Congress of the United States to equip for him two vessels "of 250 or 300 tons burden," and in 1824 even sought aid from the General Assembly of the State of Ohio. Naturally no such request was even considered by an American Congress or Legislature. In 1829 he died, and over his grave, at Hamilton, Ohio, was erected a monument surmounted by a hollow globe open at the poles, inscribed: "He contended that the Earth is hollow and habitable within."

Where Symmes got his notion that the Earth has a concave, habitable surface seems to have interested nobody. But it is interesting to consider that three "concave" cosmogonies have sprung up within less than a century on this continent whose aborigines believed in the hollowness of their "great Island." The Montagnais held the earth to be pierced through and through; that the Sun set by entering one hole and hiding inside the Earth during the night; that it rose by emerging from the opposite hole. Numberless tribes have the tradition that formerly their race lived underground, until some adventurous youth climbed upwards by some great vine to the outer surface of the Earth, and, finding it delightful and habitable, returned and brought their people out of the "concave." Indian gods fell from Heaven, through the Earth; and vanished races were those who had returned to their first homes. How much of this Symmes had picked up through fraternising with the western Indians, or whether he had ever heard any of this tradition from them, we shall probably never know.

In 1826, "A Citizen of the United States," otherwise James McBride, published, at Cincinnati, a little book called The Symmes Theory of Concentric Spheres, giving thesis and proofs.

"According to Symmes's Theory, the earth, as well as all the celestial orbicular bodies existing in the universe, visible and invisible, which partake in any degree of a planetary nature, from the greatest to the smallest, from the sun down to the most minute blazing meteor or falling star, are all constituted in a greater or less degree, of a collection of spheres, more or less solid, concentric with each other, and more or less open at their poles; each sphere being separated from its adjoining compeers by space replete with aerial fluids; that every portion of infinite space, except what is occupied by spheres, is filled with an aerial elastic fluid, more subtle than common atmospheric air; and constituted of innumerable small concentric spheres, too minute to be visible to the organ of sight assisted by the most perfect microscope, and so elastic that they continually press on each other, and change their relative situations as often as the position of any piece of matter in space may change its position; thus causing a universal pressure, which is weakened by the intervention of other bodies in proportion to the subtended angle of distance and dimension; necessarily causing the body to move towards the points of decreased pressure."

Symmes believed that the planet "which has been designated the Earth," is composed of at least five concentric spheres, with spaces between each, an atmosphere surrounding each, and each habitable upon both its surfaces. Each sphere was widely open at its poles, and the north polar opening of the outer sphere whose convex surface man inhabits, he believed to be about four thousand miles in diameter. The southern polar opening he estimated to be half again as large.

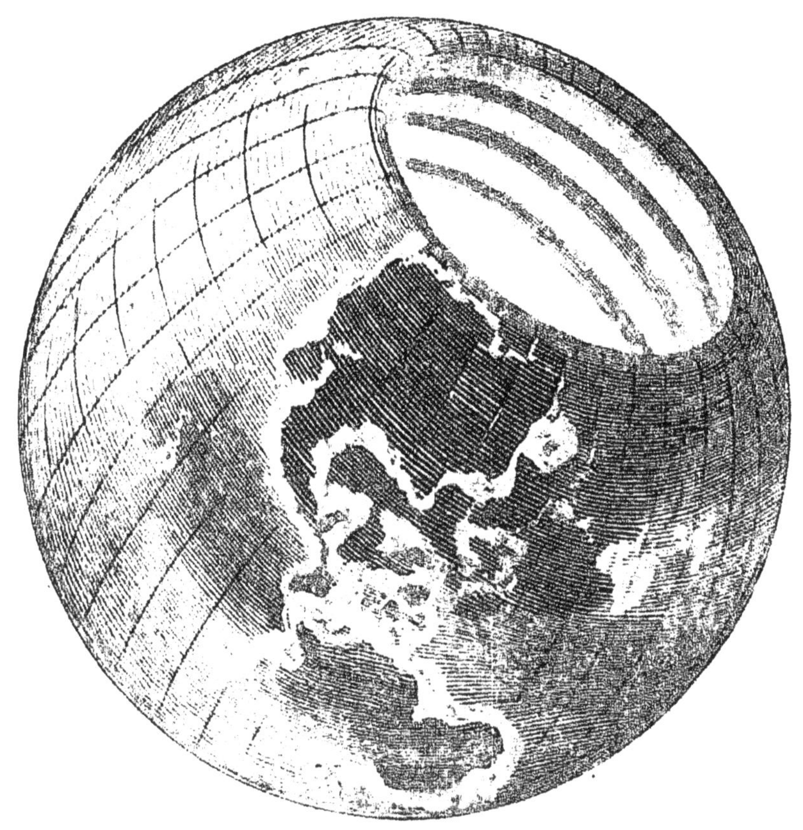

PLATE XLIII. THE SYMMES THEORY OF CONCENTRIC SPHERES
(From The Symmes Theory of Concentric Spheres, compiled by Americus Symmes, 1878)

Each of the spheres composing the Earth is according to this theory lighted and warmed "according to those general laws which communicate light and heat to every part of the universe." This light and heat might not be so bright or so intense as ours; and the probability of this is indicated, he says, in those high northern latitudes, where the "Verge" begins, by the paleness of the Sun and the darkness of the sky; yet he does not doubt that they are sufficiently warmed and lighted to support animal and vegetable life.

His "mid-plane-space" theory is interesting, and Gardner's diagram (Plate XLIV) makes it very clear. Each sphere has a cavity, or mid-plane-space near its centre--the medial line, that is, which would split its crust or shell into inner and outer layers--filled with this light, subtle, elastic aerial fluid, "partaking somewhat of the nature of hydrogen gas; which aerial fluid is composed of molecules greatly rarefied in comparison with the gravity of the extended or exposed surfaces of the sphere." It is this mid-plane-space which gives the sphere lightness and buoyancy, and the aerial fluid with which it is filled may possibly, he conjectures, serve for the support of animal life.

Clouds formed in the outer air of the planet would probably float through the vast polar openings in the form of rain or snow. The great winds or typhoons, known on the Earth, might have their force supplied by winds sucked into one polar opening, and emerging through the other, thus performing the circuit of the sphere.

He argues his hollow Earth by analogy--to hollow stalks of wheat, the hollow quills and feathers of birds, the hollow bones of animals, and the hollow hairs of our heads. This would be, he says, "the most perfect system of creative economy, a great saving of stuff." And, this early in the history of north polar exploration, and from the evidence of whalers and fisher-men in the northern seas regarding the migration of birds, animals, and fish to and from the north polar zone, he is arguing for a warm and habitable region beyond the ice-packs, "where the fresh waters furiously contend with the salt." He develops at great length the precise manner in which light and heat from our Sun might, by reflection and refraction, penetrate into every part of the interior shells. It is even possible, he suggests, that, "near the Verges of the polar openings, and perhaps in many other parts of the unfathomable ocean, the spheres are water quite through (at least all except the mid-plane-spaces or cavities), which being the case, light would probably be transmitted through the spheres."

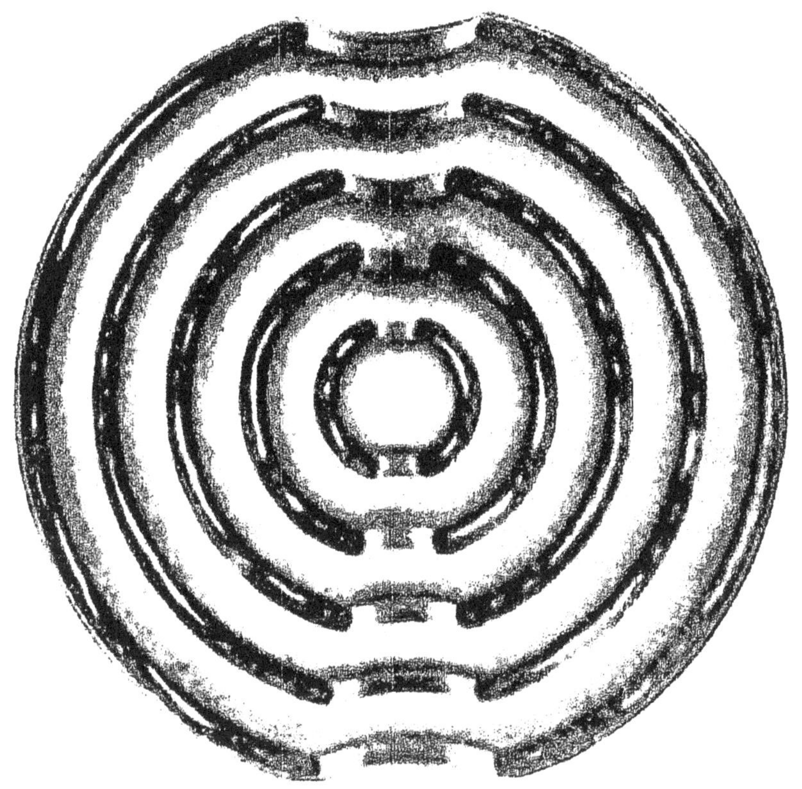

PLATE XLIV. GARDNER'S DIAGRAM OF SYMMES'S EARTH
Showing the five concentric spheres, with their polar openings at the Verges of the World. their separating atmospheres, and their mid-plane spaces.
(From A Journey to the Earth's Interior; Marshall B. Gardner, 1920)

Symmes believed that man, in his efforts to reach the North Pole, had always failed just on the "Verge"; that once past the ice barrier and headed inevitably for the interior of the hollow shell, he would find himself almost at once in a temperate zone. The path to the interior, he says, would be a tortuous one, by way of "the winding meridians of the Verge."

THE KORESHAN COSMOGONY is another "hollow Earth" theory, which was first given out in 1870 by Cyrus Reed Teed. The chart given in Plate XLV contains all the principal diagrams by which the theory is illustrated.

This second of modern American cosmogonies holds that the Earth we live upon and think we "know" to be the outer surface of a sphere, is, in reality, its concave surface; that we are actually living enclosed within a hollow shell, however much our collective senses and our collective science seem to prove the contrary. This, Teed affirms, is because we have been taught for centuries that the Earth is a globe filled with molten matter on whose cooled crust we live; that it is but a speck in infinite Space, a dot in a vast ocean of worlds, revolving on its own axis every twenty-four hours and thus creating its own days and nights in its yearly revolutions around the Sun; that the Moon shines a borrowed light; that comets appear, fly off into space, and return; that above and around and below our solar system stretch the orbits of other worlds to illimitable distances; that our Sun, the centre of our system, has a diameter of 866,000 miles, is distant from the Earth 93,000,000 miles, and has a volume or bulk 1,300,000 times that of the Earth; that the planet nearest the Sun, Mercury, is 36,000,000 miles distant from it, and 57,000,000 miles distant from the Earth, and so on until we reach the planet Neptune which is 2,800,000,000 miles from the Sun and guards the outermost boundaries of our universe.

The Koreshan cosmogony, on the other hand, "maintains and demonstrates that the universe is a unit; it is an alchemico-organic structure, limited to the dimensions of 8,000 miles, diameter. According to the great law of analogy we hold that its form is cellular, that all life is generated in a cell--omne vivum ex ovo. The earth's shell, composed of metals and minerals, is about 100 miles in thickness, constituting a gigantic voltaic pile, the basis of the great galvano-magnetic battery, furnishing the negative elements of the cell for the generation and supply of the sun's fuel. The concave surface of the earth alone is habitable. Superimposed upon the strata of the shell and emplaced in their static planes are the three atmospheres. At the centre we find the positive pole of the great battery--the central sun, around and with which the heavens revolve in twenty-four hours. All the energies of the physical universe are engendered through the relation of the positive centre to the negative circumference; a great complex battery of physical unity is thus attained and perpetuated." [1]

This shell, one hundred miles in thickness, is composed of seven metallic, five mineral, and five geologic strata. The seven metallic layers or laminæ

[1] Cellular Cosmogony, Cyrus Reed Teed, 1905, p. 172.

are "the seven notable metals," of which gold constitutes the outer rind of the shell. Beyond this is--nothing.

The inner surface of the shell is land and water, a concave expanse inhabited by every form of life. That we live on a concave surface, this cosmogony undertakes to prove by exactly the same phenomenon which "proves" the Earth's surface is convex--the disappearance of a ship "around" the world. Within the shell are the three atmospheres, of which the outermost, the atmosphere in which we exist, is composed chiefly of oxygen and nitrogen. The next or middle atmosphere is composed of pure hydrogen; and the one above of "aboran." Within this is the solar sphere, and within the whole and nucleus of all, the astral or stellar centre. Thus the starry nucleus is the centre of Space, and the metallic plates or laminæ the circumference of Space. The heavens do not surround the Earth, but the Earth, the heavens.

In and occupying these atmospheres are not only the Sun and stars, but also "the reflections called the planets and the moon. The planets are mercurial disci moving by electro-magnetic impulse between the metallic laminæ or planes of the concave shell. They are seen through penetrable rays, ultra electro-magnetic, reflected or bent back in their impingement on the spheres of energy regularly graduated as the stories in the heavens." And, later on, they are further described as "little focal points of energy, partially materialized spheres in process of combustion. Their diameter is very small. Jupiter is nothing like the concept in the usual theory. The real planets are discs of mercury in the earth, between the metallic shells. They focalise the sun's energies in the atmosphere above us. They are what their names indicate--plan-ets--little planes." Of these mercurial discs there are seven.

Comets are not great streams of fiery matter; they are tiny things, broken up bits of crystalline energies spirating about the central solar sphere. "They do not fly off into space and return. They plunge into and feed the sun."

Neither is the Sun 886,000,000 miles in diameter, nor distant from the Earth 93,000,000 miles, since it is a body contained within the concave Earth. Given the Earth's diameter of 8,000 miles, the Sun's diameter would not be over 100 miles, or its distance from the concave habitable surface over 1000 miles. "The sun, moon, stars, including Sirius, Arcturus, Procyon, all the great nebulæ and comets, in short, all the things that exist in the heavens above, are contained in the shell. They are not worlds, or systems of worlds; they are not wanderers or erratic orbs, but points of generation of energy, every one of which has a distinctly different function belonging and necessary to universal perpetuation."

PLATE XLV. CHART OF THE KORESHAN COSMOGONY
(From Cellular Cosmogony; Cyrus Reed Teed, 1898)

The revolution of the Sun and not the rotation of the Earth is the cause of day and night. Instead of appearing to rise above a convex surface, the Sun simply comes into our sphere of vision in the course of its revolution, and, at sunset, "goes out over the earth beyond the sea of hydrogen and arc of the heavens."

FIGURE 99. "All things shew great through vapoures or myste."
(From The Castle of Knowledge; Robert Recorde, 1556.)

As to the Moon, which is an interesting part of this reversed cosmogony, it is to be first of all understood that there is uninterrupted reciprocal interchange of substance from centre to circumference of the shell; from the positive pole of the great battery--the central one," to the shell itself, described before as "a gigantic voltaic pile, the basis of the great galvano-magnetic battery, furnishing the negative elements of the cell for the generation and supply of the sun's fuel." For energy, it is explained, "is the destruction of matter as matter, and matter is the result of the destruction of energy as energy."

The origin of the Moon is in the Earth's shell, a sphere of energy derived from the planets and from the energies generated in the concave crust of the Earth. "The moon we see is projected or reflected from the great concave mirror, the metallic laminæ in the circumference; this moon is a sphere of force in the physical heavens, a sphere of crystalline energy upon which is implanted the picture of the earth's surface. The visible moon is a gravosphere or X-ray picture of the crust; hence we see light and dark places upon it, produced from the earth's surface and the geologic strata.

The real moon is the laminæ of the earth's shell. The sun is the centre, the moon the circumference; the image or focalisation of each we see in the physical heavens. The moon does not shine borrowed light direct as in the Copernican system. But the sun and moon are two great lights; each shines with a light of its own, the light of the moon being derived from thousands of qualities of solar energies, after utilization, transmutation, and metamorphosis in the great shell."

The figures of Earth in this cosmogony are at first bewildering, until the eye becomes accustomed to the trick of "reverse." In the upper left-hand sphere (Plate XLV) we are looking at the "geography" of a concave surface--downwards as into a bowl. In the upper right-hand spherical figure, we are looking at "the heavens in the Earth." The central spherical figure shows the three atmospheres which are the cause of day and night. It is a cross-sectional view of the "gigantic electro-magnetic battery with the sun as the perpetual pivot and pole." It is the southern hemisphere of the "cell." The smaller spheres show--upper left and right--the summer and winter solstices; lower left, the actual position of the Earth and its poles; lower right, the orbits of the planetary mercurial discs in the Earth's shell.

In this cosmogony, the Earth is not "supported"; it is suspended; it is dependent wholly upon its centre. It is eternal; it is the footstool of God and necessary to His Own existence; but it is All; "it is the ultimate and outermost limit of expression of the divine mind." Beyond its outer plate of shining gold there is nothing.

These are two of the three modern theories of the Earth as a hollow shell, differing widely from each other, but having as a common ground the habitability of the concave surface. The first conceives the Earth to be a body composed of at least five concentric spheres or shells, with enormous polar openings through which light and heat enter from the exterior Sun. The second affirms that the Earth is a single shell containing within itself the whole universe--the atmospheres, the planets, the heavens with the stars and Moon and Sun, and that on its concave surface man lives without ever knowing that he is enclosed within his world, like a bird in a cage. The third theory says that the Earth is a single shell, habitable on both its surfaces, with polar openings and an interior Sun.

This theory of the figure of the Earth was first published in 1913, in Marshall B. Gardner's A Journey to the Earth's Interior, or Have the Poles

Really Been Discovered. Plate XLVI shows the exterior of his working model, and Fig. 100 is a diagram of the Earth bisected through its polar openings and showing the interior Sun.

According to these figures, the Earth's shell is a solid mass about 800 miles thick, with its own centre of gravity. Within as without there is land and water, their distribution inside being probably the reverse of the distribution without. That is, the Pacific and Atlantic ocean areas indicate great interior continents (perhaps the lost continents Atlantis-Lemuria-Pan-Mu!), and the space occupied by our continents are probably the places of the interior seas.

At each polar axis there is a great opening, about 1400 miles in diameter, around which both the exterior and interior waters, whose currents flow both ways, pour over "the lips of the world." Over this great curve, says Gardner, mariners might float, or flying men fly, with no more realisation--except for disturbances to their compass needles--that they were describing a half circle about a Titanic waterfall, than a voyager realises he is rounding the globe at any single stage--or total of stages--of a world-voyage. "They would only know that they had actually passed over the lip by the peculiar behavior of the magnetic needle and by the fact that they would see above them--as above them would mean toward the actual centre of the earth--the interior sun, which of course would be shining whether the voyagers came under its influence during the day or during the arctic night."

No mariner has ever rounded this hypothetical lip, entered the great "concave," and emerged to tell his tale. But, says Gardner, messages from the Earth's interior have drifted and constantly do drift out to us by way of the contrary current. He cites log after log of North Polar expeditions, from the first to the last, all of them filled with curious contradictions and "unexplainable" phenomena; the "warm current flowing from the polar regions," the migrations northwards--instead of south--of birds and animals to feed and breed; the greater wealth of animal and vegetable life in the higher latitudes of the arctic regions than in the lower; the "red pollen of plants that grow--where?" scattered on icebergs and glaciers; the trees--some of them green-leaved--washed down in the warm polar current; the "case after case where the mammoth has floated out from the interior incased in glaciers and bergs and has been frozen in crevasses in the interior near the polar openings, and then carried over the lip by glacial movements into Siberia." From the noted evidence of fossil remains, complete coniferous trees, the presence of butterflies and bees, gnats and mosquitoes, incalculable shoals of fish, the musk-oxen and reindeer, the millions of birds--including the sandpiper, the "red snow," fresh-water ice, the recurrent appearances of "extinct" species--the mammoth, the mastodon, the mylodon, to say nothing of the remains of the rhinoceros, hippopotamus, lion, hyena, arid other tropical species all around the North Polar region, he concludes a common origin, beyond the curve of the polar sea, after it has dipped below our horizon and has begun to flow, still north as we would say, yet south, into the Earth's interior.

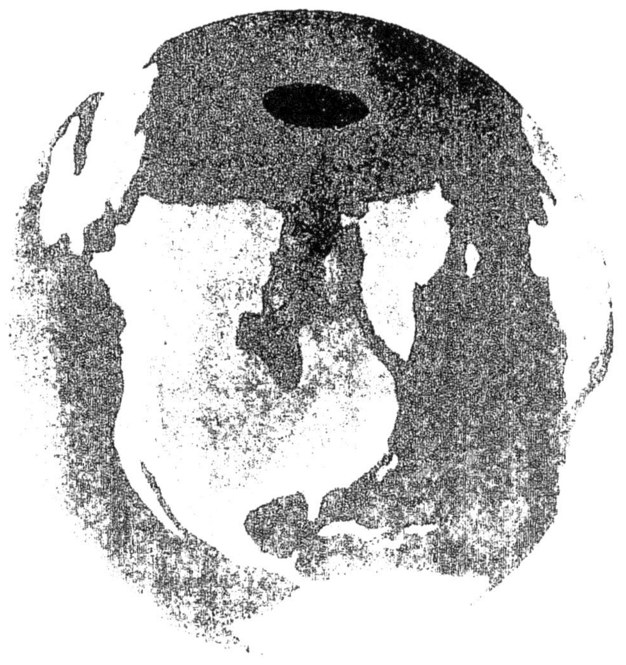

PLATE. XLVI. The Earth according to Gardner, as it would appear if viewed from space shorting the North Polar opening in the planet's interior. which is hollow and contains a central sun instead of an ocean of liquid lava. (From A Journey to the Earth's Interior, Marshall B. Gardner, 1920)

The interior Sun which warms this inner Earth may be perhaps 600 miles in diameter. It is the central nucleus of the old nebular hypothesis; but, instead of throwing off a series of rings, each of which, breaking, formed a sphere and eventually a planet revolving around the central nucleus or Sun, the original nebula, says Gardner, "did not break up into a solar system, but condensed into one planet," this Earth. The spiral nebula is the first stage, he says, of a planetary body; the shell-like nebula with its central "star" or Sun is the second stage; the oblate spheroid with its central Sun and the two openings "which are always left when the nebula cools into a planet," is the third stage. One planet, that is, is like another. As, for instance, Mars and Earth.

The "ice caps" of Mars have accounted, until comparatively recently, for the clearly discernible bright spots at its poles. Of late astronomers have begun to doubt that Martian "ice" could send light-flashes across so many million miles of space. Gardner says that what we see is no more or less than the light from Mar's interior Sun, and that now and then, in observed brilliant points like stars flashing from the midst of the polar caps, we have caught the direct cosmic ray from Mars.

The Aurora Borealis is another unexplained phenomenon--those pulsating aerial fires of the north, which have their counterpart in the Aurora Australis at the South Pole. Gardner says that the scientists themselves know that the theory of their being the result of magnetic or electrical discharges does not explain them. The nearer the Pole, the more magnificent is the display--and he quotes Flammarion on them: "This light of the earth, the emission of which towards the poles is almost continuous . . ." It is just simply that, says Gardner, the light of the Earth; the light of its interior Sun, which pours through the lips of the Earth into the northern and southern skies. Nothing but interior storms of great violence, which choke the orifices for a time with dense clouds, can hold back the almost continuous stream of light. He quotes from Nansen's Farthest North in this connection. Nansen saw one night a marvelous Aurora. A brilliant corona circled the zenith with wreaths of streamers in several layers, all tending upward towards the corona which every now and then showed a dark patch in its centre towards which all the rays converged: "The halo kept smouldering and shifting just as if a gale in the upper atmosphere were playing a bellows to it." For a time it appeared as if the celestial storm abated; then the gale seemed to increase; it twisted the streamers into an inextricable tangle, until at last everything merged "into a chaos of shining mist." There are phrases in Nansen's description of this display which delight Gardner; "bellows," "gale," "storm." As a matter of intelligent explanation, he says, the light from the central Sun was being reflected from the higher reaches of the Earth's atmosphere, and the reflection was being interfered with by a violent storm in the interior of the Earth. Great clouds were in rapid process of formation and dissipation near the polar openings, so that at one moment the rays of the central Sun shot clearly through, at the next moment they were blackened and hid.

Instead of departing for the interior of the Earth by way of Siberia, as Symmes begged to be aided to do, Gardner would pick up some Eskimos--whose ancestors, according to their own tradition, came from the "inside" where it is always light--some dogs and some sleds at God-haven, Greenland, and then proceed north along its coast to about 82° or 83°. What warm air, or warm water, the expedition would encounter would come from the north, and, if it were summer, mosquitoes would be the plague of plagues. From the coast of Grant Land or Peary Land, it would start on the last lap of the journey across the open polar sea. The Aurora Borealis would be no longer in the north, but directly overhead, and there would come a midnight perhaps that was strange day--their ship would be surrounded by an angry reddish light and a strange atmosphere. For the travellers would have passed far enough over the lips of the world to see, no longer the exterior Sun, but the inner Sun which never sets. It is no longer moving from east to west. It is stationary, or practically so, in "the centre of the world."

In that interior world, Gardner surmises, is the treasure house of all of the species of flora and fauna--and probably all of the races of man--that through millions of years have followed each other in endless procession over the exterior surface of the Earth; appearing, abiding for a while, and then passing away. Warned by great climatic changes on the outside, or by the tremors that precede great geological changes, they would have retreated, a few of the "saved," to the hidden cities of refuge within the globe. So that here would be all of the myriad "missing links" in the disconnected story of the fractured outer Earth.

The return, incidentally, to the exterior would be no easier than the departure from it. For at each orifice the contrary waters endlessly struggle to pass, and it might very well be that the traveller caught in the wrong current would not be able to make the cross to the right one on which he could float easily out.

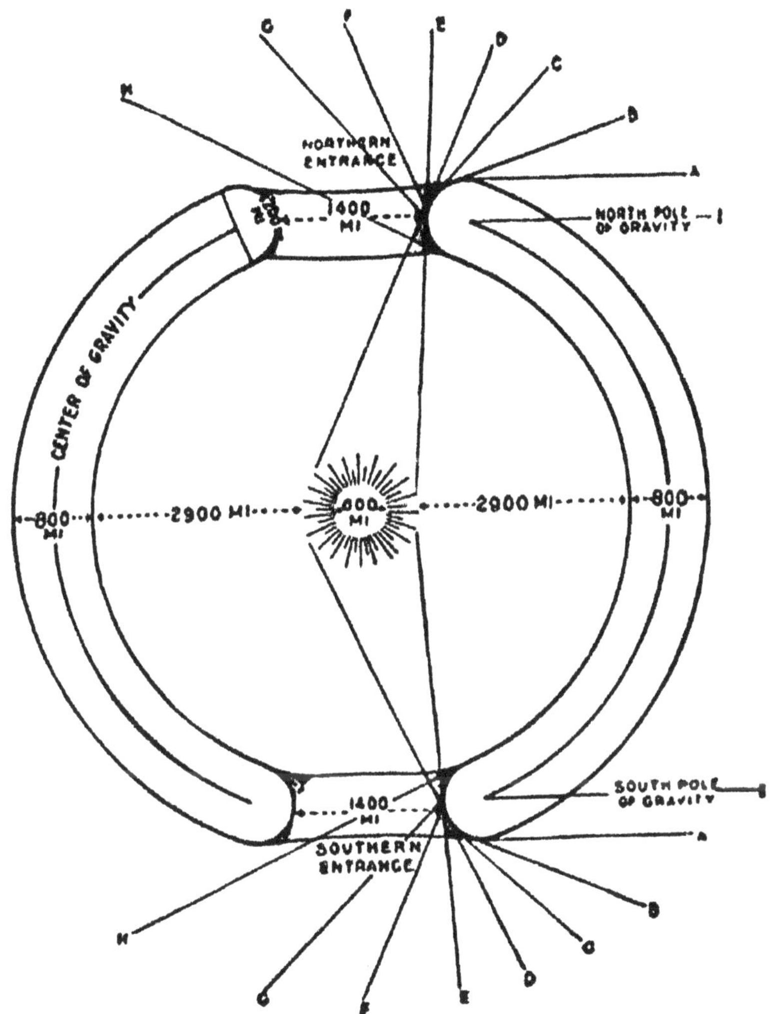

FIGURE 100. Diagram showing the earth as a hollow sphere with its polar openings and central sun. The letters at top and bottom of diagram indicate the various steps of an imaginary journey through the planet's interior. At the point marked "D" we catch our first glimpse of the corona of the central sun; at the point marked "E" we see the central sun in its entirety.
(From A Journey to the Earth's Interior; Marshall B. Gardner, 1920.)

THE TETRAHEDRAL EARTH

THE LAST FIGURE OF EARTH in this collecting of its endlessly changing forms is, so far as I know, the latest figure of Earth to be drawn; it differs in all ways from any other world-picture we have here. Plate XLVIII is a drawing of the Earth as a Tetrahedron or three-sided pyramid; it appeared in the New York World, October 24, 1926, as an illustration to a review of Théophile Moreux's Astronomy To-day. It is not "scientific"; it is just an example of how a "guess" takes a form, even in this age. It has an interesting story, this figure of Earth; and so we begin, far enough back.

"Continents rise and sink as if through some gentle act of respiration. They move in long undulations which may be compared to waves of the sea."

This sounds as if some mild mystic were speaking, but it is Elisée Reclus, French geographer, writing of The Earth in 1870. Twenty years later Clarence Dutton, American geologist, coined a term, the Theory of Isostacy, for the fast developing theory of the floatation of the earth's crust, or floating continents. Less than ten years ago Alfred Wegener, in The Origin of Continents and Oceans, advanced this theory. The continents are masses of sial or "continental rock," moving through the sima--that rock forming the substratum of the ocean bed, which he compares in its viscosity to sealing wax; it is, that is, an extremely viscous fluid, offering a very great resistance to any change of form, but inevitably yielding, under constant pressure, to the passage of the continental masses. Very simply and fantastically imaged, it is as if the continents were enormous leaves or flowers or branches springing from some great parent stalk or trunk imbedded in the very earth of Earth, and floating upwards through the ocean depths to the watery surface and far beyond it.

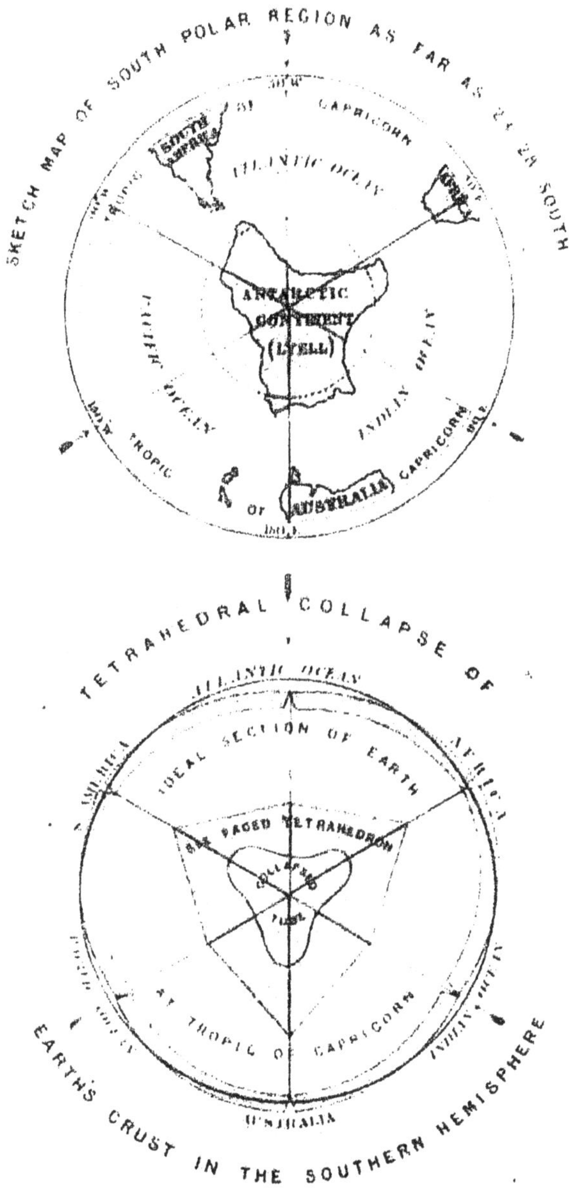

PLATE XLVII. (From Vestiges of the Molten Globe; William Lowthian Green, 1875)

And yet it is almost this very figure--the inverted pyramidal plant figure of the floating continents--which William Lowthian Green worked out in 1875 with the aid of a "model crystal," a tetrahedron with its sides depressed and its four corners thereby slightly raised. His hypothesis is that during the process of the Earth's cooling, and because of what he calls "the tetrahedral collapse of the Earth's crust in the southern hemisphere," the assumed spheroid form of the Earth (giving a minimum of surface for a given volume) tended to develop into a tetrahedron (giving a maximum of surface for a given volume), with the continents as the edges and the ocean beds as the sides. "Thus," says Green, [1] "a general view of the crystal, the six- faced tetrahedron [Fig. 20], supposed to be three-fourths covered by water attracted towards the centre of gravity of the figure, represents generally all the continents and oceans on the globe in their actual relative positions. As there are four acute solid angles on the crystal, so there are four and only four continents or masses in relief on the globe, and as there are four obtuse angles on the crystal, so there are four and only four grand depressions or oceans on the globe."

Try to find any general reference to "Green's theory"; scientists knew of it, of course, but otherwise it is as if it appeared like a comet in the sky of 1875, not to appear again for over fifty years.

Moreux spoke of it, however, in his Astronomy To-day, and thanks to the way he spoke of it, we have this last picture of a tetrahedral Earth. He takes up one by one the unsolved problems of the Earth and the heavens, and it is an amazing array of the unknown. The dozen or so movements of the Earth is a puzzle; the irregularity of those movements is a puzzle, the Earth's real centre of gravity is a puzzle, the planetary system individually and as a whole is a puzzle, the "respiration" of the Earth is a puzzle, the Earth-Moon system would be the puzzle of puzzles if it were not for the fact that the still unknown actual figure of the Earth is the puzzle that tops them all. It is more of a problem to-day than it was in 1885.

For in 1885 that which was to solve it did no more than to tangle again all the laboriously disentangled threads. The discovery of invar in that year, an alloy of nickel and steel whose expansion and contraction at ordinary temperature is almost nothing, seemed to make possible for the first time, at least in our recorded history, the accurate measuring of the supposed

[1] Vestiges of the Molten Globe; William Lowthian Green, 1875, p. 5.

oblate spheroid on which we live. The invar wire was the unerring instrument by which scientists began again the painstaking re-measuring of the Earth. "At the present time," says Moreux, "the survey of the Earth has been carried out in all possible directions, and the results have made the problem only more puzzling. It is found that, even between the same latitudes, meridian arcs are not all of equal lengths, and dissymmetry is everywhere; it becomes more pronounced still when the two hemispheres are compared; and the equator itself, instead of being accurately a circle, like the largest circle of a spheroid, has different radii of curvature at different longitudes." [1]

Since astronomers must, in all their practical calculations, make use of the mathematical elements of this globe so-called, they have, for themselves, determined on a set of average values not too far removed from the unknown real ones, which for the time serves them fairly well. But geographers and geologists, says Moreux, are not interested in this merely approximate solution of the enigma. "By considering the matter closely, they have found that certain systematic variations which occur in pendulum observations and in the value of gravity point more and more to the truth of an old theory which was long ignored. It was suggested by Green in 1875;" and then he re-states Green's hypothesis:

"According to this theory, the Earth would tend, in the process of cooling, to take the form of a tetrahedron or triangular pyramid, with four faces and four corners or coigns. The seas would occupy the depressions and form the faces of the pyramid, while the continents would be situated round the coigns and would reach out along the edges.

"The facts seem to be in considerable agreement with this supposition. Three of the coigns are in the northern hemisphere; to use the picturesque expression of Suess, they are the Scandinavian, Canadian, and Siberian 'bucklers,' the last being situated near Yakutsk. Moreover, these projecting continents are of very ancient formation, and their ramifications extend more or less uninterruptedly as far as the South Pole. The opposite faces consist of the Southern Atlantic, the Indian and the Pacific Oceans. Lastly, the fourth corner forms the Antarctic continent, to which there corresponds, on the opposite face, the frozen Arctic Ocean." [2]

---

[1] Astronomy To-day; Théophile Moreux, 1926, p. 65. 259

[2] Astronomy To-day; Théophile Moreux, 1926, p. 66.

These are the words that gave the image that produced this latest figure to be drawn of the Earth, a tetrahedron or three-sided pyramid, with four continents and four oceans, spinning in space. It is worth noting here that Green says of his "crystal model": "Crystallographers are aware that the six-faced tetrahedron with convex faces may geometrically as well as in nature and fact, approach to the form of a sphere, and that many diamonds possessing that crystalline figure are hardly distinguishable from spheres, but yet may be true six-faced tetrahedrons."

Without committing himself at all to the tetrahedral figure of Earth as established, Moreux adds that "the tetrahedral theory accounts for the inequality of the polar radii, and at the same time gives a more satisfactory explanation than any rival theory does of certain facts of astronomy which are inconsistent with the Earth's being a true ellipsoid of revolution." So, too, he says, the general plan of the Earth's relief and main lines of fractures or crumplings on its surface would, by this theory, be the logical consequence of the contracting process which began during the first of the geological eras and has continued according to the same laws ever since.

PLATE XLVIII. THE TETRAHEDRAL EARTH
(From The Sunday Magazine, New York World, Oct. 24, 1926)

Be very sure that science to-day is committed to nothing but "guesses" on the still unknown figure of the Earth. We are doing to-day, in the last analysis, no more than that first man, whoever and wherever and whenever he was, who said, "Perhaps it is like this," and set down his crude lines of an island in a sea. We know a great many facts about a great many things, and a great many things about a great many facts; and this multitude of facts and things is just exactly our confusion. The facts are facts, but they are contradictory facts; they have not fused into the one great truth about the one Earth of which we know--a little. We have girdled the globe in ships on the surface of its waters, we have rounded the unknown line of its curve under its waters, and we are making our own curves through its air as we fly above it. But no man has ever seen the Earth. It is invisible. We talk of the secrets of the frozen North; they are no more than a handful of the secrets of the Earth. It lies over the Sun and under the Moon, giving everything, but forever withholding the sum of everything--the right image of its own true, unimaginable form.

What is Earth?
A geoid.
What is a geoid?
An Earth-shaped body.
What is an Earth-shaped body?
A geoid.
What is Earth?

BIBLIOGRAPHY

A list of some of the books which were helpful in this study of man's conceptions of the figure of Earth and its relation to the Universe.

ARISTOTLE, De Coelo. Tr. by Thomas Taylor. On the Heavens. London, 1807.

------ De Mundo. Tr. by Thomas Taylor. On the World. (In the Metaphysics, pp. 585-621. London, 1842.)

BEAZLEY, C. RAYMOND, The Dawn of Modern Geography. John Murray, London, 1897-1906. 3 vols.

BERRY, ARTHUR, A Short History of Astronomy. Charles Scribner's Sons, New York, 1899.

BEUCHAT, H., Manuel d'Archeologie américaine. Paris, 1912.

BLUNDEVILLE HIS EXERCISES. London, 1606. 3rd edition.

BRINTON, DANIEL G., The Lenape and Their Legends. (In Brinton's Library of Aboriginal American Literature, No. 5. Philadelphia, 1885.)

------ A Primer of Mayan Hieroglyphics. Univ. of Penna. Publ. ser. in Philology, Literature and Archeology, Vol. III, No. 2, 1894.

------ The Myths of the New World. D. McKay, Philadelphia, 1896. 3rd edition.

BUDGE, E. A. WALLIS, The Egyptian Heaven and Hell. (In Books on Egypt and Chaldea, Vols. XX-XXII. Kegan Paul, Trench, Trubner & Co., London, 1906.)

------ The Babylonian Legends of the Creation. British Museum, London, 1921.

------ The Babylonian Legends of the Deluge. British Museum, London, 1920.

BURNET, THOMAS, The Theory of the Earth. London, 1697.

CHURCHWARD, JAMES, The Lost Continent of Mu. William Edwin Rudge, New York, 1926.

CICERO, Somnium Scipionis. Tr. by C. R. Edmonds. The Dream of Scipio. (In Of Offices or Moral Duties. Bohn's Classical Library. London, 1853.)

CODEX FERJÉRVÁRY-MAYER. An old Mexican picture manuscript in the Liverpool Free Public Museums. Elucidated by Eduard Seler. Berlin, 1901-1902.

COLUMBUS, CHRISTOPHER, Select Letters. Tr. by R. H. Major. (In Hakluyt Society Works, No. 11, London, 1847. 2nd edition.)

COOK, THEODORE ANDREA, Spiral Forms in Nature and in Art. John Murray, London, 1903.

------ The Curves of Life. Henry Holt and Co., New York, 1914.

COSMAS INDICOPLEUSTES, Topographia Christiana. Tr. by J. W. McCrindle. Christian Topography. (In Hakluyt Society Works, No. 98, London, 1897.)

CUNEIFORM TEXTS from Babylonian Tablets, etc., in the British Museum. Pt. XXII, Plate 48. British Museum, London, 1906.

DANTE, The Divine Comedy. Various editions.

DELAMBRE, J. B. J., Histoire de l'Astronomie ancienne. Paris, 1817.

------ Histoire de l'Astronomie du Moyen-Age. Paris, 1819.

DIXON, ROLAND B., Maidu Texts. (In American Ethnological Society Publications, Vol. 4. Leyden, 1912.)

DREYER, J. L. E., History of the Planetary Systems from Thales to Kepler. University Press, Cambridge, 1905.

DU BOSE, HAMPTON C., Dragon, Image and Demon. A. C. Armstrong & Co., New York, 1887.

EDDA, THE PROSE OR YOUNGER, of Snorre Sturleson. Tr. by G. W. Dasent. Stockholm, 1842.

EVERSHED, MARY A. ORR, Dante and the Early Astronomers. Gall and Inglis, London, 1913.

FLAMMARION'S ASTRONOMICAL MYTHS. Edited by John Blake. Macmillan & Co., London, 1877.

FLUDD, ROBERT, Utriusque Cosmi Majoris scilicet et Minoris Metaphysica, Physica atque Technica Historia. 1617-1629.

------ Microcosmi Historia. 1619.
------ Medicina Catholica. Frankfort, 1629.
------ Summum Bonum. 1629.

FOLKARD, JR., RICHARD, Plant Lore, Legends and Lyrics. Sampson Low, Marston, Searle and Rivington, London, 1884.

FONVIELLE, W. DE, Histoire de la lune. Paris, 1886.

GARDNER, MARSHALL B., A Journey to the Earth's Interior, or Have the Poles Really Been Discovered? Aurora, Ill., 1920. 2nd edition.

GREEN, WILLIAM LOWTHIAN, Vestiges of the Molten Globe. Edward Stanford, London, 1875.

HAKLUYT SOCIETY WORKS. 1847-

HOMER, Iliad. Various editions.

------ Odyssey. Various editions.

HOMMEL, FRITZ, Der Babylonische Ursprung der Ägyptischen Kultur. Diagram of Babylonian Universe, p. 8. Munich, 1892.

------ Diagram of Babylonian Universe. (In Aufsätse und Abhandlung, th. iii, p. 346. Munich, 1901.)

INTERNATIONALES ARCHIV FÜR ETHNOGRAPHIE. Bd. IX, S. 265. Leyden, 1896.

JENSEN, P. C. A., Die Kosmologie der Babylonier. Diagram of Babylonian Universe in Appendix. Strassburg, 1890.

JOB. The Book of Job.

JOURNAL ROYAL ASIATIC SOCIETY of Great Britain and Ireland, 1908. "The Babylonian Universe Newly Interpreted," by William Fairfield Warren, pp. 977-983.

KEPLER, JOHANN, Harmonices Mundi. 1619.

KINGSBOROUGH, EDWARD KING, Antiquities of Mexico. London, 1830-1848. 9 vols.

KIRCHER, ATHANASIUS, Mundus Subterraneus. Amsterdam, 1678. 2 vols.

------ Iter exstaticum coeleste. Norimburg, 1660.

------ Arca Noë. Amsterdam, 1675. 3 vols.

------ Physiologia Kircheriana Experimentalis. Amsterdam, 1680.

KIRFEL, W., Die Kosmographie der Inder. Bonn, 1920.

LENORMANT, FRANÇOIS, Les origines de l'histoire, etc. Tr. by Mary Lockwood. The Beginnings of History According to the Bible and the Traditions of Oriental Peoples from the Creation of Man to the Deluge. Charles Scribner's Sons, New York, 1882.

LEWIS, GEORGE CORNEWALL, An Historical Survey of the Astronomy of the Ancients. London, 1862.

LITCHFIELD, MARY ELIZABETH, The Nine Worlds. Ginn & Co., Boston, 1890.

LOCKYER, J. NORMAN, The Dawn of Astronomy. Cassell & Co., London, 1894.

LUCRETIUS, De Rerum Natura. Tr. by H. A. J. Monroe. On the Nature of Things. (In Bohn's Classical Library, London, 1864.)

MCBRIDE, JAMES, The Symmes Theory of Concentric Spheres. Cincinnati, 1826.

M'CLATCHIE, THOMAS, Confucian Cosmogony. Shanghai, 1874.

MAHABHARATA, THE. Tr. from the Sanskrit by Pratap Chandra Roy. Calcutta, 1883-1893. 18 vols.

MALLERY, GARRICK, Picture-Writing of the American Indians. Extracted from the Tenth Annual Report of the United States Bureau of Ethnology. Washington, D. C., 1894.

MASPERO, GASTON, The Dawn of Civilization. Diagram of Babylonian Universe, p. 543. D. Appleton & Co., New York, 1894.

MEAD, G. R. S., Fragments of a Faith Forgotten. Theosophical Publishing Society, London, 1906. and edition.

MEISSNER, BRUNO, Die Kultur Babylonien und Assyrien. Diagram of Babylonian Universe, Vol. II, p. 109. Heidelberg, 1920. 2 vols.

MEMOIRS OF THE AMERICAN MUSEUM OF NATURAL HISTORY. Vol. II, pp. 163-392. New York, 1900.

MILL, HUGH R., The Siege of the South Pole. Frederick A. Stokes Co., New York, 1905.

MILLER, KONRAD, Mappa Mundi: Die ältesten Weltkarten. Stuttgart, 1895-1898. 6 vols.
MILTON, Paradise Lost.

MOREAUX, THÉOPHILE, Astronomy To-day. Tr. by C. F. Russel. Methuen & Co., London, 1926.

------ L'Atlantide, a-t-elle-existe? Paris, 1924.

------ Un jour dans la lune. Paris, 1912.

MYER, ISAAC, Qabbalah. Philadelphia, 1888.

MYTHOLOGY OF ALL RACES. Edited by Louis Herbert Gray. Marshall Jones Company, Boston, 1916-1928. 13 vols.

NARRIEN, JOHN, An Historical Account of the Origin and Process of Astronomy. London, 1833.

NEWBROUGH, JOHN BALLOU, Oahspe, A New Bible in the Words of Jehovih. Oahspe Publishing Co., Boston, 1891.

NICHOL, JOHN, Thoughts on Some Important Points Relating to the System of the World. Edinburgh, 1848.

NORDENSKIÖLD, A. E., Periplus, An Essay on the Early History of Charts and Sailing Directions. Tr. by F. A. Bather. Stockholm, 1897.

OLCUTT, W. T., Starlore of All Ages. G. P. Putnam's Sons, New York, 1911.

ORCHARD, THOMAS N., Milton's Cosmogony. Longmans, Green & Co., London, 1913. See also 2nd edition, 1915.

PHILPOT, MRS. JOHN H., The Sacred Tree, or The Tree in Religion and Myth. Macmillan & Co., London, 1897.

PLATO, Timaeus and Critias. Tr. by H. Davis. (In Bohn's Classical Library, London, 1849.)

PLOTINUS, Select Works. Tr. by Thomas Taylor. (In Bohn's Philosophical Library, London, 1 895.)

PLUTARCH, On the Apparent Face in the Orb of the Moon. (In his Moralia. Various editions.)

PORDAGE, JOHN, Theologica Mystica, or the Archetypous Globe. London, 1683.

RADAU, HUGO, The Creation Story of Genesis. Diagram of the Babylonian Universe, p. 56, 1902.

RAFINESQUE, CONSTANTINE S., Wallamolum or painted traditions of the Linipe Indians, translated by C. S. Rafinesque in 1833; with a fragment on the history of the Linipi since about 1600 when the Wallamolum closes. A transcript from the original manuscript, in the MSS. Division of the New York Public Library.

RECORDE, ROBERT, The Castle of Knowledge. London, 1556.

SANTAREM, V. DE, Atlas composé de mappemondes et de cartes hydrographiques et historiques depuis le XIe jusqu' au XVIIe siècle. Paris, 1849.

SCOTT-ELLIOT, W., The Story of Atlantis and the Lost Lemuria. With Maps. Theosophical Publishing Society, London, 1925.

SELER, EDUARD. See CODEX FERJÉRVÁRY-MAYER.

SINGER, CHARLES. The Scientific Views and Visions of Saint Hildegard. (In Studies in the History and Method of Science, edited by Charles Singer, Vol. I. Clarendon Press, Oxford, 1917. 2 vols.)

SPENCE, LEWIS, Atlantis in America. Ernest Benn, London, 1925.

STEVENSON, EDWARD LUTHER, Terrestrial and Celestial Globes. Published for the Hispanic Society of America by the Yale University Press, New Haven, 1921. 2 vols.

SWEDENBORG, EMANUEL, The Earths in the Universe. The Swedenborg Society, London, 1875.

SYMMES, AMERICUS, The Symmes Theory of Concentric Spheres. Louisville, 1878.

TEED, CYRUS REED, The Cellular Cosmogony, The Earth a Concave Sphere. Guiding Star Publishing House, Estero, Fla., 1905.

TEIT, JAMES, The Thompson River Indians of British Columbia. (In Memoirs of the American Museum of Natural History, Vol. II, pp. 163-392. New York, 1900.)

UNITED STATES BUREAU OF AMERICAN ETHNOLOGY, Annual Reports, 1879.

WADDELL, L. AUSTINE, The Buddhism of Tibet, or Lamaism. Luzac & Co., London, 1899.

WARREN, WILLIAM FAIRFIELD, Paradise Found. Houghton, Mifflin & Co., Boston, 1885.

------ The Universe as Pictured in Milton's Paradise Lost. Abingdon Press, New York, 1915.

------ The Babylonian Universe Newly Interpreted. (In Journal Royal Asiatic Society of Great Britain and Ireland, 1908, pp. 977-983.)

WEGENER, ALFRED, Die enstehung der continente und ozeane. Tr. by J. G. A. Skerl. The Origin of Continents and Oceans. Methuen & Co., London, 1924.

WHISTON, WILLIAM, A New Theory of Earth. London, 1690.

WHITEHOUSE, OWEN C., Diagram of the Babylonian Universe. (In his article on "Cosmogony" in Hastings's Dictionary of the Bible, Vol. I, p. 503. Edinburgh, 1898.)

WRIGHT, JOHN K., The Geographical Lore of the Time of the Crusades. American Geographical Society, New York, 1925.

www.ingramcontent.com/pod-product-compliance
Lightning Source LLC
Chambersburg PA
CBHW041926260326
41914CB00009B/1184
9781639235025